THE
NARCISSISM
OF
MINOR
DIFFERENCES

THE
NARCISSISM
OF
MINOR
DIFFERENCES

HOW AMERICA
AND EUROPE
ARE ALIKE

AN ESSAY IN NUMBERS

PETER BALDWIN

OXFORD
UNIVERSITY PRESS

2009

OXFORD
UNIVERSITY PRESS

Oxford University Press, Inc., publishes works that further
Oxford University's objective of excellence
in research, scholarship, and education.

Oxford New York
Auckland Cape Town Dar es Salaam Hong Kong Karachi
Kuala Lumpur Madrid Melbourne Mexico City Nairobi
New Delhi Shanghai Taipei Toronto

With offices in
Argentina Austria Brazil Chile Czech Republic France Greece
Guatemala Hungary Italy Japan Poland Portugal Singapore
South Korea Switzerland Thailand Turkey Ukraine Vietnam

Published by Oxford University Press, Inc.
198 Madison Avenue, New York, NY 10016

www.oup.com

Oxford is a registered trademark of Oxford University Press

Library of Congress Cataloging-in-Publication Data
Baldwin, Peter.
The narcissism of minor differences : how America and Europe are alike / Peter Baldwin.
    p.   cm.
Includes bibliographical references and index.
ISBN 978-0-19-539120-6
1. National characteristics, European.   2. National characteristics, American.
3. Europe—Relations—United States.   4. United States—Relations—Europe.
I. Title.
D2021.B34 2009
305.809—dc22   2009007226

9 8 7 6 5 4 3 2 1
Printed in the United States of America
on acid-free paper

FOR MY SONS,
Lukas and Elias,
who negotiate both sides
of this supposed divide
with aplomb

CONTENTS

ACKNOWLEDGMENTS

I AM ENORMOUSLY INDEBTED to Michael Kellogg, a scholar in his own right, for invaluable research assistance. Without his help, I would still be scurrying down the back alleys of the Internet, trying to come up with something quantifiable on sugar consumption, per capita piano sales, newspaper readership, or who knows what. Yves-Pierre Yani, of the UCLA Department of Economics, did preliminary calculations for several of the graphs on income distribution and poverty. Jamie Barron, of the UCLA Statistics Department, refined and improved these calculations where noted, and was immensely useful in helping me sidestep the worst of my statistical mistakes. The usual provisos concerning ultimate attribution of fault apply.

Several colleagues and friends were of help with suggestions and leads to information I had overlooked, as well as wise counsel on how to phrase and structure matters. Many of them probably disagree with the argument here, and to the extent that I can, I absolve them of any implication in it. They were nonetheless too kind just to send me packing. I am indebted to Jens Alber, Joyce Appleby, Perry Anderson, Timothy Garton Ash, Peter Aterman, Michael Burda, Gøsta Esping-Andersen, Neil Gilbert, Jacob Hacker, Josef Joffe, Matthieu Leimgruber, Peter Mandler, Claus Offe, Timothy B. Smith, Lars Trägårdh, and George Weidenfeld. Frank Castles went far beyond the call of duty or collegiality. He has read the manuscript in several versions, not to mention hearing it as a lecture, and has still had the patience to guide me around numerous pitfalls. I am deeply grateful.

The inspiration to write a longish version of these ideas came during the question period at a talk I was invited to give at Jürgen Kocka's ongoing seminar on comparative history at the Free University of Berlin in April 2006. The fervor with which the students present insisted that the European social model was not only a reality, but also a crucial issue in the recent election campaigns in the new EU nations of the former East Bloc, led me to ponder how distinctive this model actually was. Versions of this material were presented in a lecture at Syddansk Universitet, Odense, and as the James Seth Memorial Lecture at the University of Edinburgh in 2007. I am grateful to Klaus Petersen, Frank Castles, and Richard Parry for those invitations.

I am also indebted to my editor at Oxford, David McBride. Presented with a manuscript containing several hundred graphs and even more statistics, it is not every editor who agrees both that it is publishable and could be pitched to a wide audience. I wish I could be certain that his training as a doctoral student in my own department at UCLA is responsible, but I fear it is likely to be native talent. I am grateful to him for sticking with the project through its various twists and turns.

Finally, my greatest debt is to my wife and colleague, Lisbet Rausing. She has worked my prose over so many times that it may finally be readable. She has subjected my arguments to so thorough a pummeling that they may now be convincing. I would like to think that she has put in so much effort on my behalf because she loves me as much as I adore her. But that would be impossible.

THE
NARCISSISM
OF
MINOR
DIFFERENCES

INTRODUCTION: EUROPE AND AMERICA, HISSING COUSINS

THE ATLANTIC GETS EVER WIDER. Not just in a physical sense, as oceans rise and coastlines recede, but also in ideological terms. Europe and America appear to be pitted against each other as never before. On one shore, capitalist markets, untempered by proper social policies, allow unbridled competition, poverty, pollution, violence, class divides, and social anomie. On the other side, Europe nurtures a social approach, a regulated labor market, and elaborate welfare networks. Possibly it has a less dynamic economy, but it is a more solidaristic and harmonious society. "Our social model," as the voice of British left liberalism, the *Guardian*, describes the European way, "feral capitalism," in the United States.[1] With the collapse of communism, the European approach has been promoted from being the Third Way to the Second Way. The UK floats ambiguously between these two shores: "Janus Britain" in the phrase of the dean of transatlanticist observers, Timothy Garton Ash.[2] It is part of

Europe, says the British Left; an Anglo-Saxon coconspirator, answer its continental counterparts.

That major differences separate the United States from Europe is scarcely a new idea. But it has become more menacingly Manichaean over the last decade. Foreign policy disagreements fuel it: Iraq, Iran, Israel, North Korea. So does the more general question of what role the one remaining superpower should play while it still remains unchallenged. Robert Kagan has famously suggested that, when it comes to foreign policy, Americans and Europeans call different planets home.[3] Americans wield hard power and face the nasty choices that follow in its wake. Europeans, sheltered from most geopolitical strife, enjoy the luxury of approaching conflict in a more conciliatory way: Martian unilateralism confronts Venusian multilateralism. But the dispute goes beyond diplomatic and military strategy. It touches on the nature of these two societies. Does having the strongest battalions change the country that possesses them? After all, America is not just militarily strong. It is also—compared to Europe—harsh, dominated by the market, crime-ridden, violent, unsolidaristic, and sharp-elbowed. Competition is an official part of the national ideology and violence the way it spills over into everyday life.[4] Or so goes the argument: a major battle of worldviews and social practices separates America from Europe.

The idea that the North Atlantic is socioculturally parted is elaborated in both Europe and America for reasons that are as connected to domestic political needs and tactics as they are to any actual differences. American criticism of Europe, when it can be heard at all, typically concerns foreign policy or trade issues. American conservatives occasionally make the old continent a symbol for what they see as the excesses of the welfare state and statutory regulation. But the longstanding European criticism of America has become more vehement and widespread and is now shared by right and left alike. Europeans are keen to define an alternative to American hegemony, now that Europe no longer needs the protection of the United States in a post-cold-war world. Beset with internal fractures and disagreements, they have rediscovered the truism that nothing unites like a common enemy.

In other words, this is not a symmetrical dispute. American anti-Europeanism exists, of course, but it pales next to its European counterpart. "There are no anti-European demonstrations," as Russell Berman writes, "no burning of French or German flags, no angry mobs with pitchforks and tractors in front of Louis Vuitton boutiques or BMW dealerships. American 'anti-Europeanism' is not an equal partner but only an anemic afterthought to the

European spectacles."[5] The renaming of french fries in the congressional caf-
eteria in 2003 (rescinded by 2006) is about as far as things have gone. Even the
characterization of the French as cheese-eating surrender monkeys was self-
caricature, with *The Simpsons* mocking American troglodytes. Occasionally,
a Richard Perle, or his equivalent, gives some Europeans a hard time for dis-
agreeing with the U.S. administration on foreign policy. Policy wonks in DC
think tanks may argue the fine points of labor deregulation, extolling alleged
American flexibility compared to European sclerosis. But they still breakfast on
microwaved simulacra of croissants without considering them emblematic of a
larger *Kulturkampf*, and they vacation eagerly in Provence. The battle is rarely
joined in reverse. When the talk is about possible gulfs across the Atlantic, one
almost never hears about differences whose tendency cuts against European
amour propre. The Europeans concerned with gun control or the death penalty have few counterparts among American observers pointing out the significant transatlantic difference in terms of the presence (strong and increasing)
of neofascist parties in Europe, contrasting to their utter absence in America.
Or detailing the well-integrated status of Muslims in the United States, their
relegation almost wholly to the social margins across the Atlantic (at least outside Britain).

Rush Limbaugh, Bill O'Reilly, and others on the American right attack
Europe, just as the European left hangs the United States out to dry. That is
no surprise. The contrast comes in the mainstream press. Where *bien pensant*
European opinion, as expressed in the *Guardian*, *Le Monde*, or *Der Spiegel*,
is heavily colored by certain preconceptions of America, their U.S. counterparts—whether the *New York Times*, *Washington Post*, or *Newsweek*—are not
analogously inclined. There is no American José Bové, no U.S. equivalent of
the European who regards the lowly hamburger as the opening shot of a battle
of worldviews that runs the gamut from McDonalds to Monsanto, from globalization to foreign aid, and who can bring the rabble into the street behind
him. "The hamburger is a particular source of hatred of America," readers are
assured by Ziauddin Sardar and Merryl Wyn Davies. "It is the single most
concentrated, or should that be congealed, symbol of the entire complex that
is America."[6] There is no American version of Harold Pinter or Margaret
Drabble, whose anti-Americanism causes her paroxysms of rage and nausea,
her prose practically frothing at the mouth.[7] A vast majority of Americans
(91%) desire closer relations with Europe. Only about a third of the French
(39%) agree, barely more than half the British (51%), though the Germans
(74%) and the Spanish (67%) are more friendly.[8]

Working-class Americans are largely unconcerned with Europe, while working-class Europeans are often quite fond of the United States. They swarm Florida's beaches and enjoy visiting a country that—less strictly governed by the *Bildungsbürgertum*—unashamedly caters to popular taste. The main contrasts come higher up the social scale. University-educated Americans are, on the whole, positively inclined toward Europe. If anything, they are deferential. Think only of the cultural cringe of U.S. academics. Yes, American right-wing intellectuals occasionally attack Europe. Yet they do so not to play to their own foot soldiers, who could not care less, but to goad the American liberal elite. Anti-Europeanism is part of the battle between right and left. In contrast, both the European left and right alike are anti-American. Each has its own reasons, whether it is the vulgarism of cultureless populism for the Right or the exploitativeness of untrammeled markets for the Left. But they are united in their dislike, and thus reassured that they have at least a European identity in common. In America, anti-European sentiments divide; in Europe, anti-American opinions unite.

One of the aspects of European criticism of the United States that puzzles Americans is how selective or even ill-informed it often is. It is a venerable tradition for Europeans to portray America without knowing much about it. Karl May was an overwhelmingly popular German author of cowboy (Old Shatterhand) and Indian (Winnetou) stories, loved by everyone from Einstein to Hitler. Travel was difficult in his day. One can perhaps forgive him for spinning his fantasies of the Wild West before ever setting foot in America in 1908, and even then, never further inland than Buffalo in upstate New York, which—despite its name—was certainly not the West of which he wrote. But when an internationally successful film director, Lars von Trier, makes a series of movies (*Dancer in the Dark*, *Dogville*, *Manderlay*) set in and critical of the United States without having ever been there, one begins to suspect something akin to willful ignorance. Not that mere knowledge has ever been a prerequisite for opinions on America. "I did not need to go to the United States to say what I said," Georges Duhamel, a French writer, assured his readers in 1930. "I could have written most of the chapters of my book without leaving Paris."[9] Reading Europe's popular press pundits, Americans often grope to recognize their country: rapster ghetto chic, laced with urban poverty or trailer park Appalachia, contrasted with gated-community golf links, iced with caloric surfeit and seasoned with prison brutality. The sociological earnestness of it all is interrupted now and then by some head-shaking Vegas weirdness for comic relief.

Equivalent Americans—otherwise well-educated people whose irrepressible desire to pronounce on Europe is matched only by their ignorance of the subject—are simply not to be found. Americans who have made a profession of observing Europe—Jane Kramer, Bill Bryson, and the like—do so affectionately, and from long experience and careful attention. Even Robert Kagan, perhaps America's most trenchant critic of Europe, lives in Brussels and knows whereof he speaks. Occasionally, conservative tub-thumpers in America criticize Europe. Politicians may strive for effect, as when Mitt Romney attacked French health care during his short-lived primary campaign in late 2007. Sometimes, a blogger or op-ed writer uses Europe's failures to make a rhetorical point. But it happens quite rarely.

Rush Limbaugh and his ilk are often thought to poison Americans' minds by contrasting godless, lazy, overregulated Europe to virtuous America. The reality is that Limbaugh and company are too provincial and self-obsessed to look far beyond America's borders—as a quick drill into the data shows. A left-wing European pendant to Rush Limbaugh is the Berlin *Tageszeitung*, the venerable mouthpiece of the aging New Left in Germany, where criticism of America is a staple on the menu. If we search Limbaugh's and the *TAZ*'s sites for the terms America and Europe, and synonyms, we discover that Limbaugh speaks 13 times as often of America as he does about Europe. The *TAZ*, in contrast, speaks of Germany only 1.5 times as often as it does of America. Indeed, it mentions America almost as often as does Limbaugh.[10] In other words, while Europe is a peripheral concern for the American Right, America is an obsession of the European Left. American views of Europe can perhaps best be described as indifference served up with lashings of nostalgia. Europe is the world left behind, sometimes under traumatic circumstances, and one which registers only peripherally on the radar. For Europeans, in contrast, opinions have run hot and contradictory from the moment of first contact: admiration for the possibilities of the new, disgust with how it was actually working out. Perhaps Americans are less interested in Europe than Europeans are in America. But if Americans do not wax eloquent about the old world, at least they do not utter much that is inaccurate or distorted.

The dispute between America and Europe does not pose only the two shores of the North Atlantic against each other. The fight is joined equally within the now expanded Europe. The new nations of the EU have often adopted similar policies and strive for much the same social, economic, and political goals as its old members.[11] Yet, reacting to the overweening statism of their own old regimes, they also have favored a more neoliberal economic model. In many instances they have rejected European models of welfare statism and looked to Anglo-American ideals of a less regulated capitalism.[12] Early in the transition from Communism, Hungarian and Czech reformers were more neoliberal than Reagan and Thatcher.[13] The Baltic states, though admiring Scandinavia, have been radically free-market reformers.[14] True, the new nations have tempered their neoliberalism in recent years. Yet tax policy in, say, Estonia, with its low flat rates and streamlined system of collection, would be the dream of any American conservative. Debates between Europe and America thus do not pit just the United States against Europe. They also frame a struggle at the heart of the enlarging EU itself.

Although such disputes across the Atlantic have been prompted by disagreements over foreign policy, they touch on something more fundamental and enduring. European criticism of America is, after all, as old as the country itself. Arguably, what we see today is a contemporary incarnation of a long-standing controversy that pits two different models of society against each other as a binary choice. Let me count the ways America and Europe are thought to differ: economic, social, political, cultural, ecological, and religious. America believes in the untrammeled market; Europe accepts capitalism but curbs its excesses. Because the market dominates, the environment is run down in the United States, cared for in Europe. "America has always grown by playing out its soils, wasting its oil, and by looking abroad for the people it needed to do its work," Emmanuel Todd, a French prophet of collapse, assures us, adding that Europeans, as erstwhile peasants, approach nature in a gentle, Gaia-like way.[15]

Americans are competitive and anomic; Europeans are solidaristic. Initiative and merit may be better rewarded in the United States, but those who cannot compete on the open market are more likely to fall to the bottom. In Europe, a safety net prevents such misery, even as it may limit the altitude of high fliers. Because social contrasts are greater in America, crime is more of a problem than in Europe. American society is more violent. Social measures either do not exist in America or are more privatized than in Europe. Education, for example, is often described as stratified and largely privatized, while in Europe it is universally accessible and state-financed. The lack of universal health insurance in America means that average life expectancies are low and the uncared for die in misery. Americans toil relentlessly, while Europeans trade income for leisure. As one book on the subject puts it, if Europeans are lazy, Americans are crazy.[16] Europeans are secular; Americans are much more likely to believe in God and accept a role for religion in public life.

On the occasions when the American Right attacks Europe, it, of course, spins a variant on the same dichotomies: Europeans are lazy and defeatist; Americans are entrepreneurial and optimistic. Europeans are corrupt and irreligious; Americans are honest and pious. Europeans are infected with Islamic fundamentalism because they are ineffective against immigration; Americans are building a fence between themselves and Mexico, or are successfully integrating their immigrants—depending on which conservative position on immigration is being espoused.

The two societies are thus thought to differ radically: competition versus cooperation, individualism versus solidarity, autonomy versus cohesion. As Jeremy Rifkin, an American writer who shares a certain technological pessimism with much European opinion, puts it: "The European Dream emphasizes community relationships over individual autonomy, cultural diversity over assimilation, quality of life over the accumulation of wealth, sustainable development over unlimited material growth, deep play over unrelenting toil, universal human rights and the rights of nature over property rights, and global cooperation over the unilateral exercise of power."[17]

European criticism of America has been voiced for over two centuries now, and the themes of such attacks have been heard before in different guises. A long tradition of cultural conservatism in Europe has lambasted the supposed attributes and effects of the modern world. During the nineteenth century, both the European Left and Right criticized modernity from its own vantage—whether as cosmopolitan, rootless, and anomic seen from the agrarian romanticism of the Right or as ruthless, exploitative, and mercantile in the opinion of the Left.[18] The new world was forced to be modern whether it wanted to or not. But many Europeans thought they had a choice. Modernity, and the ongoing debate over whether and how Europe might participate in it, has long played a role as a Rorschach test in European culture—something onto which Europeans have displaced their fears and misgivings about the change they faced.

Today, America represents the tea leaves in which Europe reads its fearsome future. When, for example, Germans—citizens of the world's most dynamic export economy—attack globalization (which is to say, their ability to sell their excellent products everywhere) as a form of *Amerikanismus*, then clearly America is not being attacked for what it is (a rather sclerotic and half-hearted player in the global economy, which, by virtue of the size of its internal market alone, will never be as interested in globalization as many European nations), but as a proxy for an otherwise inchoate fear of the world markets. When Europeans criticize America, it is often a shorthand way of expressing worries about the modern world in general. China, India, Japan, and Korea are often the real objects of suspicion. America is the devil they are familiar with, not one of the unknown unknowns. And, in any case, the dispute is really more about what sort of modernity Europe wants and what its identity in a globalized world is to be. Portraying America as the Other against which Europe defines itself is thus part of an ongoing dispute within the continent over the nature of its own society, its role in the world, and the direction of its future.

It is in this light we best interpret the small library of books published over the past few years, debating whether a sociocultural Rubicon separates (continental) Europe from the (Anglo-) American barbarians.[19] America's unregulated capitalism is a danger to Europe, warns Todd.[20] The notion of a unified West has lost whatever meaning it once had, adds Claus Offe, the German sociologist.[21] A recent letter-writer to the *Financial Times* agrees, although placing the UK on the side of the Continentals. A common language should not, this writer claims, obscure the distance between the UK and the United States: Americans carry guns, execute prisoners, go bankrupt, drive large cars, and live in even larger houses. Their men are circumcised and their working class is poor. The humanist and secular Europeans, by contrast, enjoy socialist hospitals, schools, and welfare systems. They pay high taxes, live longer, and take the train.[22] "The proposition that there is something hateful in the very nature of America, that its myths present life-threatening danger to the rest of the world, appears quite natural," Sadar and Davies, our hamburger pundits, conclude.[23] One ponders what unspoken motives inspire such letters, articles, and books. Andrei Markovits, author of one of the most interesting recent books on the subject, suggests that anti-Americanism helps fire the engines of pan-European nationalism. Europeans have less in common than the aspiring empire builders of the EU would like. But at least they can agree on being different from the Americans.[24] Or can they?

Much has been made of transatlantic differences in popular books and in the press. But these outpourings, however heartfelt, are troublingly deficient in fact and substance. Polemic and vituperation abound; caricature, rather than portrait, is the dominant genre. It is time to examine more closely what it is we do know. This book is an essay in numbers. In it, I consider if and how Europe differs from the United States. I present a broad palette of comparative and quantifiable data, a kind of statistical Baedeker juxtaposing the two sides of the Atlantic.

There is an old joke about a man looking for his lost car keys at night under a street lamp. A passing pedestrian helps him search for a while, and then asks whether he is sure that this is where the keys were lost. "Oh, no," replies the would-be driver, "I lost them over there." "Then why are we looking here?" asks the pedestrian. "Because this is where the light is." So, too, the statistical evidence available for both sides of the Atlantic severely restricts where we can probe. Subjects that could be illuminated by quantifiable evidence are often badly served by the data we have. And in any case, quantification only takes us so far. Not all differences can be identified by numbers. But at least statistics allow us a first pass over the terrain and give us the opportunity to compare reliably. Blinkered but demonstrable, quantification releases us from the clutches of anecdote and impression into the realm of fact and verifiability. The point of this book is not to engage in subjective evaluations of qualitative differences or similarities. The world's bookshelves already groan under the weight of such attempts. It is instead to look dispassionately at the quantitative evidence, such as it is. My ambition is not to settle the debate over transatlantic differences once and for all (as if that could ever be achieved). Instead, I hope to apply a swift and well-aimed karate chop of fact and figure to unsettle the prejudices and dislodge the mistaken assumptions that have become common currency in periodicals, popular books, talk shows, and conversations on both sides of the Atlantic.

Beyond those popular debates, each facet of the alleged contrasts between Europe and America can marshal an army of scholars well-versed in the details: whether social policy experts, criminologists, educational researchers, students of health care, environmentalists, or those who study religion. I cannot possibly hope to do each of these fields justice, nor to keep their practitioners from thinking that their specialty has been mauled. I can only beg their indulgence and plead the difficulty of presenting so broad and synoptic an account of so large a part of the world. My concern is not with the finer details of these specialized fields, but with the popular perceptions of difference across the Atlantic and the way that these perceptions inform the middlebrow press, TV reportage, the blogosphere, and the attitudes of those Americans and Europeans who know enough about each other to form an opinion. It is not just one aspect of the transatlantic relationship or another that I want to examine, but its entire gestalt. There is—if I can put it this way—an ideological totality to the major fault line that has been identified as running down the North Atlantic. Each aspect is seen as reinforcing and affirming the others. To tackle just one or two of these in detail would get us nowhere. A statistical bird's-eye view may.

To foreshadow my conclusion, the evidence in this book shows two things. First, Europe is not a coherent or unified continent. The spectrum of difference within even Western Europe is much broader than normally appreciated. Second, with a few exceptions, the United States fits into the span of most quantifiable measures that I have been able to find. We may therefore conclude either that there is no coherent European identity, or—if there is one—that the United States is as much a European country as the usual candidates. We might rephrase this by saying that both Europe and the United States are, in fact, parts of a common, big-tent grouping—call it the West, the Atlantic community, the developed world, or what you will. America is not Sweden, for sure. But nor is Italy Sweden, nor France, nor even Germany. And who says that Sweden is Europe, any more than Vermont is America?

Sigmund Freud coined the phrase "the narcissism of minor differences" to account for the intense energy invested in parsing divergences that, to an impartial observer, might seem trivial and inconsequential. The psychological wellspring of such behavior, Freud reasoned, was the hope of affirming internal group solidarities against an outsider who was perhaps not as "other" as his would-be enemies would have liked. His foreignness therefore had to be narcissistically elaborated in lavish detail. Among Freud's examples of such supposedly minor differences were those between Spaniards and Portuguese, North and South Germans, the English and the Scots. If he had left it at that, we might be able to agree with him that this was but "a convenient and relatively harmless satisfaction of the inclination to aggression." We could, that is, if we were willing to let, say, the Highland clearances in Scotland and Bismarck's wars of unification between Prussians and, among others, Bavarians slip into that twilight world where past bloody strife between fierce enemies has faded in memory to become but historical allusion among current allies. But Freud's other examples of what he considered minor differences are less trivial. They demonstrate the gravity of the issues actually at stake: Communists and their bourgeois opponents in Soviet Russia, and (in a book published in 1930) Christians and Jews. Freud was not a political philosopher, nor did he elaborate this theme at any length. We need not, I think, accept his examples of minor differences as very telling. And yet we stand to benefit from his insight into differences whose objective divergence is so slight that it does not actually justify the ferocious devotion put into elaborating them.[25]

Not everyone will welcome this book's conclusion, that unrecognized affinities span the Atlantic. In Europe, it may be read as a neocon apologia for America, one that does not even have the courage of its own convictions, namely that the United States is, and wants to be, different. It may be seen as arguing that things are not so bad in America, and therefore as a book that cuts corners on the truth. American conservatives may find it unsettling that less separates Europe and America than they think—or want. However, it is above all, I suspect, American liberals who will be troubled by this book. They may be annoyed by what they interpret as support of the status quo. American liberals appreciate having an idealized image of Europe at hand to criticize domestic American policy. If Europeans enjoy having an ugly America to buff the sheen of their own continent's qualities, liberals in the United States like to have a virtuous Europe—and above all, a Europe that is different from America—as the target to aim for when calculating their own policy ambitions and trajectories.

I would urge my audience to contemplate the possibility that the potential reactions I have sketched out here to this book say more about the reader than the read. I wrote the book in the belief that recent U.S. foreign policy has so poisoned relations between Europe and America that it has affected more general perceptions of what differences actually divide the North Atlantic. The debate has degenerated into ideological posturing, motivated by local politics and tactics. Vast cauldrons of rhetorical soup have been boiled from meager scraps of evidence. It is time to bring some empirical meat to the table. To argue, as this book does, that the differences across the Atlantic are not as great as commonly thought is not to discount European achievements, nor gloss over American shortcomings. It is to aim for an accurate portrayal of the two sides of the Atlantic. And it is to suggest that a clear-eyed view reveals that the commonalities across this divide are greater than the differences. Indeed, it may well be that the cultivation of whatever divergences remain is, as Freud warned us, narcissistic. In any case, it is highly likely that the election of Obama and his new administration in Washington, ameliorating eight years of transatlantic antagonism, will lend plausibility to the arguments put forth here.

Readers may argue that different figures could be found for some of the data presented here, or that the picture I sketch is unbalanced. That the United States profoundly differs from Europe is a "fact" so often stated that it has become just that: part of what we intuitively think we already know. The story of radical difference is too often the conceptual prism through which we view both Europe and America: a philosophical starting point rather than a question to be examined. This book thus aims to start a debate that has not yet taken place, or rather, one that has been held in an atmosphere of too little data.

To the best of my ability, I have collected and examined the available evidence. But my ambition—to write a brief, evidence-based account comparing the United States and Europe—has proven unexpectedly difficult. Few comparable statistics exist. All too often, the numbers deal with only a small assortment of nations, and rarely do they span the Atlantic. The ones I present here are those that I have found. I am not a statistician. Few of those who engage at a popular level in this debate are. I have therefore not sought to go beyond amassing and presenting the standard available data gathered by reputable organizations. Occasionally, I have created my own comparisons, but only where the data seemed to be robust and comparable. Most of the time, I have ventured only where the statistical light shines, which is far from everywhere.

The book's data come mostly from a handful of organizations that devote significant effort to presenting internationally comparable figures: the World Health Organization, the United Nations, UNESCO, UNICEF, the International Monetary Fund, the World Bank, Eurostat, the Sutton Trust, the World Values Survey, the International Labour Organization, the International Agency for Research on Cancer, the International Association for the Study of Obesity, the World Resources Institute, the International Energy Agency, the International Social Survey Program, and, above all, that astounding emporium of facts and figures, the OECD. To their efforts, I owe whatever rigor the following may possess. But unlike the scholars whose acknowledgments are rife with the usual pieties, I'm not going to absolve them of the weaknesses. The flaws, shortcomings, and inadequacies of the data are also theirs. At least, they have taken a significant first step in gathering evidence. But in this ever-globalizing world, we need far better and more comprehensive data to understand differences and similarities across national boundaries.

No doubt, objections can be raised to many of the statistics presented here. But these objections go both ways. For example, American unemployment figures do not include the many young men in prison and are thus understated. In a similar way, Swedish unemployment figures would be higher (and more truthful) if they included many of those who are counted as disabled. (If you believe the raw figures, Swedes are the most disabled people in the industrialized world, with over a fifth of all adults incapable of work.) In America, 0.7% of the population is incarcerated, in Sweden a mere 0.08% (figures from 2005–06). In America, 10.7% of the adult population is disabled (figures from the late 1990s); in Sweden, the figure is twice as high (20.6%). If the United States had Swedish incarceration rates and counted the surplus prisoners as unemployed, the American unemployment rate for 2005 would rise from 5.1% to 5.8%. Alternatively, if we were to assume that Sweden had American levels of disability and counted the other Swedes on disability benefits as unemployed, the Swedish unemployment rate would rise from 7.4% to 17.3%.[26] In point of fact, McKinsey calculates the actual unemployment rate in Sweden to be around 17%.[27] Different nations cook the books in different ways.

Another example: a substantial fraction (ca. 13% in 2005) of American foreign aid goes to two countries in the Middle East: Egypt and Israel. Though it easily disappears in quantitative comparisons, this observation should be part of any accounting of American foreign aid: it is prompted by geopolitical as well as humanitarian motives. Equally, so should the fact that for historical, strategic, and geopolitical reasons, almost two-thirds of British and French foreign aid goes to their former colonies in sub-Saharan Africa. In comparison, 40% of German aid and 25% of American goes to sub-Saharan Africa.[28] A quarter of French aid returns to its source as funds intended to allow recipient nations to pay back loans extended by France in the first place, and the statistically single best predictor of French aid is whether the recipient country is francophone.[29] One could go on picking holes in the available statistics until no trustworthy figures remained. For better or worse, I have accepted the numbers presented by the international organizations as the best we have and worked with them accordingly. At the end of the day, as many mistakes will have been made in one direction as in the other. The overall trend is what will carry conviction. As is so often the case in scholarship, one can have precision or breadth, but not both at the same time.

The comparisons that follow assume that each country is equally interesting and pertinent, whether a large one, like the United States or Germany, or a small one—Denmark, say, or the Netherlands. The comparisons are not, as a statistician would put it, weighted according to the demographic importance of the country. Norway, with fewer than five million inhabitants, does not vanish against the massive bulk of the United States. Of course, when we look for lessons that can be learned from other nations, size is not always irrelevant. What works in tiny, homogeneous Iceland may not be suitable for more fragmented America—or Switzerland, for that matter. But nor is size everything. Just because one country is smaller, or larger, than another does not automatically eliminate the value of drawing comparisons between them. When economists debate the virtues of deregulation, for example, the sizes of the respective economies do not figure prominently in their considerations. Certainly, the intellectual and social policy importance of the Scandinavian nations can best be understood in this way. Were it not for the implicit assumption that these small countries have something to teach the rest of the world, it would be hard to explain their grip on the imaginations of sociologists, political scientists, and public policy makers. Small, distant, and obscure, they nonetheless punch above their weight in social policy discussions. They are taken seriously in their own right and not judged just by their geopolitical clout. I make a similar assumption here. When we seek to identify commonalities and weigh differences, we talk about ways of organizing societies, types of nations, or styles of citizenship, not just about the sheer brawn of demography, GDP, and firepower. Small nations may, in this respect, have as much to contribute as their larger peers.

Before plunging into this book, a final methodological caveat is required: the data assembled here are the latest figures I have been able to find that include both Western Europe and the United States. In most cases, I have examined the immediately preceding annual numbers to ensure that the latest year is not just a statistical blip, but represents a stable value of some duration. The vast majority of numbers presented come from the last decade. Occasionally, I have been forced to rely on slightly older ones. This means that the picture sketched here, though as up-to-date as possible, is nonetheless a snapshot of relations between the score of countries under consideration. It is a picture frozen in time, not an account of an ongoing relationship. However much the two shores of the North Atlantic approximate or are distanced from each other right now, the longer story may be one of moving closer together—or farther apart. I argue that Europe and America are closer now than is commonly thought. But it may be that, nonetheless, they are moving away from each other. While others claim that they are far apart, it may be that they are actually coming closer. I will come back to this question later, rather than getting further involved in matters of method before presenting my findings, but the issue should be kept in mind during what follows.

As I now turn to compare Europe and America, I will speak only of Western Europe as it largely overlaps with the 15 states that made up the EU before its recent expansion. When it is available, I include data from a few nonmembers (Norway, Switzerland, Iceland) since my subject is Western Europe, not the EU as such. Limiting the focus to Western Europe is the fairest approach. Were I to include the new members of the EU as well, Europe and the United States would be even less distinguishable and my argument would be won almost by default. The recently arrived EU nations are not only more likely to agree with the United States on foreign policy than is old Europe. The new Europeans also act more like Americans. They are more religious, more skeptical of an interventionist state, and more laissez-faire in their economic practices. As it expands, the new EU is also becoming more heterogeneous, and in that sense, too, more like America.

ONE
THE
ECONOMY

LET US BEGIN WHERE EVERYTHING STARTS, with the economy and the labor market. This is perhaps where contrasts are thought to be sharpest. America—so the proponents of radical differences across the Atlantic argue—worships at the altar of what West German chancellor Helmut Schmidt once called *Raubtierkapitalismus*, predatory capitalism, where the market sweeps everything before it and the state exerts no restraint. The result is what another German chancellor, Gerhard Schröder, called *amerikanische Verhältnisse*, "American conditions," plucked straight out of a play by Bertolt Brecht: America's labor market is untrammeled and cruel, jobs are insecure and badly paid. Americans live to work, while Europeans work to live. That is the story. But is it true?

America's core ideological belief is often thought to be the predominance of the market and the absence of state regulation. "Everything should and must be

pro-market, pro-business, and pro-shareholder," as Will Hutton, a British col-
umnist, puts it, "a policy platform lubricated by colossal infusions of corporate
cash into America's money-dominated political system...."[1] Hutton stands in
a long line of European critics who have seen nothing but the dominance of
the market in America.[2] There is some truth to the American penchant for
free markets. But the notion that the Atlantic divides capitalism scarlet in
tooth and claw from a more domesticated version in Europe has been overstated. When asked for their preferences, Americans tend to assign the state
less of a role than many—though not all—Europeans. Proportionately fewer
Americans think that the government should redistribute income to amelio-
rate inequalities, or that the government should seek to provide jobs for all, or
reduce working hours. On the other hand, proportionately more Americans
(by a whisker) than Germans and almost exactly as many as the Swedes think
that government should control wages, and more want the government to control prices than Germans. Proportionately more Americans believe that the
government should act to create new jobs than the Swedes, and about as many
as the Germans, Finns, and Swiss. The percentage of Americans that thinks the
state should intervene to provide decent housing is low. But it is greater than
the percentage of Germans and Swiss. And when it comes to government support for new technologies, Americans are more mercantilist than the British,
Italians, Swedes, Dutch, Germans, Danes, Swiss, and even the French. They are
more in favor than the Germans, Swiss, Finns, Danes, and Dutch of government helping industry to grow. On support for declining industries to support
jobs, they back government support proportionately more than the British,
Swiss, Swedes, Norwegians, Dutch, Western Germans, Finns, and Danes.[3] In
other words, Americans are more laissez-faire than Europeans. But they are
not off the scale of statutory intervention. They do, however, seem to prefer
having government play a role in the productive end of things, rather than act-
ing to redistribute the outcome.

Attempts to measure the degree of economic freedom, or what we might
call the reign of the market, place the United States only toward the top of the
European spectrum, below the UK and Switzerland. But such comparative ex-
aminations also show a relatively narrow span between the least free economy
(Greece) and the most (Switzerland) (figure 1). The American state directly
controls the economy only lightly by European standards. By the OECD's definition of public ownership, the United States comes in lower than any of our
other nations, which is to say somewhat under the UK and Denmark. But it
is only fractionally further from the European mean (2.2 standard deviations)

[margin note, handwritten] America in certain cases actually supports gov't intervention more than many European countries

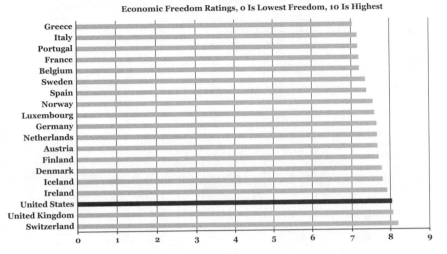

1. Economic Freedom

Economic Freedom Ratings, 0 Is Lowest Freedom, 10 Is Highest

than the high extreme, Italy (2.09 standard deviations).[4] And if one looks at the OECD's quantification for state control, the United States ranks above Iceland and closer to the European mean (0.57 standard deviations below) than Italy (1.8 standard deviations above) (figure 2).The span within Europe itself is thus greater than that between the United States and Europe. (Standard deviations allow us to measure how dispersed a set of data is, and thus to express how far one data point is from the average relative to the rest of the data.)

Switching from industry to real estate, the American state owns about 30% of all land in the nation. As a landowner, it thus stands as close to the sparsely populated Nordic countries, Sweden, Norway, and Finland, where the state owns almost half of all land, as it does to other European countries, where far less land is held publicly (figure 3). This outcome derives not just from the United States being a late-settled nation. Yes, in Australia and New Zealand, Crown ownership of land is also high (over half and about a third of total land, respectively). But no comparable public ownership of land seems to exist in South America, whose nations were settled under broadly similar circumstances. High public ownership of land in the United States is one of the reasons, as we will see, why America has a comparatively generous percentage of its territory set aside as nature reserves. It is a direct statutory intervention into what would otherwise have been private property to achieve a public good, and thus in spirit similar to Europe's occasional nationalization of industries. Government land ownership was how much of higher education was

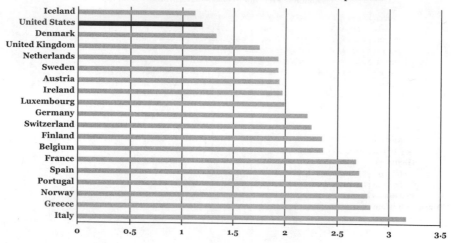

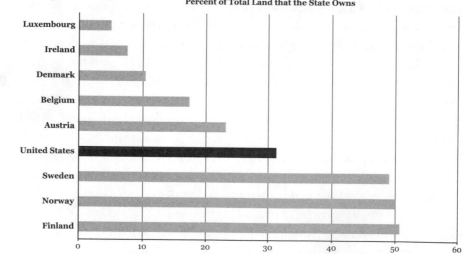

financed in the United States, including arguably the best public university in
the world, UC Berkeley. It was also how the Americans built their railroads in
the nineteenth century. Ten percent of the total public territory was used to
finance four transcontinental rail lines. In total, to finance railroads, government at various levels staked some 180 million acres, an area slightly larger
than the combined size of Germany, the UK, Austria, and the Netherlands.
This pushed government participation in railway building in the United States
to higher proportionate levels than even in Prussia.[5]

In some respects, the World Bank's rankings of the ease of doing business put America highish compared with European nations. Among the
ones under the glass here, it is the easiest country to start a business in, after
Ireland, and to employ workers, and it is the best at protecting creditors.[6] On
the other hand, in terms of dealing with licenses, it is bested by Denmark,
Iceland, Sweden, Germany, and France. Registering property is easier in
Iceland, Norway, and Sweden. Austria, Finland, Luxembourg, and Iceland
are less troublesome places to enforce contracts. Free trade is more widely
practiced in Norway, Finland, Sweden, Germany, Iceland, Austria, and the
Netherlands. And the difficulties of paying taxes and closing a business put
the United States toward the bottom of the European spectrum for business-
friendliness. Indeed, in the amount of time businesses have to spend prepar-
ing and paying their taxes, the only European countries more onerously bu-
reaucratic are Portugal and Italy.[7]

An exhaustive study of similar topics came to the same conclusion: although labor is lightly protected in the United States, for other forms of
economic regulation, the UK and often Ireland, and sometimes Denmark,
score even lower.[8] American business executives claim to spend more time
dealing with red tape than their colleagues in Finland, Sweden, Iceland,
Luxembourg, Ireland, Belgium, Switzerland, Austria, the UK, Italy, Norway,
Spain, and France.[9] America's regulatory style, sometimes described as "adversarial legalism," is characterized by dispersed and decentralized authorities, complex legal rules, and heavy participation of courts and lawyers. The
impositions set by this regulatory apparatus are similar to those found in
Europe. But administrative frictions generated by the American system
and its complexity are often much higher.[10] All in all, it is fair to conclude
that the United States is not quite the streamlined, market-slavish, efficient
entrepreneurial fantasy of the stereotypes. Nor, conversely, that Europe is
the feather-bedded, hyperregulated, business-hostile, sclerotic mess that
American conservatives imagine.

When the World Bank turns its attention to trade logistics (the ability of countries to connect firms, suppliers, and consumers to global supply chains in an effective manner), which presumably is a practical proxy of market thinking, Singapore unsurprisingly tops the heap. More unexpectedly, Germany, the UK, the Netherlands, Sweden, Switzerland, Ireland, Belgium, and Denmark, and even Austria, all rank higher than the United States. Only Finland, Norway, France, Italy, Spain, Portugal, Luxembourg, and Greece are less attuned to international competitiveness.[11] A Pew Research Center report on attitudes to globalization in 2007 found that, although 70% of Americans support free markets, an even higher percentage of Britons, Italians, and Swedes do. Proportionately fewer Americans back expanding international trade than the citizens of all the European nations surveyed.[12] Fewer Americans consider free trade an advantage than Europeans do, except those from Germany, Austria, Norway, France, and Finland. More favor limiting the import of foreign products to protect the national economy than anyone but the Portuguese.[13] Fewer Americans have confidence in business and industry than the Irish, the Norwegians, Swedes, Spaniards, and Danes.[14] In sum, the United States checks in somewhere at the middle of the European pack, even when it comes to something that we are asked to consider as quintessentially and exclusively American as the belief in free trade and free markets. "Devotion to the free market has never been particularly strong in American politics," John Gray, the English political philosopher, notes, "even on the Right. The idea that it is peculiarly American is belied by American history, in which protectionism and populism have been more enduring traditions, and the power of government has been vigorously used to deal with economic crises."[15]

In America, the labor market is less regulated than in many European nations, at least outside the English-speaking fringe. But even here there are surprises. Labor is lightly regulated, though only, according to one attempt to quantify matters, a bit less so than in Denmark and the UK (figure 4). In Denmark, in turn, regulation is approximately one-third as onerous as in Portugal. It is hard to quantify such matters—or even to know what is true. Danish, Icelandic, and Swiss bosses, for example, believe that they have more flexibility in hiring and firing than their American colleagues.[16] Countries that, on paper, are flexible may have strict de facto regulation, imposed through union strength, say. Conversely, highly regulated countries may differ significantly in how strictly measures are enforced. The Portuguese labor market, for example, though seemingly akin to the Spanish, has actually been much

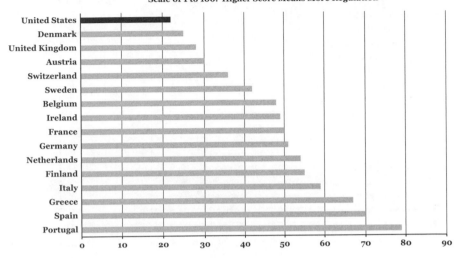

4. Labor Regulation

Scale of 1 to 100. Higher Score Means More Regulation

more flexible and blessed accordingly with lower unemployment.[17] One system of labor regulation (in the United States and the UK, for example) may permit workers to be easily fired, while another (Germany) allows employers significant leeway in reassigning workers to new tasks, though they can be made redundant only with difficulty. Hours of work, rather than the number of workers, can be adjusted. Core workers can be retained, even in unregulated systems, while peripheral ones are fired. Labor regulations are more complicated and multifarious than commonly appreciated.

When attempts are made to quantify regulation of the labor market, the difference between the United States and the European extremes pales in comparison to the breadth of the internal European spectrum itself. "[V]ariation in the institutional combination of labour market regulation is higher within Europe than between European and non-European countries," as one of the best surveys of the subject puts it.[18] American bosses can fire workers more easily than their European counterparts, though again, the difference between the United States and the low end of the European spectrum is narrower than between the low and the high end of Europe—with a ratio of over eight to one between Portugal and the UK (figure 5). As for regulations on hiring, the United States is well within the European spectrum, with Austria, Belgium, Switzerland, Denmark, and the UK equally good or bad, depending on your point of view (figure 6).

5. Firing Flexibility

Scale of 1 to 100. The Higher the Index, the More Firing Is Regulated

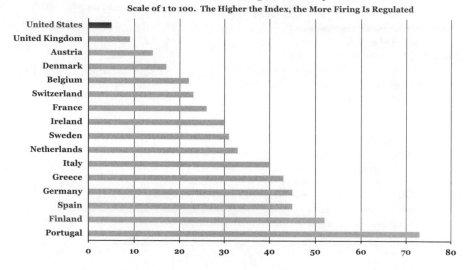

6. Hiring Flexibility

Scale of 1 to 100. The Higher the Index, the More Hiring Is Regulated

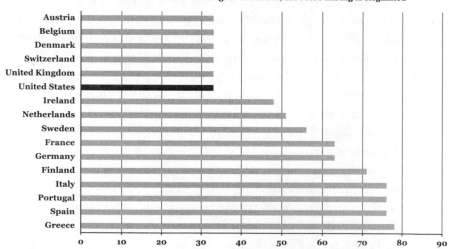

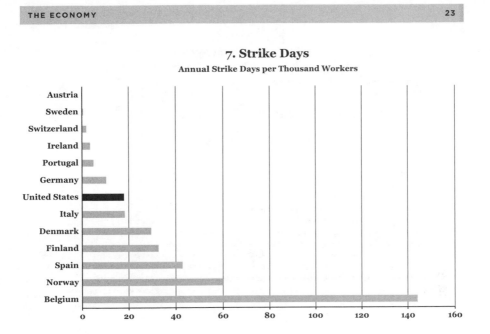

7. Strike Days

Annual Strike Days per Thousand Workers

Union membership is low in the United States, but within the European span, and higher than in France. Proportionately more American workers report being active in a labor union than is true in France, Italy, Spain, Switzerland, and Germany.[19] Labor relations in America are not scarred by many strikes (figure 7). Proportional to its labor market, Belgium lost over six times as many days in 2003 and 2004 to strikes, and even Norway, exemplar of consensus, sacrificed well over three times as many. Collective bargaining, on the other hand, covers a much higher proportion of workers in Europe than America. A mere 14% of U.S. workers were thus included in 2000, while in the UK, with the lowest rates in Europe, the figure was over twice that. Austria, with the highest numbers, was thrice the English rate.[20]

"Surely civilization depends on the idea of public space and a duty and responsibility to each other," argues a Tory tabloid, the *Daily Mail*. "The American Dream depends on the very opposite: winner takes all."[21] And yet, American workers have managed to wrest reasonable compensation from the capitalist system. Measured as a percentage of GDP, they are paid better than any European workers except the Swiss (figure 8). Accounting for differences in purchasing power, American employees are beaten only by the Luxembourgeois.[22] If we look at average earnings of production workers, things are more sober. In purchasing power equivalents, the average American makes more than average workers everywhere in Europe other than Germany,

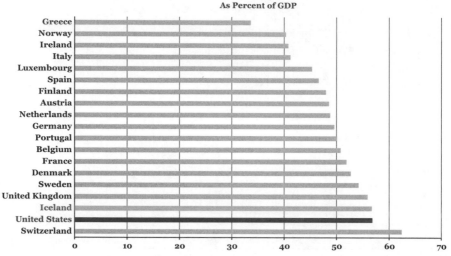

8. Wages
As Percent of GDP

Norway, Switzerland, the UK, and Luxembourg—in other words, Americans are toward the top of the European scale.[23]

If you look solely at the federal standard, minimum wages in the United States are at the low middle of the European pack. In Greece, Portugal, and Spain, the worst-paid workers receive lower wages (figure 9). These sums are adjusted for purchasing power so that they account for differences in cost of living. Shown here are the figures for 2005, when the U.S. federal minimum wage was $5.15 per hour. In July 2009, however, it will have risen 40% to $7.25. If we look instead at the state minimum wages in the United States, the picture improves. Well over half the states have higher minimums than the federal standard, and these bear comparison with Europe (figure 10). Indeed, the minimum wages of Washington, Oregon, Connecticut, and Vermont are higher than any European equivalent for which we have figures, other than Luxembourg's. Moreover, few American workers are paid minimum wages in the first place. Only 1.4% of American employees made do with minimum wages in 2004, compared with 15% of the French and 5% of the Portuguese (figure 11). True, America has a higher percentage of workers who make do on a relative definition of low wages (below 65% of median earnings) than in any Western European nation.[24] This follows from the broader spectrum of wage inequality found in the United States. But, to judge by the comparatively few American workers on the minimum wage, that is not the same thing as being at rock bottom. We will return to the question of relative and absolute poverty.

9. Minimum Wages

Real Hourly Minimum Wages in US $ PPP

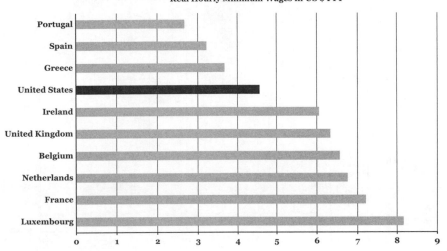

10. State Minimum Wages

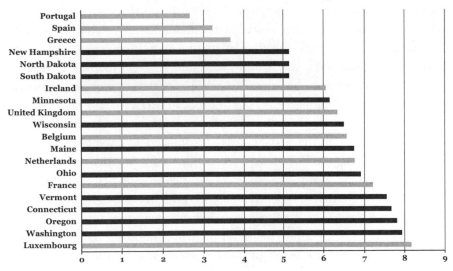

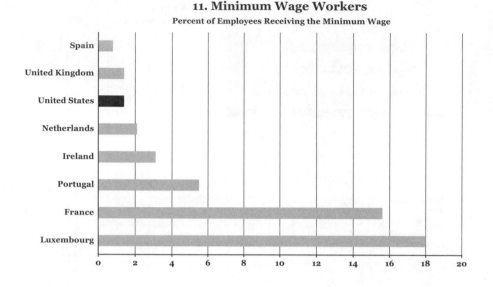

11. Minimum Wage Workers

Percent of Employees Receiving the Minimum Wage

Nor are Americans hired only in part-time McJobs. In fact, fewer Americans work part-time than workers in most European countries (figure 12). Only Finland, Portugal, Spain, and Greece have fewer. (And even McDonald's and Starbucks offer fringe benefits—health insurance and the like.) According to the OECD's figures, permanent employment—work contracts of indefinite duration—is more the rule in the United States than in any Western European nation other than Ireland.[25] The average length of Americans' job tenure (7.4 years) is low by European standards, but only six months shorter than the Danes' and five months shorter than the British.[26] At the top of the labor market, American CEOs keep their jobs longer than their European peers, for about nine years.[27] Job creation and job destruction are much the same in the United States as in several European countries, about equal to the Italian and lower than the French and Portuguese figures.[28] Serious work accidents in America's untrammeled capitalist system are comparable to European figures. The percentage of workers unfortunate enough to be killed on the job is higher in Belgium, Spain, Italy, Greece, and Austria. The Portuguese rate is more than twice as high (figure 13). In terms of years of life lost to injury for the whole population, the U.S. results are not as good, but still better than those for Finland and Luxembourg, the same as Iceland's, and only a notch worse than France's.[29]

In terms of leisure, Americans fare badly. Workers in the United States are not guaranteed a minimum vacation time by law. And their holidays are shorter

12. Part-Time Employment
As Percent of Total Employment

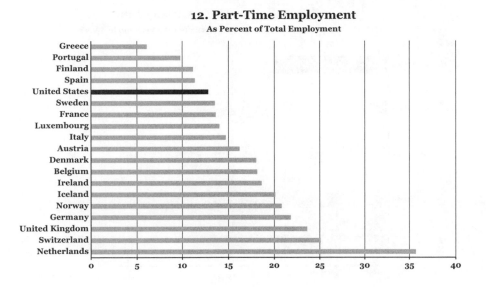

13. Fatal Work Injuries
Rate of Fatal Injuries per 100,000 Workers Employed or Insured

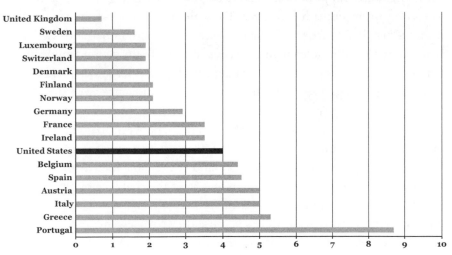

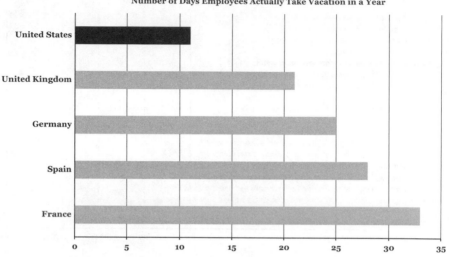

14. Vacation Time Actually Taken

Number of Days Employees Actually Take Vacation in a Year

than in Europe, averaging some 10 days annually. That compares unfavorably to 20 in the UK, and even higher figures elsewhere (figure 14). But the number of national holidays Americans are entitled to is comparable (figure 15). Five nations have as many (10), nine have fewer, three have more. Nonetheless, despite the myth of the always-working American, the actual average time put in at the job is only in the upper half of a very flat scale. That holds if you measure it by minutes per day, where the Germans work the same number and the Danes work more.[30] And it holds if you measure it as the hours worked annually per person, where in 2006 the Finns, Italians, Portuguese, Icelanders, and Greeks worked longer (figure 16). Despite its statistical omniscience, even the OECD cannot quite manage consistent figures, so if you look instead at average hours actually worked in 2006, whatever the difference between that and the previous figure may be, the Americans come in high, below only those perennially hardest working Europeans, the Greeks, and at the same level as the Italians.[31] *La dolce vita*, indeed. The fewer hours put in at the coal face by Europeans is due, in some measure (about one-third), to a preference for leisure. But, to a greater extent, Europeans work less because they have fewer choices: many are unemployed or have been slipped off into early retirement. As one observer puts it, the unemployed 30-year old Italian male who sits at home expecting his mother to cook and wash for him is not expressing his desire for leisure. He (and his mother) are victims of a sclerotic labor (and housing) market.[32]

15. Public Holidays
Days per Year

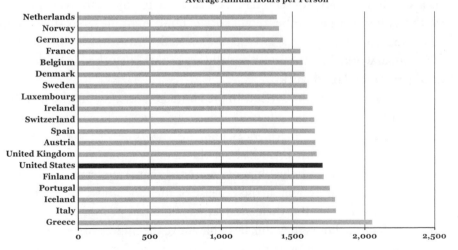

16. Working Time
Average Annual Hours per Person

If we look at time diary studies, Americans work more on weekends than Germans and the Dutch, but the Italians do so even more. Since the Germans and Italians (among the countries looked at in this particular study) work more in household production than do Americans, their total work hours, though still lower than the Americans', are less distinct than if one looks just at formal working hours.[33] The German lawyer, in other words, has neither maids nor gardeners. Instead, his wife cleans their house and irons his shirts, while he mows the lawn and washes the car. Immigration, both legal and not, has made more and cheaper labor available in Europe, and middle-class Europeans today use hired-in services much more than did their parents. But to judge by these latest and most sophisticated numbers, a difference still persists. Hired help remains comparatively scarce and expensive in Europe. Labor taxes prevent people from working longer at what they were trained to do while employing someone else to do the housework. Not surprisingly, the tradeoff between market and household work affects women especially. If we count both forms of activity together, figures from the 1990s suggest that Europeans and Americans worked almost the same number of hours per week (around 60 in all cases), with a slight edge to the Americans. American men did a little more housework (two hours more) than their European peers, but the big difference was found among the women. Female Europeans on average did almost 10 hours more household labor weekly than American women, who in turn shifted a large number (eight) of the hours of home labor they saved to the market instead.[34] Yes, as is so often noted, Europeans choose leisure over formal work. But one could equally argue that they choose household drudgery over salaried work.

And who are the Stakhanovites? In the United States, they are the wealthy. Men in the top income quintile work, on average, over 20 hours a week more than those at the bottom. America's poor men work less than the poor in Sweden, France, and Switzerland, about the same as those in Germany, and only half as much as in Italy.[35] It is often argued that Americans' high GDP output per worker is bought at the expense of the long hours they put in at the job.[36] That may be. But their productivity, in terms of what they put out during each of the hours they toil, lies a bit above the middle of the European spectrum (figure 17). Among others, the Germans, the Danes, and the Swedes are less efficient workers, and the French and the Dutch are about the same. And that is despite the discovery by a recent survey that the typical American

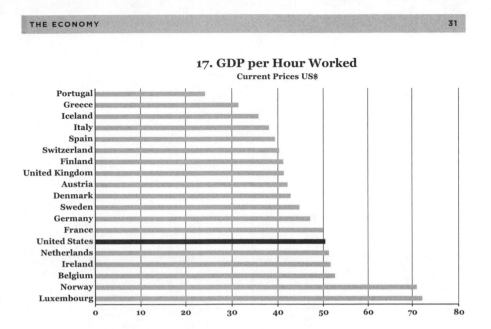

17. GDP per Hour Worked
Current Prices US$

worker spends over two hours a day of work time doing other things than working, mainly Web surfing, writing personal e-mails, socializing, and spacing out.[37] Perhaps unsurprisingly, when surveyed about the stress of their jobs, proportionately fewer Americans fussed than any Europeans other than the Irish, Spaniards, Portuguese, Danes, and Swiss.[38] And, in any case, Americans do not appear to be natural Stakhanovites. Fewer of them agreed strongly with the proposition that work should come first, even at the expense of spare time, than any Europeans other than the Swedes, and more disagreed than anyone.[39]

So what are Americans doing if they are not vacationing, but also not working? We do not know, but their pace of life is quite leisurely, compared with Europeans'. One attempt to quantify this used various measures, like the speed at which the post office sold stamps and the accuracy of clocks in banks. It concluded that only in easygoing (but longer-working) Greece was the pace of life more relaxed than in the United States (figure 18). Another attempt measured the average pace of pedestrians in major cities: New York was less hectic than Stockholm and London, though more rushed than Berlin, Dublin, Madrid, and Copenhagen (figure 19). Whatever the frailty of such attempts to attach numbers to a slippery concept, these studies at least agree in broad terms that Americans are less harried than many Europeans. Vacationing may not be the only thing that matters.

18. Pace of Life
From Slower to Faster

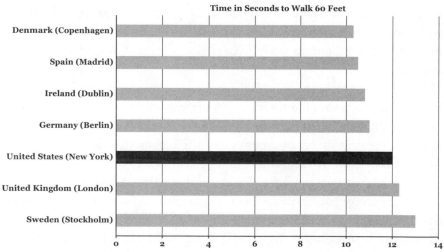

19. Pace of Life
Time in Seconds to Walk 60 Feet

And if we broaden our horizons to look beyond mere leisure to true happiness, here, too, the results are possibly unexpected. Happiness, which used to be the province largely of philosophers or psychologists, has increasingly been tackled by economists, perhaps in the hope of dispelling the aura of dismalness attached to their discipline. Until recently, the scholarly consensus (associated with the work of Richard Easterlin) has been that there may be an overall correlation between prosperity and happiness: wealthy nations tend to be happier than impoverished ones, and the rich within countries more content than the poor. But equally, it appears that above a certain threshold of prosperity (about $15,000 GDP per capita), absolute material well-being no longer plays an important role, aspirations increase, and relative position in the hierarchy of affluence now determines subjective well-being. This pessimistic conclusion—which implies that public policy is powerless to deliver lasting increases in happiness—has now been challenged by economists who claim that greater absolute prosperity, measured both within and between nations, in fact produces greater satisfaction and happiness.[40] That has not prevented cultural critics from finding a worm in the apple. A surfeit of prosperity, they caution, may make us miserable. They argue that the successful capitalist market, with its ever-growing array of choice, far from making us content and satiated, leaves us anxious and unsatisfied.[41]

If Americans are not only wealthier than most others in the developed world, but also living beyond their means, going into debt to consume more than is possible on their already ample incomes, are they among the most miserable? Alas for the pessimists, the answer is decidedly not. Whether rightly or not, they are content with their lot. According to the World Database of Happiness, based at Erasmus University in Rotterdam, only the Danes are happier, while the Swedes, Dutch, Luxembourgeois, and Norwegians are approximately as content. All other Europeans are less serene, and the Portuguese are the gloomiest of all.[42] Some confirmation of the accuracy of this assessment can be found in survey data demonstrating that, while about 6% of Americans think that the world is wholly evil, a full quarter of the Portuguese do. Conversely, while about 13% of Americans regard the world as entirely good, only 2% of the Portuguese have an equally sunny outlook. Four times as many Portuguese (13.2%, the highest number in Europe) as Americans are existential pessimists, convinced that life serves no purpose.[43] More Americans feel that they have a great deal of freedom of choice and control than any Europeans other than the Swiss, with the Swedes neck and

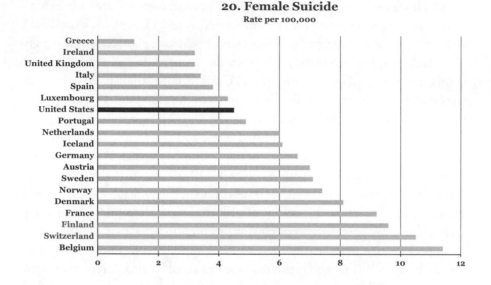

20. Female Suicide
Rate per 100,000

neck.[44] That American optimism is not just hot air is suggested by comparative suicide rates. Americans are less prone than most Europeans to kill themselves. If we look at the rates for women, only the Greeks, British, Italians,
Spanish, and Luxembourgeois do themselves in less often. The Belgians and
the Swiss, at the other end of the spectrum, commit suicide well over twice
as often. Mercifully, the Portuguese appear unwilling to back their gloomy
outlook with action (figure 20). Suicide rates for men are much higher than
for women in all our countries, but the hierarchy among nations remains
virtually the same.

Returning to the everyday realities of economics, the American tax system
is comparable to its European equivalents, with one exception: its overall tax
take is low, though the same rate as the Greek. But that is just if we measure it
as a percentage of GDP. If, instead, we look at the actual sums the American
state collects per citizen, then it does better than seven of our nations, including Switzerland, the UK, and Germany (figure 21). Rates of U.S. income tax,
which is usually considered the single most important levy, are at the middle
of the European spectrum, measured as a percentage of GDP. They are higher
than those in France, the Netherlands, Spain, Germany, Portugal, and Greece
(figure 22). The progressivity of taxes in America is quite high by European
standards. Income taxes are more progressive in America than in the Nordic
nations and in four of our other countries (figure 23). In 2005, the richest 10%

21. Total Tax Revenue
Per Capita (PPP)

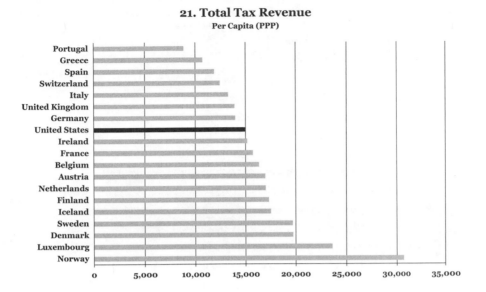

22. Income Tax
Taxes on Income and Profits, % of GDP

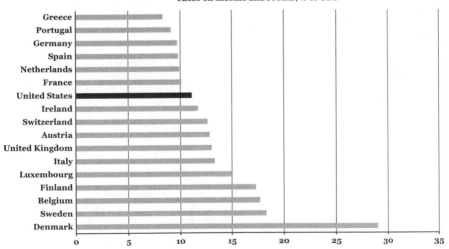

23. Income Tax Progressivity
Kakwani Index

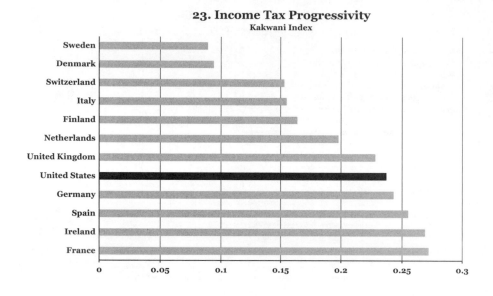

24. Taxation of the Wealthy
Share of Taxes Paid by the Richest 10%

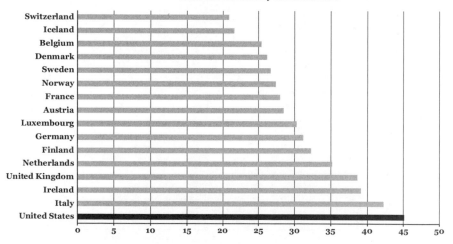

25. Property Tax

Property Tax Revenue (% of GDP)

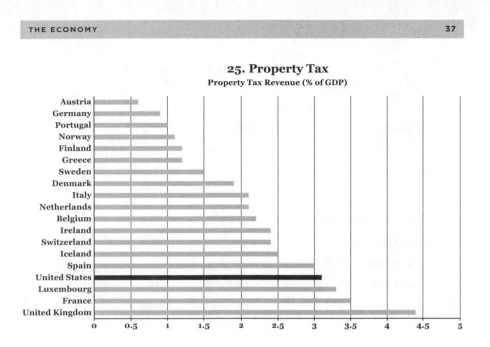

of Americans paid a larger share of total taxes than any of their European peers (figure 24). The United States relies less on regressive consumption taxes, which hit the poor hardest, than any Western European country and more on the income tax than any but Denmark, Iceland and, by the tiniest of margins, Switzerland.[45]

One difference between the United States and the high-tax nations of northern Europe is this: the American poor are largely exempted from taxes, indeed often given state monies via tax credits, while their Scandinavian peers are granted social benefits, but are taxed on income like everyone else. Hence, the U.S. tax system is at once less demanding and more progressive than the Continental European, while at the same time social benefits are stingier. As a rule of thumb, as income taxes are levied on an ever-larger swath of earners and as their rate increases, their progressivity has to decline. Robin Hood may have helped the poor of Sherwood Forest by taking from the rich. But if governments seek to aid the majority of their citizens in modern circumstances of comparatively equal income distribution, they cannot rely only on what they extract from the best-off. Most redistribution takes place via social spending, largely paid for by taxing the same groups that receive the bulk of benefits.

Property taxes, measured as a percentage of GDP, are higher in the United States than anywhere in Europe other than France, Luxembourg, and the UK (figure 25). In a nation with a relatively high level of property ownership, this

26. Home Ownership
Percent of Households

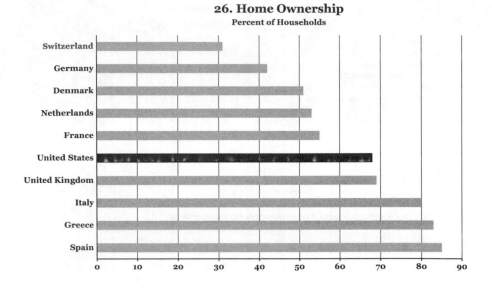

27. Corporate Taxes
Effective Tax Rates on Corporate Capital in %

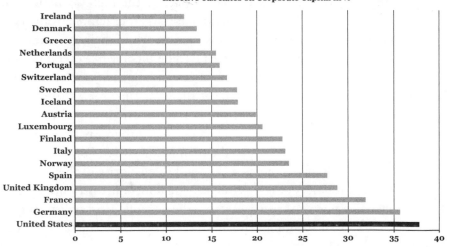

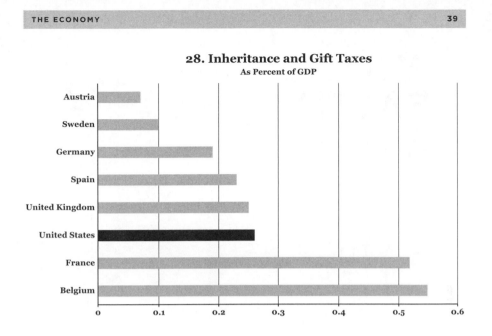

28. Inheritance and Gift Taxes
As Percent of GDP

means that most Americans, but especially the more well-off, again pay unexpectedly high taxes (figure 26). U.S. corporate taxes are middle of the pack if measured as a percentage of GDP, but higher than in any European country if judged by their average effective rate (figure 27). American inheritance and gift taxes are middle of the European spectrum, higher, for example, than in Austria, Germany, Spain, and the UK (figure 28). And in 2004, Sweden passed what in the United States would count as a right-wing reform, and abolished inheritance and gift taxes altogether.

TWO
HEALTH
CARE

THE U.S. ECONOMY DOES DIFFER from Europe's: a less regulated labor market, but also an economy that is more hemmed in than might be expected. By European standards, America has hardish-working people, a state that collects fewer tax dollars, and workers who are paid well even if their holidays are short. In social policy, the contrasts are more moderate. Europeans commonly believe that the United States simply has no social policy—no social security, no unemployment benefits, no state pensions, and no assistance for the poor. As Jean-François Revel, the political philosopher and *académicien*, summed up French criticism, the United States shows "not the slightest bit of social solidarity."[1] Will Hutton similarly assures us that "The structures that support ordinary peoples' lives—free health care, quality education, guarantees of reasonable living standards in old age, sickness or unemployment, housing for the disadvantaged—that Europeans take for granted are conspicuous by their absence."[2]

And, in fact, the United States is the only developed nation, unless one counts South Africa, without some form of national health insurance, which is to say a system of requiring all its citizens to be insured in one way or another. This lack of universal health insurance is the one fact that every would-be comparativist working across the Atlantic knows, and the first one to be hoisted as the battle is engaged. One of the first attempts to quantify and rank health care performance, by the World Health Organization in 2000, gave the American system its due. Overall, it came in below any of our comparison countries, three notches under Denmark. In various specific aspects of health policy, it did better. For disability-adjusted life expectancy, it came in above Ireland, Denmark, and Portugal; on the responsiveness of the health system, it ranked first; on a composite measure of various indicators summed up as "overall health system attainment," it ranked above seven Western European countries. Even on the measure of "fairness of financial contribution to health systems," where we might have expected an abysmal rating, the United States squeaked in above Portugal. That is, of course, damning with faint praise, especially given that in this particular aspect of the ranking—a well-meaning but other-worldly attempt by international bureaucrats to rake the entire globe over the teeth of one comb—Colombia came in first, outpacing its close rivals, Luxembourg and Belgium, while Libya beat out Sweden.[3]

One of the most corrosive critiques, by the Commonwealth Fund, gives the U.S. system very bad marks in comparison to an eccentric group of peer nations (the English-speaking world plus Germany). Interestingly, from the vantage of the American discussion over how to reform health care, the Canadian system—often held up as the socialized foil to America's market-driven approach—is as awful, though the Canadians can console themselves that they pay about half as much for equally dismal results.[4] What follows is not intended to defend America's inequitable system, nor to deny that health insurance reform is urgently needed. It is, rather, to look at whatever figures exist and to ask what the outcome is of the vast sums that America spends on health care. The U.S. system, it turns out, is neither equitable nor efficient. But nor is it entirely ineffective.

Although having no national health insurance, America spends large amounts of money on health care. Even if we look only at *government* spending per capita, the United States ranks comfortably within the span of European nations. Indeed, only Iceland, Norway, and Luxembourg surpass it (figure 29). America's Medicaid and Medicare organizations, the governmental health care systems for the poorest citizens and for all elderly, together form the largest publicly financed health system in the world. It comes as no surprise that, in terms of private spending

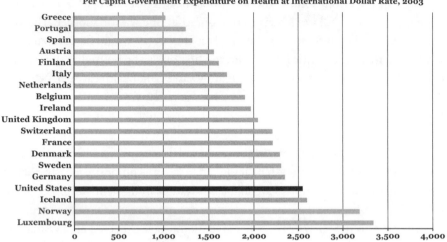

29. Governmental Medical Spending
Per Capita Government Expenditure on Health at International Dollar Rate, 2003

per capita, the United States outstrips Europe. And since that is not instead of public spending, but in addition to it, total health outlays put the United States in the lead, shadowed at some distance by Norway, Switzerland, and Luxembourg (figure 30). On average, European countries spend about half of what the United States does on health care. American spending on drugs, in contrast, is not as off the scale as these figures might suggest. Measured as a percent of GDP, Americans spend less on pharmaceuticals than the Italians, Portuguese, and French.[5]

What does the United States get for its style of health care expenditure—heavy and unequally distributed? First, American health care administration is ponderous, but not top-heavy without compare. It lags in adopting computerized record-keeping, and its fragmented structure generates needless paperwork. But the percentage spent on administration and insurance (7.5%) is only moderately greater than in France (6.9%).[6] Second, for its outlays, the United States gets relatively decent infrastructure. The density of physicians is lower than Western Europe, a fraction below the UK, and comparable to Luxembourg, Ireland, and Finland.[7] The number of hospitals in America is also in the bottom half of the European spectrum, with Denmark, Sweden, the Netherlands, Spain, and Portugal ranking lower (figure 31). The number of hospital beds per capita is low, but within the European spectrum. Sweden has even fewer.[8] Medical technology, however, is well-supplied. The number of MRI units and CT scanners per capita in America is second to none—well over twice the OECD average for the former.[9] Sophisticated procedures are

30. Total Medical Spending
Per Capita Total Expenditure on Health at International Dollar Rate, 2003

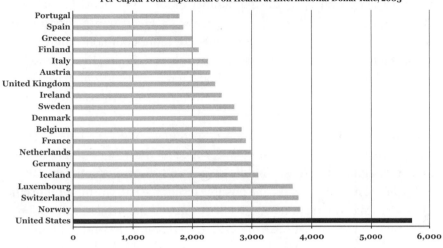

31. Hospitals
Per 100,000 Population

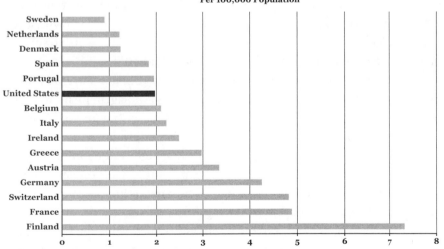

routine. More cardiovascular operations are performed in America per capita than anywhere in Europe, and the number of kidney patients in dialysis or with transplants is equally off the European scale. Heart transplants are more routine only in Belgium, liver transplants are more common only in Spain and Belgium, and bone marrow transplants only in Belgium, France, and Italy, though for lung transplants the United States is merely middle of the European pack. Perhaps it is fitting that only Italian women give birth via Caesarian section more often than their American sisters.[10]

But what does this style of health care spending not get the United States? The fundamental unfairness, of course, concerns the 15% of citizens—most often from among the lower-middle classes and disproportionately minorities—who are not covered. As one possible result, the nation's infant mortality rate is high. Six American newborns per thousand die, while in the poorest-performing European nations (the UK, Luxembourg, Ireland, and Austria) only five babies per thousand are lost (figure 32). No doubt, high rates of teenage pregnancy in America and the social problems faced by many young and especially minority mothers are part of the story. But it is hard to believe that the lack of health insurance and, more generally, unequally distributed medical resources are not another part. Some investment in free prenatal care might give dramatically improved results. If infancy is perilous in the United States, the next four years are not good either, but mortality from ages one to five is below levels in Portugal, Ireland, and Belgium, and only fractionally above that of Denmark and Norway.[11] Infant mortality, combined with a very high homicide rate, help explain why the United States has worse results for premature mortality than any Western European nation.[12]

In terms of life expectancy, however, the United States stays within the European spectrum for both sexes. Finnish, Irish, and Belgian men can expect to die at the same age (75), the Portuguese a year earlier (figure 33). Danes die on average as early as Americans, even though they enjoy universal health care. Since calculations of life expectancies at birth are affected by infant mortality, the picture changes if we look at life expectancies later on, at 65 for example. At that age, American men can expect to live as long as or longer (16.8 years) than their peers in the UK, Portugal, Spain, Norway, the Netherlands, Luxembourg, Italy, Ireland, Greece, Germany, Finland, Denmark, Belgium, and Austria.[13] If we look at other figures, the picture is also more differentiated than what is revealed by simple figures on life expectancy at birth. Healthy life expectancy at birth for American women is 71.3 years, 8.5 years less than their gross life expectancy, which takes no account of years lost to disability. Dutch women lose the same number of years to ill health and disability, Danish

32. Infant Mortality
Per 1,000 Live Births

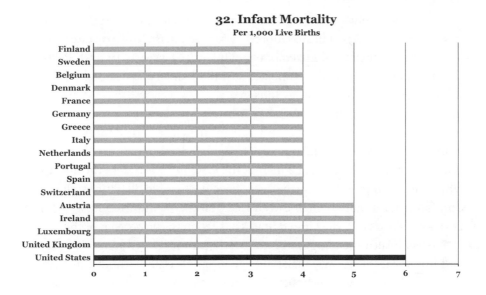

33. Male Life Expectancy
Average Age at Death

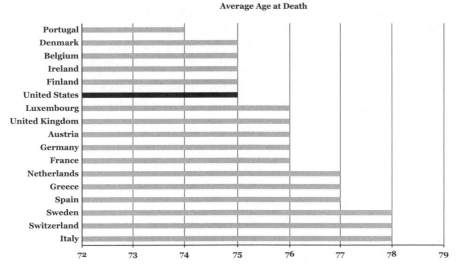

women only a month and a half less. French, Austrian, and Portuguese women lose more years.[14] Age-adjusted mortality for men in the United States is lower than in the Netherlands, Luxembourg, Finland, Denmark, Ireland, Portugal, and Belgium.[15] Measured in terms of so-called amenable deaths (deaths due to treatable conditions) things look worse, however, and have deteriorated in recent years. Amenable mortality in the United States accounts for a bit less than a quarter of all deaths under 75 in men, and a third for women. Ten years ago, in 1997–98, the American amenable death rate for men was lower than that in Ireland, Portugal, Finland, the UK, and Austria. In the meantime, while the death rates from such causes have declined in all nations, they have done so faster in Europe than the United States. The most recent study, from 2002–03, shows that the United States has fallen to the bottom of the pack.[16]

Not all health spending translates neatly into increased longevity. Cornea and hip replacements may make old age more pleasant without extending it. As we shall see below, health spending outcomes are not exhausted by comparative ages of death. That American hospital stays tend to be short is harder to evaluate. Is this the heartlessness of the market? Or is it efficiency and a desire not to institutionalize patients needlessly? That all the Scandinavian countries and France rank even lower gives hope that the latter is true. Americans seldom go to the doctor (on average four times a year), and no doubt the many who are not insured pushes that figure down. But the Swiss and the Swedes are even less frequent visitors. Americans go to the dentist more often than the British and the Luxembourgeois. Their use of hospitals is low on the European scale, but above that of the Dutch, Spaniards, Irish, and Portuguese.[17]

For other aspects of health care, the contrasts across the Atlantic are less dramatic, indeed often nonexistent. American vaccination figures are comparable to those in Europe, whether for diphtheria, tetanus, pertussis, hepatitis, or measles. All results place the United States in the European middle range.[18] Everyone knows that Americans are fatter than Europeans. The numbers collected by the International Association for the Study of Obesity show that an additional 10% of American men are obese compared to the plumpest European nations— Austria, the UK, and Germany (figure 34). But how long will this front-runner status hold? Looking at the figures on those who may become tomorrow's obese, namely the overweight, we find that there are proportionately more overweight Europeans than Americans. Indeed, the only nation with a lower percentage of overweight men (i.e., those with a BMI between 25 and 30) than the United States is France (figure 35). Possibly, there is no straight march through the ranks from the overweight to the obese. Historical statistics suggest otherwise. Take

34. Adult Male Obesity
Percent with Body Mass Index of 30 or More

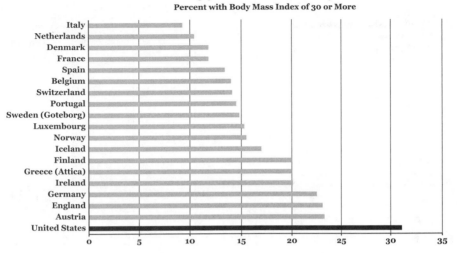

35. Overweight But Not Obese Men
Percent with Body Mass Index between 25 and 29.9

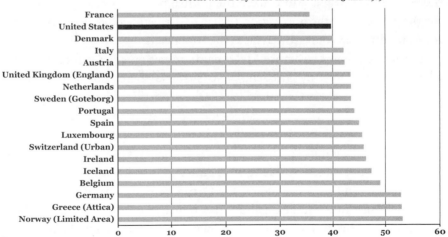

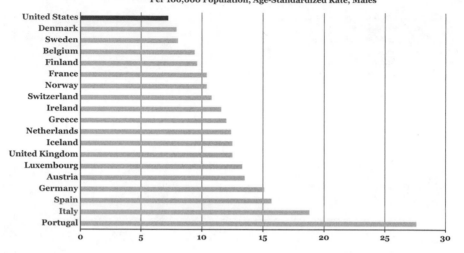

36. Stomach Cancer Incidence
Per 100,000 Population, Age-Standardized Rate, Males

the Swedish case. The incidence of overweight adults has risen from 31% in the 1980s to 40% in the late 1990s, peaking at 44% in 2002. Concurrently, the number of obese adults in the population has risen from 5% through the early 1980s to 10% in 2002, the latest year of this particular series.[19] Perhaps these growing numbers—doubling in two decades—of the obese are recruited directly from those of normal weight. More likely, the normal become overweight, the overweight, obese. If so, the implication is that—barring major changes in habit— the Europeans may soon grow as fat as the Americans.

The United States has more McDonald's restaurants per capita than anywhere else, followed by Sweden.[20] No surprise there. But if that makes Americans fat, it doesn't seem to have other, equally serious consequences, like stomach cancer. The American incidence for men, in age-adjusted terms for proper comparability, is the lowest of our group and about one quarter of the highest, found in Portugal (figure 36). Diabetes is a disease associated with obesity. But mortality due to it in America is well within the European norm, coming in below the figures for Denmark, Italy, and Portugal (figure 37). Americans' intake of sugar per capita is high by European standards, about 17% more than the closest competitors, Switzerland and Denmark. Their consumption of fat, however, falls within the European spectrum, below that of Switzerland, Spain, France, Belgium, Austria, and Italy.[21]

Nor do European and American eating habits differ much in the aggregate. The total per capita caloric supply in America is a tad above that of Italy, Greece, and Portugal (figure 38). Americans eat less fish than the Scandinavians

37. Diabetes Mortality
Diabetes Mellitus Deaths per 100,000 Population

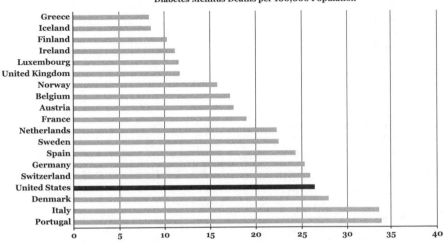

38. Calorie Supply
Per Capita (Kilocalories/Person/Day)

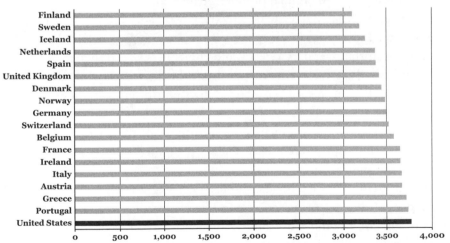

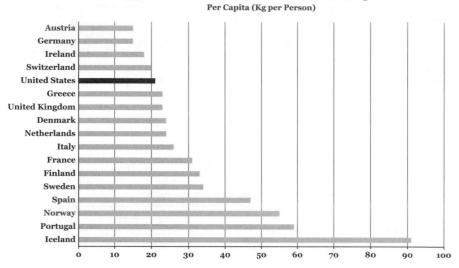

39. Fish and Fishery Products Consumption
Per Capita (Kg per Person)

and the Mediterraneans, but more than the Germans, Austrians, Swiss, and the Irish (figure 39). They consume a large amount of meat, surpassed only by the Danes.[22] Perhaps surprisingly, both the British and the Germans fall toward the bottom half of the carnivorous spectrum. But in terms of their overall consumption of animal products, Americans and the Mediterraneans are proximate in their habits, with only the Greeks and the Italians eating less (figure 40). The protein intake per capita of Americans is below that of the Portuguese, Irish, Icelanders, Greeks, and French. They are beaten in the quantity of fruits and vegetables they eat only by the Mediterraneans, the Danes, and the Dutch.[23] In some respects, Americans live more healthily than Europeans. They drink moderately. Only high-tax Scandinavians and Mediterranean wine-drinkers are more abstinent, and far from all of them (figure 41). They smoke sparingly, with about one-third fewer people lighting up than in Greece or Germany (figure 42).

To the extent that diet, habits, and lifestyle affect the prevalence and consequences of disease, Americans come off relatively healthily, compared to Europeans. For a number of cancers, incidence rates, in age-adjusted terms, are higher in the United States than any European nation: breast, uterine, and prostate cancers, melanoma, Hodgkin's and Non-Hodgkin's lymphoma.[24] For the rest, they are within the European spectrum, though for some they are worse only in one or two European nations: colon and rectum, kidney, lung,

40. Animal Products
Calorie Supply From (%)

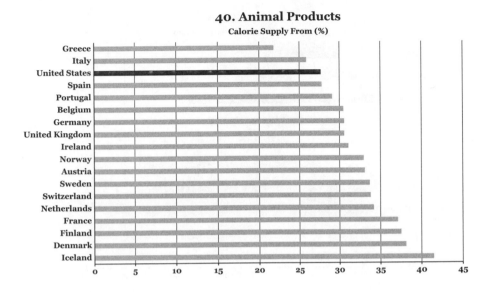

41. Alcohol Consumption
Pure Alcohol Consumed in Litres per Capita

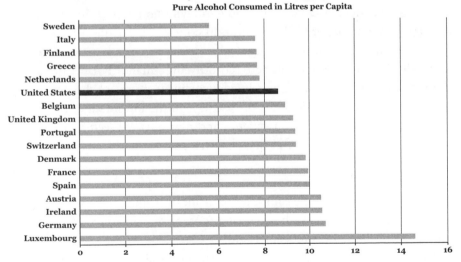

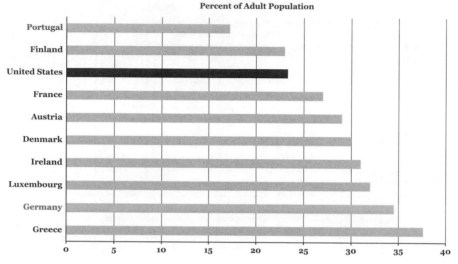

42. Smokers
Percent of Adult Population

pancreatic, multiple myeloma, thyroid, and leukemia. Interestingly, however, in almost all cases where the U.S. incidence rates are high, mortality is substantially lower. Only for nasopharynx cancers, leukemia, and ovarian cancer are the American mortality rates worse within the European rank order than is the case for incidence. For non-Hodgkin's lymphoma, both incidence and mortality are worst. For bladder cancer, in contrast, the United States ranks high, with only five nations having worse incidence rates, but for mortality, it has dropped to the bottom, bettered only by Finland. For breast cancer, the United States has the highest incidence, but in terms of the percentage of women who actually die of the disease, it is in the lower half of the group. Similarly steep drops between incidence and mortality are seen for cancers of the colon, kidney, larynx, oral cavity, pharynx, pancreas, prostate, thyroid, and for Hodgkin's lymphoma.

Looking at overall cancer rates shows a similar effect. Incidence rates for American men are higher than for any Europeans (figure 43). But mortality rates are quite moderate, with a lower percentage of male cancer deaths to be found only in Finland, Sweden, Iceland, Greece, and Switzerland (figure 44). Either those Americans diagnosed with cancer are dying of other unrelated causes, or the care they receive must be beneficial. Possibly, too, the incidence rates are high because Americans are more accurately diagnosed. For prostate cancer, for example, widespread screening may lead to earlier detection and

43. All Cancers (except Non-Melanoma Skin), Incidence

Per 100,000 Population, Age-Standardized Rates, Males

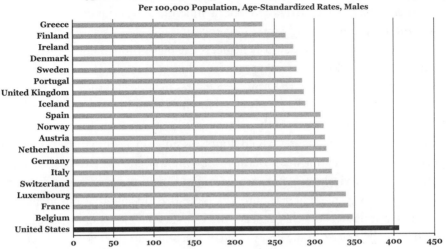

44. All Cancers (Except Non-Melanoma Skin), Mortality

Per 100,000 Population, Age-Standardized Rates, Males

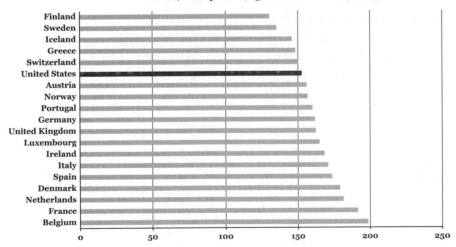

enhanced five-year survival rates, without actually improving longevity. But for other cancers, that particular effect is much less pronounced. Either way, the American numbers say something encouraging about the quality of U.S. health care, even as it scandalously neglects the many uninsured.

Indeed, the chances of surviving cancer are better in the United States than in many European countries. The American figures include also those who are uninsured, and thus likely to be poorly cared for. If they could be factored out, thus allowing a strict comparison of the effectiveness of medical treatment across the Atlantic, the European figures would doubtless suffer in a comparison. For a variety of cancers, including many of the most common, the United States has the best five-year survival rates: prostate, colon and rectum, bladder, and thyroid. Breast cancer is graphed here (figure 45). Note that this figure is not incidence but the survival rate. For other cancers, the U.S. survival rates are the same as the two or three best-performing European nations: brain, uterine cervix and corpus, esophagus, lung, melanoma, and ovary. For yet other cancers, it is slightly below the three or four best European nations: testicle, Hodgkin's disease, kidney, larynx, oral cavity, pancreas, and leukemia. Survival rates for liver cancer are at the center of the European spectrum; for stomach cancer and multiple myeloma in the bottom half. The only disease for which survival rates are significantly worse than in Europe is non-Hodgkin's lymphoma, and even here the U.S. figures are equal to the Dutch and above the English and Portuguese.[25]

The results presented here are from the mid 1990s and merely compare the readily available statistics. But more sophisticated studies of comparative cancer survival rates that have become possible only within the last decade confirm them: survival rates for most cancers are significantly better in the United States than in Europe, despite the absence of national health insurance. For the four major killers (colorectal, lung, breast, and prostate cancer) all European nations have worse survival rates.[26]

The United States has rates of mortality for heart disease that are in the middle of the European spectrum, less than in six of our countries.[27] Correspondingly, years lost in the United States as a result of heart disease are similarly positioned (figure 46). More specifically, only the French, Luxembourgeois, Spanish, and Italians die less often of heart attacks, the Icelanders at about the same rate.[28] For strokes, an illness that strongly reduces with preventive medication, the United States has a low mortality. The Swiss are at the same level, while in all other European countries more people die from strokes than in America. The Greeks and Portuguese have stroke rates about three times as high as the United States (figure 47). In no European

45. Breast Cancer Survival Rates

Relative Survival Rate of Women after 5 Years (%)

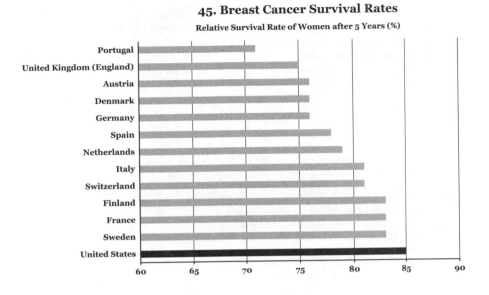

46. Heart Disease

Average Years of Life Lost (%)

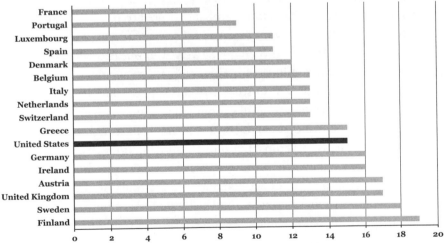

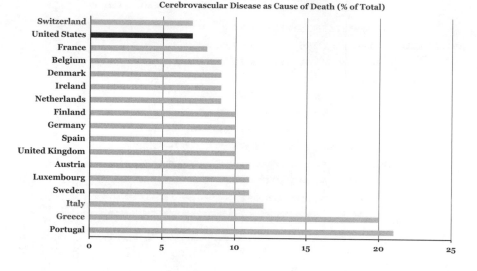

47. Stroke Mortality

Cerebrovascular Disease as Cause of Death (% of Total)

nation are fewer years of life lost on average to strokes than in the United States.[29] Deaths due to circulatory diseases are middle of the pack (figure 48).

The incidence of cosmetic surgery in the United States is also low by European standards. Per capita, more people surgically alter their looks in France, Finland, and Sweden than in the United States. That the rate is almost seven times as high in Switzerland is probably related to medical tourism. But even the Spanish figure is over twice the American (figure 49). For diseases of the soul, Americans are also comparatively well-off, though problems of diagnosing and evaluating in readily comparable terms make it hard to find many studies. When the WHO sought to measure the incidence of mental disorders at primary care settings in various cities, people in Seattle (picked as the American venue) were found to become mentally ill at slightly higher rates than northern Italians in Verona, but only about half, or less, as often as those in Paris, Manchester, Mainz, Groningen, Berlin, or Athens.[30] Studies of entire countries (phrased in terms of age-standardized disability-adjusted life years) do not paint as favorable a picture. But the United States remains within the European spectrum. More Americans proportionately suffer from unipolar depressive disorders than any Western Europeans; bipolar disorders are at the same or a lower rate. The United States comes out high for post-traumatic stress disorder, but the same as all European nations for panic disorder and middle of the pack for schizophrenia.[31]

48. Circulatory Disease Mortality

Annual Deaths per 100,000 Population, Standardized Rates

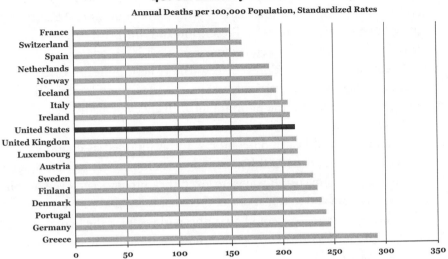

49. Plastic Surgery

Per 100,000 Population

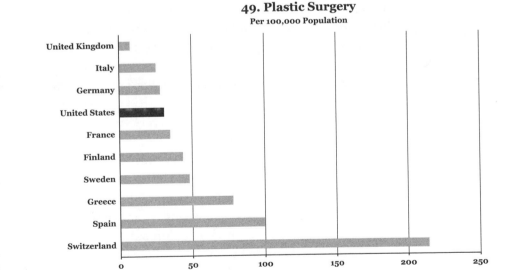

For health care, in summary, we have a mixed bag. Fifteen percent of Americans have no health insurance. This is not only a question of equity and morality, but also one of efficiency. Prevention and timely care are more cost-effective than treatment in an emergency room, which is where many uninsured receive whatever attention they get. The American health care system has often and rightly been criticized for being inefficient and unfair. The uninsured get a raw deal and the poor are most likely to be badly treated. But beyond this, something more is going on. Excepting infant mortality, a transatlantic comparison of health outcomes is not as lopsided as one might expect. Indeed, the American health system delivers impressive results, though it does so at a premium cost. If you were given the outcomes surveyed here in an anonymous form and told that one of these nations did not have a national health insurance system, you would not unhesitatingly pick the United States. Looking at the most consistently poor results, you would be most likely to choose Denmark or the UK.

This may explain why even those who are enthusiastic about European health care sometimes shy away when push comes to shove. The American journalist T. R. Reid, after having expounded on how Europe sets the standard that America must follow, comes to an inadvertently revealing conclusion on his experiences with the British National Health Service: "Looking at the waiting lists at British hospitals for major operations, and the long-term survival rates for cancer and other major diseases, I think I'd rather be in the United States than in Britain if somebody in my family contracted a serious disease," he admits. He then recovers to damn with faint praise. "But for flu, colds, rashes, intestinal complaints, eye exams, and the occasional broken bone or sprain, the NHS doctors performed on par with any treatment we have had in the United States. And all for free."[32] In other words, Reid praises the NHS for providing minor care at the expense of the British taxpayer to well-heeled foreigners. He goes on to complain that British doctors would not give him an annual physical exam nor a PSA test for prostate cancer—routine in the United States and elsewhere—because the NHS did not consider it cost-effective. And indeed, the NHS, though a British holy grail, delivers unimpressive care. In the 2007 results of the Euro Health Consumer Index, it ranked 17th out of 29, beating only Greece, Italy, and Portugal in Western Europe and trailing such newcomers as the Czech Republic and Estonia.[33] Critics who want to shame the U.S. health care system are well advised to use more effective systems as benchmarks, like the German, or especially the French, which interestingly shares many assumptions and characteristics with the American.[34]

The American health care system is unjust, expensive, and inefficient. The uninsured suffer. And it spends twice as much as other nations for similar results. One would not want to be born a poor child in the United States, nor would one want to be uninsured. But the overall average outcomes of the American system are surprisingly comparable to those in Europe, especially given that so many Americans remain uninsured. Why are American health outcomes reasonably—or often, very—good, even though not everyone has insurance? Perhaps health care does not matter as much to our eventual fates as the medical establishment would have us believe. Perhaps those with insurance are receiving so much better care than Europeans that their results balance out the sad fates of the uninsured. More likely, even in the absence of universal insurance, most Americans—however unfairly, inefficiently, and circuitously—are receiving at least basic care. That means, in effect, that the American system is—broadly speaking—achieving the sorts of results one might expect from a universal system of health care, but at a far greater price. We will come back to the reasons for this seemingly peculiar social policy choice later.

THREE
THE
REST OF
THE WELFARE
STATE

IF WE TURN TO OTHER FORMS of social policy, how does the United States care for its old, its poor, its unemployed, and its disabled? Here, most outcomes place the United States in the lower half of the spectrum, but within European norms and standards. The primary weakness of American social policy is its reluctance to deal resolutely with poverty. If we measure outcomes before redistribution, the United States starts with an economy that produces less poverty than most European nations. According to one calculation, only Finland and the Netherlands have lower "natural" poverty rates.[1] But after taxes, social benefits, and other mechanisms of redistribution have worked their magic, the American poverty rate (as measured relatively, i.e., as a fraction of median income) is higher than anywhere in Western Europe. We will come back in more detail to the question of poverty and inequality. In what one might call the middle-class entitlement aspects of the welfare state, however, America is less of an anomaly.

50. Public Employment
Public Employees per 100 People

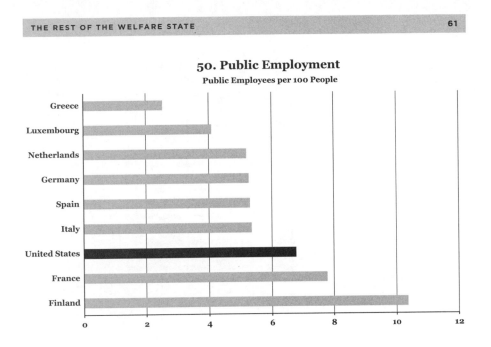

As is widely known, the American state is more modest in size and scope than its European peers. Yet as an employer of civil servants, it ranks in the middle of the European scale (figure 50). France and Finland employ proportionately more civil servants, but at least five other countries, including Germany, hire fewer. Correspondingly, the percentage of America's GDP spent on government employee salaries is higher than in six of the nations we are examining.[2] The size of the American state, as measured by government expenditure as a percentage of GDP, also fits into the European span. Ireland and Switzerland spend less (figure 51). For most social policies and benefits— which together make up what is usually called the welfare state—the picture is analogous: the United States ranks low, but within the bottom half of the European spectrum. All figures given here and elsewhere (unless otherwise indicated) are phrased in internationally comparable terms. Sometimes this means benefits rates are measured as a percentage of median income, allowing a sense of what proportion of a standard of living is maintained. Sometimes they are calculated in Purchasing Power Parity (PPP) terms, which means that differences between the cost of living in poorer and richer nations have been factored in.

Social assistance is miserly in the United States, but better than the equivalent benefits in Italy and Greece.[3] Unemployment benefits in America are higher than in some European nations. Greece, the UK, Italy, and Iceland spend

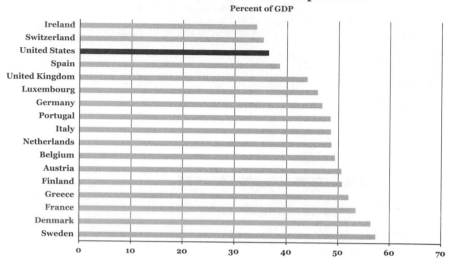

51. Total Government Expenditure
Percent of GDP

less than the United States on unemployment, measured per capita (figure 52). The amount of salary replaced by initial rates of unemployment benefits puts the United States at the low end of the European range, at the same level as Greece, Italy, and the UK, and above Ireland (figure 53). If measured as the percentage of an average industrial wage for married couples, the American benefit rates fall at the center of the European scale.[4] One recent attempt to quantify benefit generosity places American unemployment payments below Belgium, the Scandinavian nations other than Finland, Switzerland, and the Netherlands, but above all others in Europe.[5]

The duration of unemployment benefits in America is short, but no worse than in the UK or Italy.[6] For long-term unemployment, the American benefit replacement rate drops: only Greece and Italy rank lower (figure 54). But this is comparatively unimportant since for many years now, proportionately fewer American workers have been unemployed compared with many Europeans (figure 55). In 2005, only Denmark, the Netherlands, Luxembourg, Britain, and Ireland had fewer people out of work. Even if all the men locked in American prisons were counted instead as unemployed, the United States, with a recalculated unemployment figure for 2005 of 5.76%, would trade places with only one European nation: Austria. Moreover, the American unemployed remain without work for substantially briefer times than their European peers. The average spell of unemployment for American men is less than a third as long as

52. Public Spending on Unemployment Benefits
Per Capita, US$ PPP

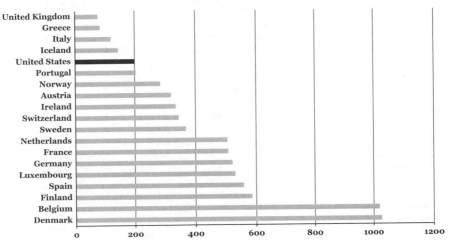

53. Unemployment Benefit Replacement Rate
Initial Replacement of Net Earnings While in Work (%)

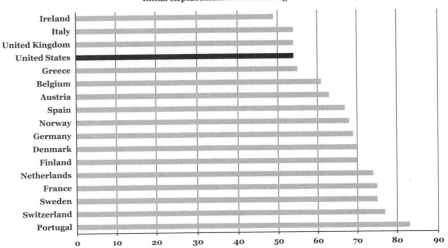

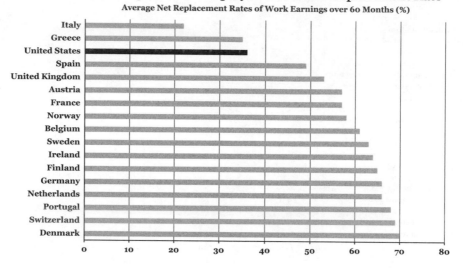

54. Long-Term Unemployment Benefit Replacement Rate
Average Net Replacement Rates of Work Earnings over 60 Months (%)

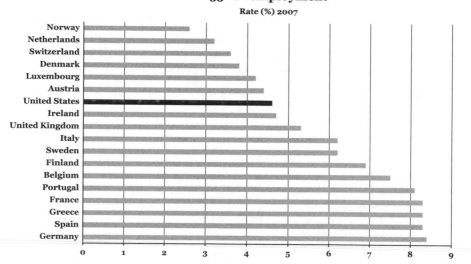

55. Unemployment
Rate (%) 2007

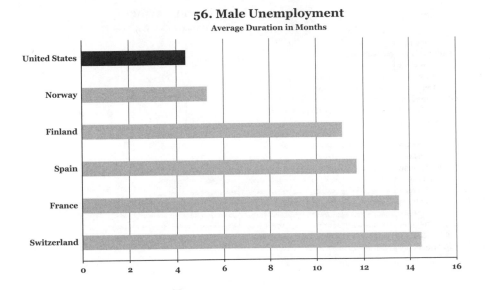

56. Male Unemployment
Average Duration in Months

that for the Swiss or French (figure 56). Compared with Europeans, far fewer American workers have been out of the labor market for over a year. In all of Europe, only Iceland has better results. Indeed, the number of long-term unemployed Americans is proportionately less than a fifth as large as the equivalent number of Germans (figure 57).

American spending on disability benefits per capita is higher than in Greece and Portugal, and is practically at the same level as France, Italy, Ireland, and Germany (figure 58). Yet, comparatively few Americans are disabled in the first place. Only in Italy are there fewer handicapped per capita (figure 59). Of course, these figures are to some extent an artifact of the welfare system itself and the ability of recipients to game it, or the wish of the authorities to disguise what would otherwise be higher unemployment rates. How else can one explain why the Swedes—otherwise so healthy, robust, and long-lived— should be incapacitated more than anyone else in the industrialized world? The average Swedish woman was ill 46 working days in 2007, the equivalent of nine full weeks.[7] On survivor's benefits, the United States spends more per head than all European countries other than Italy, France, Belgium, and Luxembourg. Measured as a fraction of GDP, only Portugal is added to this list.[8]

It is commonly known that the American state does not help out much in terms of family provision. Parental leave is not statutory, and there are no guarantees that women can reclaim their jobs after pregnancy. Family allowances

57. Long-Term Unemployment

12 Months or More as % of Total Unemployment

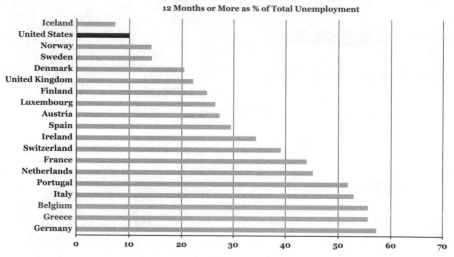

58. Public Spending on Disability Benefits

Per Capita, US$ PPP

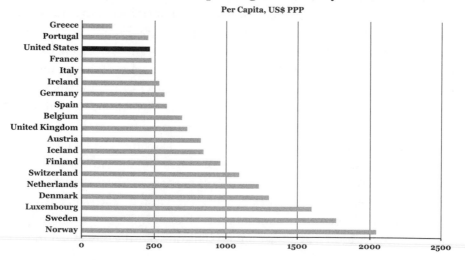

59. Disabled People
Percent of Population Aged 20-64 Who Are Disabled

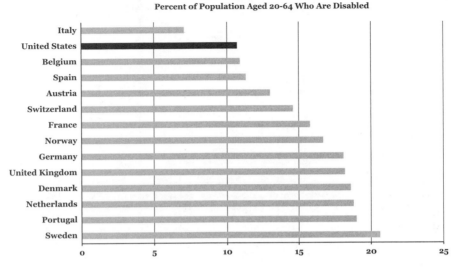

as such do not exist. On the other hand, if one counts resources channeled via the tax system as well as outright cash grants and services, and if one measures them as a percentage of GDP, for family benefits the United States ranks higher than Spain, Greece, and Italy, and only marginally below Switzerland.[9] Public spending on child care (day care and preprimary education) puts the United States into the middle of the European spectrum (figure 60). Total spending on preprimary care per child is higher in the United States than anywhere but Norway.[10] Child-care fees, as a percentage of an average wage, are lower in the United States than in Belgium, the UK, Ireland, France, Portugal, Spain, Luxembourg, and Switzerland. The net costs of child care in the United States are at the center of the European spectrum.[11] The percentage of very young children (under three) who are in formal child-care arrangements is higher in the United States than anywhere in Europe other than Denmark. The American figures are in the European middle range for children between three and school age—lower than Scandinavia, but higher than Austria, the UK, Ireland, and Greece.[12] The percentage of Americans who work flexible schedules (45%), which may relate to their child-care obligations and is generally taken to be an example of progressive workplace policies, is almost twice the average rate in Europe (25%).[13]

Pensions offer a mixed picture. For the average percentage of former earnings that state pensions replace for women, the United States is in the lower

60. Public Spending on Child Care
Including Pre-Primary Education, as % of GDP

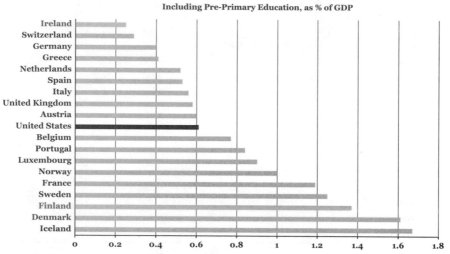

half of the European spectrum, though above Ireland and the UK (figure 61) Public spending per head on pensions puts the United States above the UK, Ireland, Iceland, Finland, Spain, Portugal, and the Netherlands.[14] That accounts only for what the state does for retirement. Many people save for their old age. If you look at the average disposable income of the retired as a percentage of what the still-active receive, only in Austria, Germany, and France do the elderly fare better than in the United States (figure 62). But that does not mean that the American pension system is uniquely privatized. Measured as a percentage of GDP, the holdings of private pension funds are larger in Iceland, the Netherlands, Switzerland, and the UK than in the United States.[15]

More broadly, data from the Luxembourg Income Study, the most extensive of its kind, shows that the amount of transfer income received by American households bears comparison with European sums. A smaller percentage of Americans receive social transfers from the state than is the case in Europe, at least outside the Mediterranean. About half of all American households do, which is much the same as in Italy, Spain, and Greece, but substantially lower than the 80-some percent of people who receive social benefits in Sweden and Finland. Average social transfers per household are therefore low, about $5,200 PPP. That puts the United States above only Greece. But if instead we look at the median sums received by those U.S. households that actually get

61. Female State Pensions

Mandatory Pensions as % of Pre-Retirement Gross Income, Women

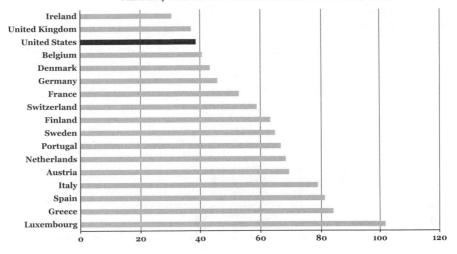

62. Retirement Income as % of Earlier Income

Percentage of Disposable Income of Those 65+ to Those 18-64

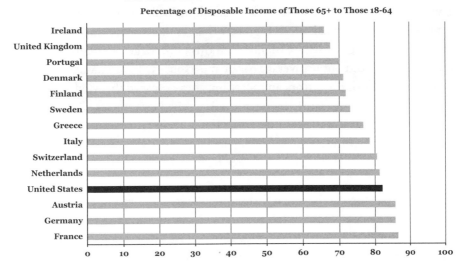

63. Median Social Transfer Income
For Households with Social Transfers, US$ PPP

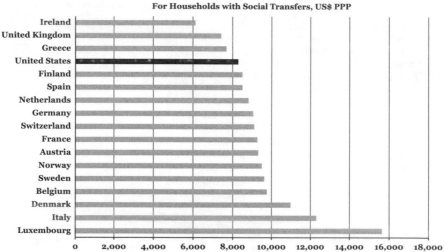

social transfers, the outcomes are more presentable, some $8,280 PPP annually. That figure comes in above Greece, Ireland, and the UK, and in the same league as Spain and Finland (figure 63).

As a fraction of the total economy, American public social expenditure narrowly makes it into the European norm, sneaking in above Ireland (figure 64). But because the American GDP is greater than in most European nations, the per capita spending figures are higher than this rank suggests. In terms of how much money is paid out on average for each person, the United States ranks in the lower middle of the European spectrum, above most of the Mediterranean and Iceland and in the same league as the UK, the Netherlands, and Finland (figure 65). The Swedes allot almost twice the American fraction of their GDP to social policy. But the actual spending per citizen in the United States is only about 30% less than in Sweden. A larger fraction of less is not as much more as it seems.

This comparison can be taken further. Public social spending in America—that is, monies channeled through the state—is on the low end of the European spectrum. But that is not the only measure of what the welfare state does. The total social policy effort is larger than cash directly redistributed by the state. For one thing, generous as cash benefits may be in some nations, they are significantly clawed back by Europe's high reliance on indirect taxes, as well as by direct taxes levied on those benefits. In other words, a Swedish mother may

64. Public Social Expenditure
Percent of GDP

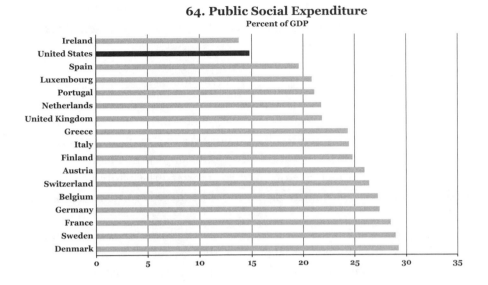

65. Public Social Expenditure
Per Capita, US$ PPP

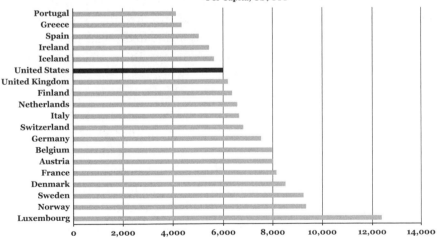

gratefully use her generous child allowance to buy a stroller. But she is actually paying for much of it herself, as the state collects its 20% value-added tax, as well as other taxes on her income.

Furthermore, much of what government does for its citizens takes the form not of cash, but of services—health care, child care, education, and the like. If we aggregate all the activities of the welfare state, including services as well as cash benefits, and factor in taxation clawbacks (in other words, if we look at net benefits), the results are not what we might expect. In one study, which included fewer nations than our sample, the Netherlands devoted the smallest percentage of GDP to transfers, the United States was tied with Finland in second-to-last place, while the UK was only a smidgen more generous.[16]

Beyond that, a complete accounting of welfare effort cannot focus only on what the state does through social policy. Other avenues of redistribution are also important: voluntary efforts, private but legally mandated benefits, and taxes. If we include all these, the American welfare state is more extensive than is often realized. By taking account of all these various components of social policy redistribution—public, voluntary, and mandatory—the total social policy effort made in the United States falls, once again, into the middle of the European spectrum.

That is not to say that all forms of social policy are strictly comparable, or that there are no consequences to different ways of distributing resources. Voluntary efforts are often more inequitably distributed than statutory ones, and they may well suffer more than legally mandated social policy during economic downturns. And size isn't everything. There are clearly differences of emphasis and adequacy between America and the best-developed European welfares states: above all, access to health insurance, but also the employment-based nature of many U.S. benefits (sickness pay, for example) that makes them highly variable in their availability. The lack of much maternity support is equally a major difference. Significant regional variations are also found within the United States, with widely varying benefit rates and few national standards. (Of course, the same holds true for any continent-wide study of European welfare policy.) Nonetheless, it is also the case that a nation's overall welfare effort cannot be measured simply by cash handouts from the state. If we look at the total net redistribution of income in the United States, the American welfare state looks much like its European peers, at the center of the spectrum, with six countries more generous and half a dozen less so (figure 66). Indeed, if we calculate net total social expenditure in PPP

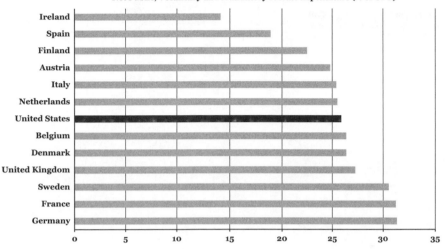

66. Total Social Spending

Net Public, Voluntary and Mandatory Private Expenditure (% of GDP)

terms per citizen, as we did in figure 65 for public social expenditure alone, no European country, barring possibly Luxembourg, spends as much as does the United States.[17] Comparing American and European welfare states (as indeed comparing Europe with other developed nations, in Asia, for example) means identifying different styles of policy rather than a simple binary choice between absence and presence.

FOUR
CRIME

IT IS COMMONLY CLAIMED that American society is crime-ridden and violent. Horrendous numbers of murders are committed, almost twice the per capita rate in 2004–05 of the nearest competitors, Switzerland, Finland, and Sweden (figure 67). The death-by-assault rates in America are over three times the nearest European comparisons, Finland, followed by Portugal.[1] That is without question. Such mayhem cannot be due simply to gun ownership, since by some accounts the Finns and the Swiss have a higher percentage of armed households than the Americans (figure 68). Firearms ownership, though highest in the United States per capita if measured by individual citizen, is not as far beyond the European numbers as one might expect from the horror stories of South Central or the South Bronx. According to the Graduate Institute of International Studies in Geneva, Americans own 97 firearms per hundred people, the Finns 69, the Swiss 61, the Swedes 40.[2] Another survey, published

67. Murder Rate

Per 100,000 Population

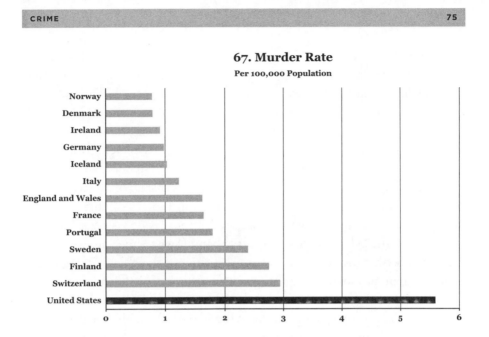

68. Gun Ownership

Percent of Households with Firearms

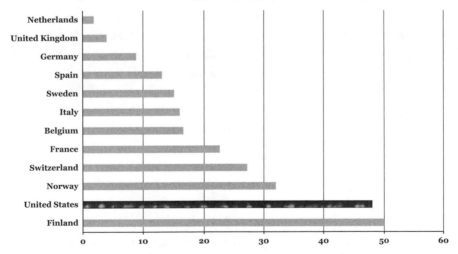

by Tilburg University in the Netherlands, the Dutch Ministry of Justice, and two United Nations Institutes, reveals that percentage-wise there are more firearms in the hands of the residents of Zurich, Vienna, Stockholm, Rome, Reykjavik, Oslo, Madrid, Lisbon, Helsinki, and Athens than in those of New Yorkers. Indeed, the burghers of Helsinki, Berlin, Lisbon, Rome, Vienna, and Zurich own proportionately as many or more handguns as New Yorkers.[3]

To the extent that gun ownership and hunting overlap, the distinctions between the United States and Europe also fade. Svenska Jägarförbundet, the Swedish Hunters Association, has a membership (200,000) that is proportionately almost twice as high as what the National Rifle Association claims (4 million). The Schweizer Schiesssportverband (Swiss Shooting Association) has a membership (85,000) that is relatively as high as the NRA's. Its arguments against current proposals to regulate gun ownership in Switzerland more strictly sound many of the same themes that are heard in the United States, down to the slogan about people, not guns, doing the actual killing. The smaller Pro-Tell Society defends gun ownership as part of Switzerland's liberal tradition.[4]

In Switzerland, of course, men often keep their military weapons at home. Arguably, the Swiss firearms associations do not have to be as active as the NRA for the simple reason that they have achieved what American gun enthusiasts can only dream of: not only the right but the obligation for all men to keep firearms. The military obligation does not, however, account for the Finns' affection for firearms, though three wars with the Russians in a century might. Finland and Switzerland have both the highest murder rates in Europe and the highest gun ownership rates. This suggests some relationship between the two figures. On the other hand, on average, four times as many murders are committed per firearm in America as in Switzerland.[5] Crime is more often committed with a gun in America than in Europe. Six percent of assaults and threats in the United States involve use of a gun, while in Europe only Northern Ireland has numbers as high. The closest other European competitors (at 4%) are Switzerland, the Netherlands, Italy, and France. But Europeans are pretty handy with a blade. Only Luxembourg, Greece, Finland, and Denmark have proportionately fewer knife assaults than the United States.[6]

In the developed world, American murder rates are in a class by themselves. Nor is there any doubt that the United States locks into prison a far higher percentage of its population than any of its peers (figure 69). Indeed, the American figure is well over four times the Luxembourgeois, British, and Spanish rates, which are the highest in Europe. The average length of jail sentences, however, is within the European spectrum, lower than Spain's and only a tad higher than Portugal's (figure 70). Policing levels are quite normal by northern European

69. Prison Population

Per 100,000 Population

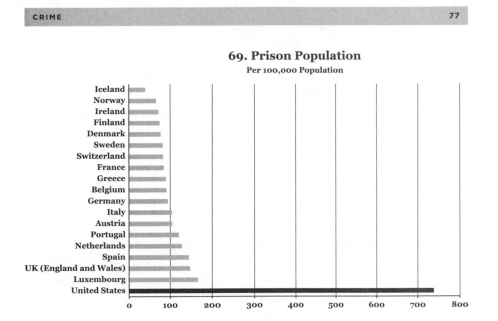

70. Average Prison Time

Average Length of Time Actually Served in Prison after Conviction, in Months

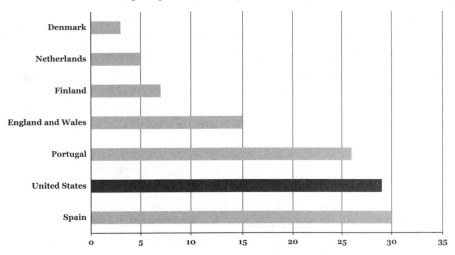

standards, which in turn are half those of some Mediterranean countries like Portugal and Italy (figure 71). And the U.S. police seem to do a reasonable job. The percentage of Americans who consider the police good at controlling crime in their area is higher than in any European country, bar Finland. More Americans feel very safe walking alone after dark than any Europeans other than most of the Scandinavians and the Dutch. The Austrians and Swedes feel as secure as the Americans, the Swiss, and French about as much, the British, Belgians, Germans, Greeks, Italians, Luxembourgeois, Irish, Spanish, and Portuguese quite a bit less so. New Yorkers feel as safe at night as the residents of Vienna, Amsterdam, and the Scandinavian capitals. Proportionately, many fewer New Yorkers worry about being attacked than do the residents of Berlin, Athens, Rome, Madrid, or London.[7] In a recent poll conducted by YouGov and the *Economist*, Americans ranked crime as the least of their worries, while the British named it as their second-most-pressing concern, after only immigration. Similarly, a smaller percentage of Americans worry about being victims of a burglary during the coming year than anyone but the Danes or the Finns.[8]

The murder rate and the number of prisoners in America are both off the European scale. That is without doubt. Homicide and incarceration, however, affect but a minuscule minority in all nations, and the average citizen's experience of crime is colored by more mundane offenses. In those terms, America is—despite its reputation—actually a peaceful and quiet place by European standards. As one team of scholars puts it, violence, not crime, is the American problem.[9] Whether American society owes its relatively law-abiding nature to the many criminals locked in jail we do not know. Americans tend to be polite to each other. In *Reader's Digest*'s anecdotal survey of polite behavior in different cities, New Yorkers scored better than anyone, a nose ahead even of the residents of Zurich (figure 72). Although they have lots of lawyers, Americans are less litigious than many Europeans, such as the Germans or even the supposedly consensual Swedes, not to mention the Austrians (figure 73).

U.S. property crime rates, as measured by the percentage of the population victimized, are toward the middling high end of the European spectrum (figure 74). The British and the Italians suffer more. Car theft rates are toward the low end, less than one-fifth the Italian rate and higher only than in Austria, Switzerland, Finland, Germany, and the Netherlands (figure 75). American burglary rates are highish, but below the Danish and British. The incidence of theft is the same as or better than in six Western European countries, and pickpocketing is above only the levels in Sweden, Scotland, Finland, and Portugal.

71. Police Personnel

Per 100,000 Population

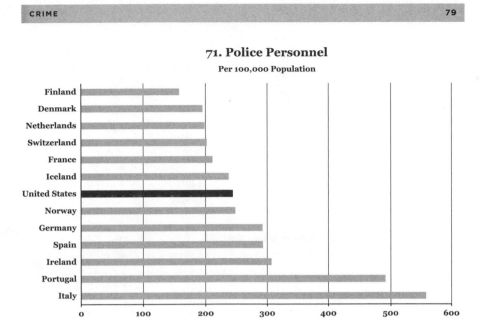

72. Courtesy

Percent of People Who Passed Reader's Digest's Courtesy Tests

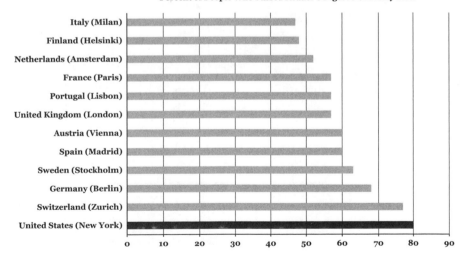

73. Litigation Rate

Legal Cases per 1,000 Population

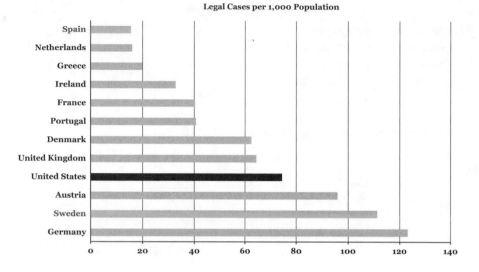

74. Property Crime

Population Victimized (%)

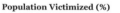
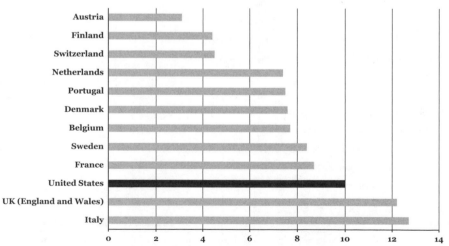

75. Car Theft

Population Victimized (%)

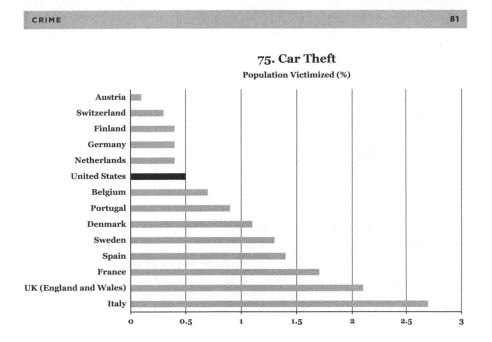

Robberies are also toward the bottom of the European scale.[10] *Readers' Digest* ran an admittedly impressionistic survey of the rate at which apparently lost mobile phones were returned in major cities; New York acquitted itself better than any city other than Stockholm.[11]

Assault is in the middle, on par with the rates in Sweden and Belgium (figure 76). Rape levels are high, but sexual assault rates are low. Only Belgium and Portugal are lower; Austria suffers three times the American rate (figure 77). Such numbers are tricky, however. Obviously, the distinctions between these two crimes are nebulous and likely to be differently interpreted across cultures. In some statistics, rapes may be counted among sexual assaults. A more recent account of sexual assault places the United States at the top of the scale for 2003–04, the same level as Iceland and one notch above Sweden. But the same study's figures for 1999 put America at the bottom of the scale, above only Portugal and Belgium, at the same level as Denmark, and at about one-third the Swedish rate.[12] Perhaps a more accurate measure is the percentage of women who have been victimized by a criminal sexual incident of some kind or another. By that standard, American women are less often harmed than any European women other than the Belgians, French, and Portuguese.[13]

American children fared badly in UNICEF's recent survey of their well-being, though better than the British. They suffer high levels of death and injury from accidents. But in terms of other forms of violence that the young are especially

76. Assault
Population Victimized (%)

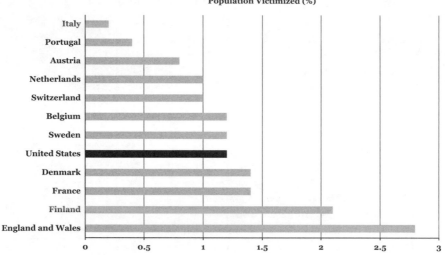

77. Sexual Assault
Population Victimized (%)

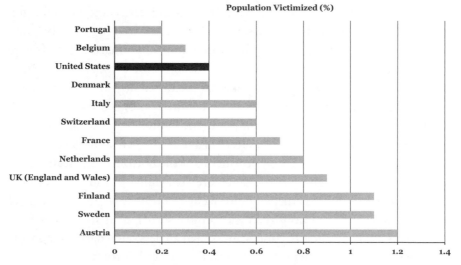

subject to, they were middle of the pack. They fight less than in any European nations other than Sweden, Finland, Portugal, Germany, and Switzerland (figure 78). And the likelihood of being bullied is at the center of the European spectrum, below France, the UK, Germany, Switzerland, Austria, and Portugal.[14]

American drug use is highish for some drugs. Cannabis and cocaine are used a bit more often than in the UK, the closest European competitor. But otherwise American consumption falls within the European spectrum.[15] Amphetamine use is lower than in the UK and Ireland, and only a bit higher than in Spain and Denmark. Ecstasy use is lower than in Ireland, the UK, Spain, and the Netherlands (figure 79). Opiate abuse is in the center of the European spectrum (figure 80). As for the precautions taken by citizens to protect themselves against crime, Americans no more live in barricaded fortresses than do Europeans. Proportionately more Americans have watchdogs than Europeans. But they build high fences less often than the French, British, and Belgians, have fewer window grilles than the British, have as many burglar alarms as the Norwegians (and many fewer than the British), and install fewer special door locks than the Dutch, English, and Germans (and about as many as the Italians and Austrians).[16]

"American business ethics are abysmally low and require the toughest of policing," Will Hutton warns us.[17] Yet the white-collar crime rate is at the middle to the low end of the European spectrum. The French suffer over six times the American rate of bribery. Indeed, bribery levels are lower only in Sweden and the UK (figure 81). Corrupt public officials are as likely to solicit bribes in Switzerland and Belgium as in the United States, and more so in Germany, Austria, Denmark, Portugal, France, and Greece.[18] France, Ireland, and Belgium, as well as all the Mediterranean nations, appear more corrupt than the United States (figure 82). The World Bank estimates the United States as less troubled by graft than Greece, Portugal, Italy, Ireland, Germany, France, and Belgium, and the same as Spain.[19] According to the UN's figures, fraud is over eight times as common in Germany as in America, and over four times as frequent in England and Wales. Even Denmark has more fraud than America (figure 83). Consumer fraud is more widespread in Iceland, Denmark, Sweden, and Greece than America.[20]

The EU adds another supranational arena for corruption. It also brings together different national styles of governance, with different tolerances for crime. The number of prominent European public figures who have recently been killed—by their own hand or others'—because they were implicated in corruption within the EU is startling and without compare across the Atlantic:

78. Young People Fighting

Percent of Teens Involved in Fighting during Previous Year

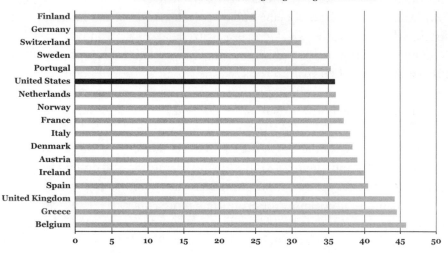

79. Ecstasy

Use within Past Year (%) of Adults

80. Opiates
Annual Percent of Adult Population that has Abused Opiates

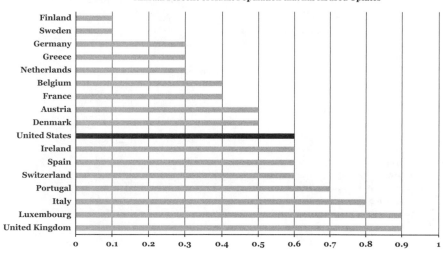

81. Bribery
Population Victimized (%)

82. Corruption
Corruption Perceptions Index, 10 = Highly Clean, 0 = Highly Corrupt

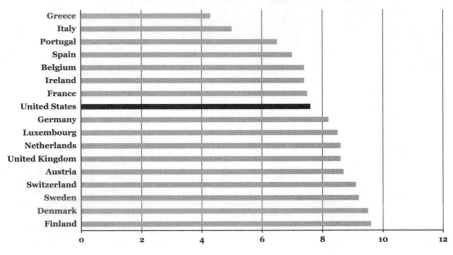

83. Fraud
Frauds Committed per 100,000 Inhabitants

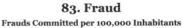

Carl Algernon, Gabriele Cagliari, André Cools, Camillo Crociani, Robert Feliciaggi, Raul Giardini, Wolfgang Hüllen, Thierry Imbot, Jacques Lefebvre, Jürgen Möllemann, Antonio Quatraro, Alain van der Biest.[21] American executives judge the domestic business costs of common crime and violence to be no worse than do their colleagues in Belgium, France, Ireland, the UK, Italy, the Netherlands, and Spain. For organized crime, they are more sanguine than their peers in the Netherlands, Spain, and—no surprise—Italy.[22] The total American crime figures are in the low middle of the pack. Indeed, only relatively small countries—Finland, Austria, Switzerland, and Portugal—are less crime-ridden than the United States (figure 84).

The robbery rate in America is highish, below only the Portuguese and British figures (figure 85). But the percentage of citizens who are victims is far lower—only Austria has fewer, and Finland's rate is the same as the United States' (figure 86). In other words, in the United States there are many robberies but fewer victims. A violent underclass preys on itself, but the average citizen is unlikely to be disturbed. No more than in Europe does American crime saturate society as a whole. It tends to be confined to pockets of misery. And indeed, our comparison here points to what is arguably the main difference between the United States and Europe: the continuing presence in America of an ethnically distinct underclass, as one of the unresolved tragic legacies of slavery.

Take out the black underclass from the statistics, and even American murder rates fall to European levels. America remains a fairly violent society, but no more than some European countries. Its nonblack murder rate is lower than the overall levels of homicide in Switzerland and Finland, and it squeaks in under even the Swedish level (figure 87). It goes without saying that "black" is here a proxy for the poverty, unemployment, and exclusion of big-city ghettos, not a racial marker. If statistics allowed us to factor out the murders committed in America's worst neighborhoods, the effect would be even more dramatic, since we would be eliminating also those committed by other excluded ghetto minorities. America's problem is not violence or even murder as a kind of generic issue spread throughout society. What sets the United States apart from European nations are the social pathologies of inner-city ghettos and, of course, the society that has not yet seen fit to solve this problem.

If we were able to adjust our statistics correspondingly for other crimes, American crime rates would descend from the middle of the European spectrum toward the bottom. Conversely, were we to have an analogously dispossessed underclass in European societies—and this is increasingly becoming the

84. Total Crime
Population Victimized by Crime in Total (%)

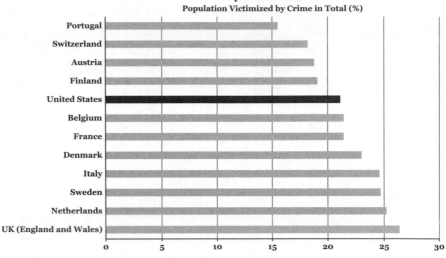

85. Robbery
Per 100,000 Population

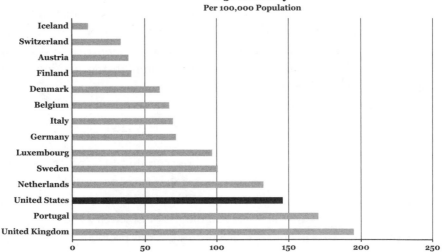

86. Robbery Victims
Population Victimized (%)

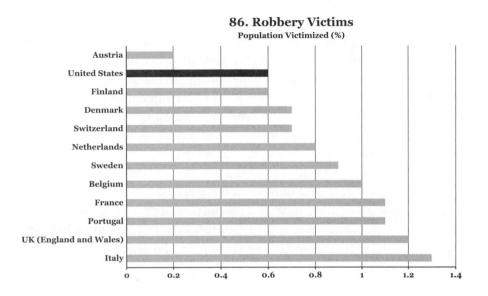

Austria	
United States	
Finland	
Denmark	
Switzerland	
Netherlands	
Sweden	
Belgium	
France	
Portugal	
UK (England and Wales)	
Italy	

0   0.2   0.4   0.6   0.8   1   1.2   1.4

87. Non-African-American Murder Rate, 2005
Per 100,000 Population

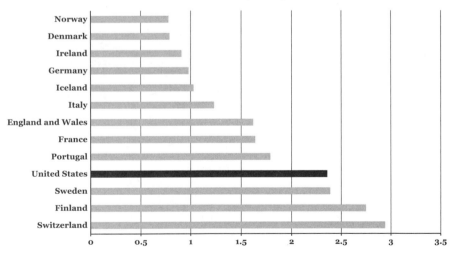

Norway	
Denmark	
Ireland	
Germany	
Iceland	
Italy	
England and Wales	
France	
Portugal	
United States	
Sweden	
Finland	
Switzerland	

0   0.5   1   1.5   2   2.5   3   3.5

case—crime rates would (and depending on European abilities to assimilate outsiders, will) rise significantly. Blacks in America commit seven times the number of homicides as whites.[23] In Sweden, where we have reliable figures, crime is similarly overrepresented among outcast groups. The "new Swedes," as the foreign-born are called, are twice as likely to commit crimes of any sort, and those from sub-Saharan Africa over four times. Foreigners are over four times more likely to commit attempted murder and murder.[24] As Europe takes in more immigrants, legal and illegal, the danger arises that they might become a dispossessed underclass and that crime rates across the Atlantic might increasingly converge. Already now, while only 6% of inmates in U.S. jails are from abroad, foreigners make up over one-quarter of prisoners in Germany and Sweden, one-third in Italy, the Netherlands, and Spain, a bit under half in Austria, Belgium, and Greece, and over two-thirds in Switzerland and Luxembourg.[25]

FIVE
MORE
BROADLY

EUROPEANS OFTEN REGARD AMERICA as a country of bigness: big people, big cars, big houses. People we have already touched on; cars will come. American housing standards do fall in the upper half—but still well within— the European scale. Two rooms per inhabitant is the U.S. average. Residents of Luxembourg, the Netherlands, the UK, and Belgium have more (figure 88) The Irish have a higher percentage of their households occupying at least five rooms, the English and Spanish are very close runners-up.[1] For social or public housing, transatlantic discrepancies pale before even more impressive disparities within Europe itself. Approximately a fifth of all accommodation in England and France is public housing, but those are by far the highest figures in Europe. In Italy, it is only 7%. In Spain, the fraction of the public housing stock of all dwellings is even less than in the United States, namely 1%. According to figures from the OECD, social housing scarcely exists at

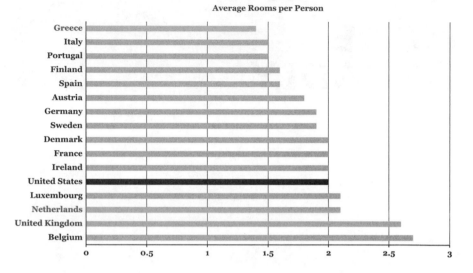

88. Living Space

Average Rooms per Person

all in Portugal, at least to judge from the sums the government spends on it. Sweden, a country with a somewhat smaller population, spends well over 500 times as much. In any case, the range of state spending on housing in those nations with figures high enough to register as a fraction of GDP varies from 0.1% in Austria and Luxembourg to 14 times that in the UK.[2] It is hard to call a penchant for social housing a defining European characteristic. Moreover, despite the absence of much public housing in the United States, the poorest fifth of tenants in America pay less of their income for housing than their peers in Sweden or Switzerland, and only a bit more than in the UK.[3]

America is often considered a stingy helper of Third World nations in distress. It is true that American foreign aid, in the form of direct cash grants, is not impressive if measured per capita. Nor is that of Austria or the Mediterranean nations, except France, which are all lower (figure 89). But if we take a broader measure that also includes indirect assistance through tariff and trade policies, investment, ease of migration, security, and technological interchange, the United States helps the Third World more than the Mediterranean nations, more than France, Belgium, and Ireland, and only a smidgen less than the UK (figure 90). In a recent measure of the quality of the job done by governmental agencies distributing aid to the underdeveloped world, America ranked below the best-performing national institutions (the UK, Norway, Sweden, Switzerland, Portugal, Belgium, and Italy), but above those of Austria, Ireland,

89. Development Assistance
Per Capita (2002 US$)

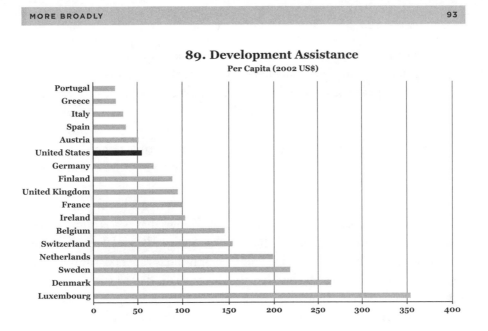

90. Total Foreign Aid
Scale of Commitment to Development in Poor Nations

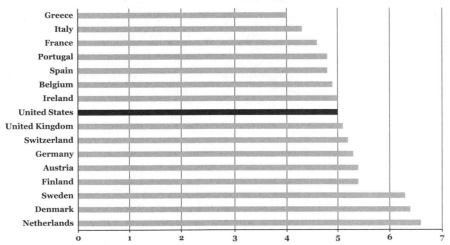

the Netherlands, Denmark, Finland, Germany, and Spain.[4] Unexpectedly, a higher percentage of Americans have a great deal of confidence in the UN than any Europeans other than the Italians and the Luxembourgeois.[5] On the other hand, only the Finns are less likely to agree that international bodies should have the right to enforce solutions for problems like environmental pollution, though the Danes and Spaniards are in the same league.[6]

Americans are often thought to take little interest in the world around them, except perhaps when invading it. The paucity of Americans with passports is often held up as an indication of disinterest. Eighty-five percent of American tourism and travel is domestic. If it follows that 15% is international, Americans join the company of the Greeks, Spaniards, and French, among whom, respectively, only 12%, 13%, and 17% of holidays are taken abroad. And that does not take into consideration the distance needed to travel before the Great Abroad begins. That more than 99% of Luxembourgeois vacations of four nights or more were enjoyed outside the nation's borders does not surprise; where else could they possibly have been taken?[7] For purely topological reasons, international travel is a different enterprise for residents of big countries. Assuming that for a European to leave Europe is an effort roughly analogous to that of an American exiting the United States, the figures become more comparable. In 2006, 9.7 million Western Europeans visited the United States and 13 million Americans visited Europe. Thus, in the realm of travel, Americans were proportionately more interested in Europeans than the other way around. The same year, significantly more Americans (30 million) traveled overseas (other than to Mexico and Canada) than overseas visitors came to the United States (22 million).[8]

Quantifying the purported American indifference to the rest of the world presents difficulties. But here is a try. Using the online archives of four major newspapers, the *Frankfurter Allgemeine Zeitung (FAZ)*, the *New York Times*, the *Guardian*, and *Le Figaro* (unfortunately, the search engine of *Le Monde* does not permit a similar analysis), we used the frequency of the conjunction "but" and its equivalents in the other languages as a proxy for the total number of words in these respective organs. That was our denominator.[9] We then investigated the relative frequency of the following words or their equivalents: "Paris," "Berlin," "Washington," and "Moscow." The results reveal that the *New York Times* writes about Paris about as frequently as the *Guardian* and somewhat less than the *FAZ*. It is slightly less interested in Berlin than the *Guardian* and about half as much as *Le Figaro*. It is about 30% less interested in Moscow than the *FAZ*, about as interested as *Le Figaro*, but almost twice as much so as the *Guardian*. It is more interested in London than the *FAZ* but less than *Le Figaro*. The *New York Times* writes more frequently about Paris than the *FAZ* does about Washington, and only a bit less than *Le Figaro* and the *Guardian* do. If we look at coverage of two major foreign policy figures, Vladimir Putin and Kim Jong Il, the *New York Times* has been more interested in the Russian president than has the *Guardian*, but much less so than the *FAZ* and *Le Figaro*. It has published articles more frequently about the North Korean leader than any of the other newspapers. Word counts, of course, provide only a rough measure of interest, but given the limitations of the search engines, it was the best possibility on offer. From this sketch, drawn admittedly with a thumbnail, we see approximately equal interest for the outside world among these newspapers.

I can hear the objections already: Maybe the *New York Times*, and maybe New Yorkers, but what about all those corn-fed provincial Americans who don't know the difference between Vienne and Vienna? Let us run the same test on a sampling of decent regional newspapers: in the United States, the *Dallas Morning News*, the *Baltimore Sun*, the *San Francisco Chronicle*, and the *Atlanta Journal-Constitution*; in France, *Le Progrès*, *La Dépêche du Midi*, and *Lyon Capitale*; in Germany, the *Aachner Nachrichten* and the *Stuttgarter Nachrichten*. The selection is of necessity limited by the few Web sites that will allow the sort of search we are attempting. We have not included any English newspapers since there is no longer a functioning regional press in that country.

One result is that the German regional press is more interested in the great abroad than the French. No surprise there. The French papers paid a little more attention than the American to Berlin, and somewhat less to London. The German papers bested both the French and Americans in attention devoted to Washington and Paris, respectively. The average attention of the French and Americans to Moscow was almost exactly equal, while the Germans took more notice. The same holds for their respective interest in Putin. On the North Korean leader, in contrast, the American papers were significantly more alert than any of the European ones.

If we compare the American provincial press to *Dagens Nyheter* (the results for *Svenska Dagbladet*, the alternative, were eerily similar), the mouthpiece of the Swedish chattering classes, a group that prides itself on its cosmopolitan graces, this is the outcome. Interested in Putin you would be better off reading *Dagens Nyheter* than any of the U.S. press, and if Kim Jong Il caught your fancy, you would be better off only if you read the *San Francisco Chronicle* or the *Baltimore Sun*. That speaks well of the Swedish paper. On the other hand, if you were more generally interested in the other nations whose capitals we have used as proxies for the amount of coverage they receive, then the advantage lies with the *Dallas Morning News* or the *San Francisco Chronicle* if Paris was the concern. If interested in London, you would be better off with the *San Francisco Chronicle* and the *Baltimore Sun*. If Moscow, with the *Dallas Morning News*. But if Berlin is the focus, then the U.S. provincial press cannot compete with *Dagens Nyheter*. In other words, American regional papers are as interested in the world as their French counterparts, less so than the German, and a nose behind the Swedish national press. As always, the deep ravines we are led to expect turn out to be but gently rolling hills.

Yet so insistent are the European chattering classes on burnishing their own credentials as worldly and sophisticated at the expense of Americans that one wonders about the underlying psychological needs craving fulfillment. When it writes of America, the European press often pulls a Borat: sophisticated Europeans report on American yokels for other sophisticated Europeans. This is, of course, a gratifying trick if no one calls you on it. But it is a mistake to assume that it cannot be repeated in reverse. Sooner or later, we will see an American writer performing a Baudrillard on Europe, publishing a book on European weirdness in all its glorious multifariousness: *Schuhplatteln* (a relentlessly commercialized form of folk dancing) on prime-time Bavarian or Austrian television; the hermetically sealed holiday resorts that keep Germans or Brits at home even while abroad; the Eurovision Song Contest; Lourdes as the site where the Catholic Church practices medicine; *Lederhosen, Trachten* and *Dirndlen* worn by grown-ups; naked weather announcers on Italian TV; the erotic lure of fancy cars in German singles ads; Blackpool; Kurt Waldheim; Padre Pio; Liechtenstein; Armin Meiwes, the cannibal of Rotenburg; reality TV; Europeans' universal and supremely smug contempt for Roma; Heino; Norway's dry counties; football hooligans; the Common Agricultural Policy; *Butterreisen*; the Mediterranean songbird hunt; *Hello* magazine; Silvio Berlusconi; Appenzell Innerrhoden, the Swiss canton forced finally in 1990 to grant women the local vote; *Heimatlieder*; binge drinking; Page 3 girls; the cult of Diana, and so forth. Hans Magnus Enzensberger's *Europe, Europe* is a brilliant portrayal of the sometimes bizarre extremes tucked behind the placid facade of Europe, but—published in 1987—needs updating.

SIX
EDUCATION
AND THE
HIGHER
PURSUITS

IT IS GENERALLY RECOGNIZED that higher education in America is in comparatively good shape, with the main competition coming from the UK. With less than 5% of the world's population the United States accounts for 40% of global research and development spending, produces 63% of all highly cited scientific publications, employs 70% of the world's Nobel Prize winners, and is home to three-quarters of both the top 20 and top 40 universities in the world.[1] Spending figures reveal the reasons why. As a proportion of total outlays on universities, government spending is lower in the United States than in any European nation (figure 91). But, as we have seen when looking at overall social spending, monies channeled through the state do not tell the whole story. Total spending on university education in America, measured as a percentage of GDP, is not merely high by European standards. It is some 60% above the nearest competitors, the Scandinavians, and more than twice

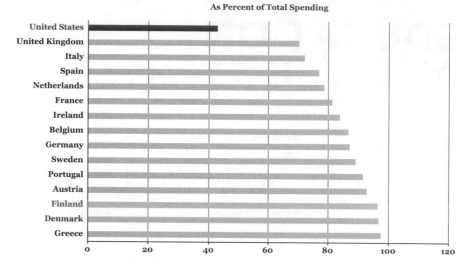

91. Public Spending on University Education

As Percent of Total Spending

the level of Germany, a country that once boasted universities as good as any (figure 92). It is worth remembering, too, that the U.S. GDP is itself bigger than Europe's. Americans therefore not only spend proportionately more on universities. In absolute terms, the gap becomes greater. A higher percentage of Americans have graduated from university than in any European nation. America's adults are, in this sense, better educated than Europe's (figure 93). Despite this, the amount of continuing education that Americans undertake is above that of the Germans, Swiss, and Belgians, among the narrower range of countries surveyed in this case.[2]

The United States is in the middle of the European pack for state spending on primary and secondary schools, and for overall state educational spending (figure 94). But total educational spending, public and private, measured as a percentage of GDP, remains higher in the United States than anywhere in Europe (figure 95). Primary and secondary school teachers are reasonably well paid by European standards, in the upper middle of the spectrum (figure 96). And proportionately more Americans have graduated from secondary school than in any European country.[3] For primary schools, American average class sizes are in the upper middle half of the European scale, and in the center for secondary schools. (Figure 97)

Contrary to popular belief in both Europe and the United States, American primary and secondary school pupils perform as well academically as many

92. Total Spending on University Education

As a Percent of GDP

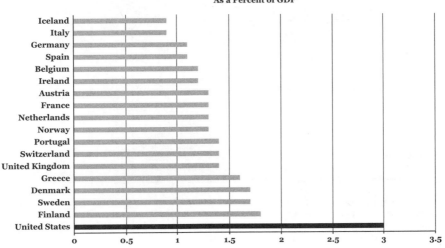

93. University Education Attainment

Percent of Adult Population

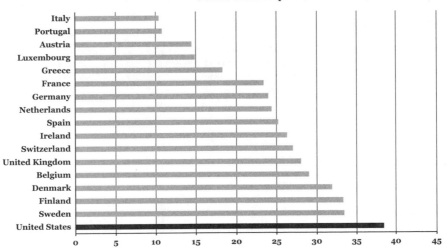

94. State Spending on Education

As Percent of GDP

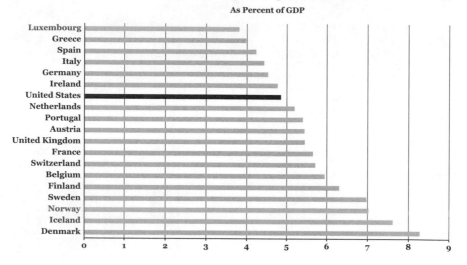

95. Total Education Expenditure

Total Public and Private Expenditure on Education as % of GDP

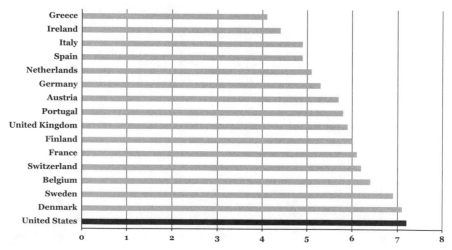

96. Primary Teachers' Salaries

After 15 Years Teaching (US$ PPP)

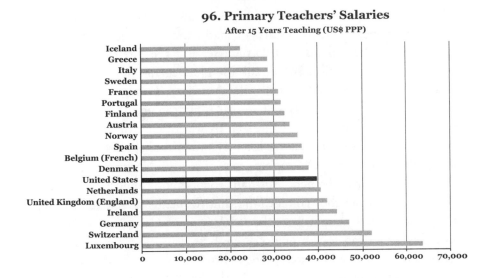

97. Class Size

Lower Secondary Education

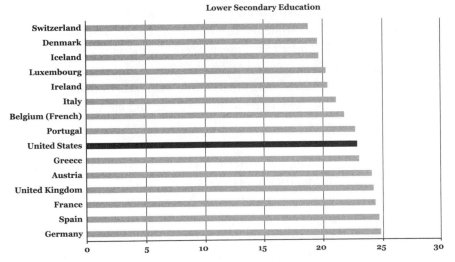

of their European peers, as measured by the 2006 Program for International Student Assessment (PISA) results. In math, they could do better, ranking only above the Italians, the Portuguese, and the Greeks.[4] In science, however, American pupils also outrank the Norwegians, Spaniards, and the Luxembourgeois.[5] For reading skills, the Austrians, Danes, Icelanders, and Germans have slipped below as well, so that American pupils rank at the center of the European spectrum (figure 98). By way of confirmation, the 2006 Progress in International Reading Literacy Study ranked American fourth graders at the center of the European scale: above the Norwegians, Belgians, Icelanders, Spaniards, French, Austrians, Scots, and English.[6] The 2007 TIMMS comparisons showed much the same for math and science, although for a more limited sample than the PISA studies. Compared to Western Europeans, American fourth graders were bested in their math knowledge only by their English and Dutch peers, eighth graders only by the English. In science, both groups were beaten only by the English.[7] Such mean scores for each country, however, do not tell the whole story. How many students are really good or hopelessly incompetent? In the PISA tests for science, the United States had proportionately more low achievers than any Western European country other than Italy and Portugal, although it ranked only a bit lower than Luxembourg, Norway, Greece, and France. At the opposite end of the scale, America had proportionately more top-scoring pupils than any European nations other than the UK, Germany, Finland, and the Netherlands.[8]

These figures deal with students. If we look at schools and their performance, disparities in the United States are moderate, although Europeans commonly believe that in America good and bad schools are starkly separate. The *Independent*, for example, warns its British readers against emulating America lest one result be schools "grossly divided along race and class lines."[9] Yet the figures indicate otherwise. For the 2003 PISA math scores, variations between schools in the United States were moderate. America clustered toward the Nordic end of the spectrum, not with the highly stratified Central European or Mediterranean countries (figure 99). An American pupil from a blue-collar background is slightly more than twice as likely as his peer from a white-collar family to score in the bottom quarter of the PISA science tests. This result is the same as in the UK and Luxembourg. It is lower than the social stratification found in the Netherlands, France, Germany, Belgium, and Austria.[10] For reading, the gap between scores for pupils from occupationally privileged and unprivileged families is wide in the United States. It is wider still in Portugal, the UK, Belgium, Luxembourg, Germany, and Switzerland.[11] Family cultural

98. Reading Scores
2003 PISA

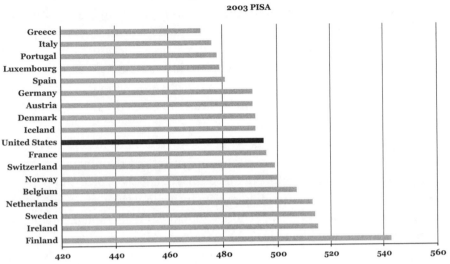

99. Variance Between Schools
Student Performance, 2003 PISA Math (%)

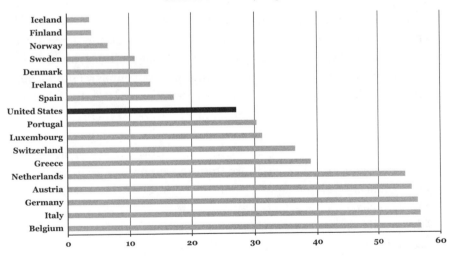

attainment (parents with university educations) had a more positive influence on pupils' math scores in the United States than anywhere in Europe. But parents finishing secondary school had no more effect on math scores in America than in six European countries. And cultural capital, measured in terms of those households with more than 200 books, had less influence in the United States than in seven European nations. In other words, secondary-school students' results are determined by family cultures in much the same way both in the United States and in Europe.[12]

Europeans often believe that good U.S. schools are private and serve only an elite. Yet American education is no more privatized than many European systems. This holds for enrollments in primary schools, where the percentage of American students attending private institutions is at the center of the European scale.[13] For secondary schools the same is true, though the figures are harder to pin down (figure 100). Data from the World Bank, graphed here, distinguishes only between state and private secondary-school pupils. Belgium and the Netherlands, in this accounting, have a far higher percentage of children attending private schools, many of which are religious. But the bulk of private schools in countries like the Netherlands and most of Scandinavia are, in fact, funded indirectly via government taxes through what Americans call a voucher system, often with a fee supplement. While the American Left resists vouchers as capitulating to the market in an area where the public good should hold sway, many Social-Democratic-minded European nations have introduced them. If we distinguish instead by three categories—what the OECD calls public schools, government-dependent private schools, and independent private schools—the picture looks somewhat different. The United States then has a higher percentage of upper-secondary-school pupils attending public school than any European country other than Switzerland, Italy, Ireland, Greece, and Denmark. On the other hand, it also has a higher percentage of pupils in independent private schools than anywhere in Europe outside of Spain and Portugal, among the countries for which there are figures.[14] The percentage of educational expenditure from private sources for primary and secondary education is comparatively modest in the United States, lower than in the UK, Switzerland, and Germany.[15]

What results emerge from the American educational system? First and foremost, by European standards, a high percentage of young Americans are either in education or employed—their energies, in other words, are gainfully occupied. Only in the Nordic countries (other than Sweden), Ireland, and the Netherlands are more youngsters actively learning or working (figure 101). Proportionately

100. Private Secondary Schools
Children Enrolled in (%)

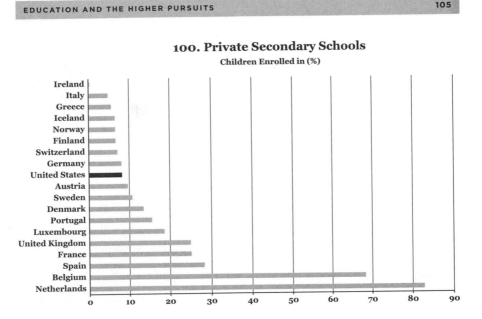

101. Footloose Young
15-29 Year-Olds (%) Not in Education and Unemployed

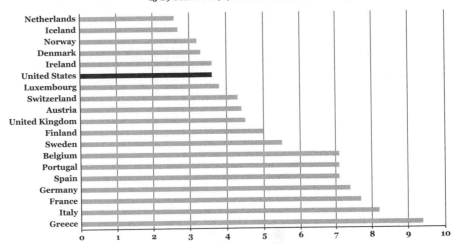

102. Illiteracy

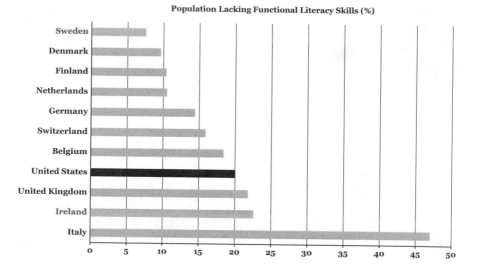

Population Lacking Functional Literacy Skills (%)

more young people leave secondary school without a qualification in 10 European nations than in the United States.[16] The percentage of illiterate Americans is average by European standards (figure 102). Proportionately more British and Irish, and more than twice as many Italians, cannot read or write. Average literacy rates in the United States are at the middle of the European scale. The American score on prose literacy falls below only the Netherlands, Finland, Norway, and Sweden, though it is also true that the range between good and bad readers in the United States is broad, as is the case also in the UK and Portugal.[17]

Americans do not need to read, Simone de Beauvoir was convinced, because they do not think.[18] Thinking is hard to quantify, reading less so. And read the Americans do. There are more newspapers per head in the United States than anywhere in Europe outside Scandinavia, Switzerland, and Luxembourg (figure 103). The circulation of these newspapers is higher per capita than in most of the Mediterranean and in Ireland and Belgium.[19] Another source, quantifying the copies of newspapers per capita, ranks the United States above all West European countries except the Scandinavian nations, other than Denmark.[20] And more Americans have read one of these papers during the last week than the French or the Spanish.[21] The United States is also well equipped with libraries. With its amply endowed universities, it is no surprise that the supply of books per capita in America's university libraries is higher than in any European country other than Finland, Denmark, and Iceland.[22] The long tradition of

103. Daily Newspaper Titles
Number per Million Adult Population

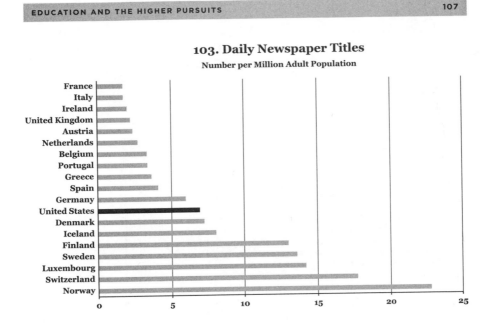

municipally funded public libraries in the United States means that also average American readers are better supplied with library books than their peers in Germany, Britain, France, Holland, Austria, and all the Mediterranean nations (figure 104). They also make better use of these public library books than most Europeans. Average Americans borrowed 6.4 books each in 2001, more than their peers in Germany, Austria, Norway, Ireland, Luxembourg, France, and throughout the Mediterranean.[23] Not content with borrowing, Americans also buy more books per head than any Europeans for whom we have numbers (figure 105). Proportionately more Americans claim to read a book per month than anyone but the Swiss, Swedes, Germans, and Irish.[24] And Americans write more books. Per capita, they come in at the high end of the European spectrum as authors, measured in terms of volumes in print (figure 106).

As one might expect, on average Americans watch more television than most Europeans. But not all: the British watch more and the Italians are a hard-running third (figure 107). Proportionately fewer Americans watch more than two hours TV daily than the Portuguese, Norwegians, Danes, Finns, Dutch, Irish, Germans, and British.[25] And, yes, Americans go to the movies more often than most—but not all—Europeans.[26] The Icelanders are even more devoted cinema buffs.

Comparative snobs may counter that Americans like only popular culture— their books are trash, their films are from Hollywood. This is a long-

104. Public Libraries
Number of Books per Capita

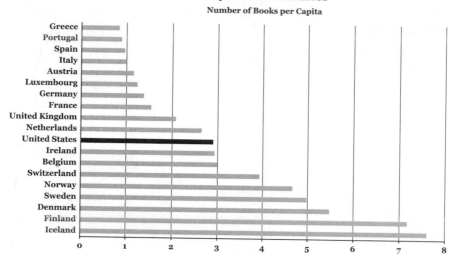

105. Books Sold
Per Person

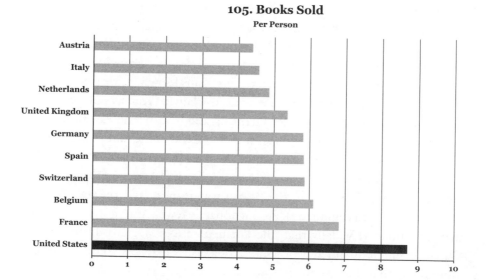

106. Book Titles in Print
Per 1000 Population

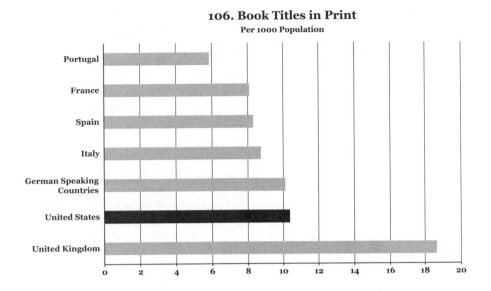

107. Television Viewing
Per Capita per Week in Hours

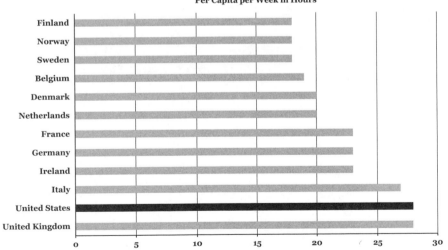

standing complaint, shared widely among Europeans of all ilks. A year after his unprompted declaration of war against the United States in December 1941, when he might have had other reasons to criticize the country, Hitler lamented America's paucity of opera houses, even though—as he grudgingly admitted—its citizens may have had more refrigerators than the Germans.[27] Accurate, internationally comparative figures on opera houses are, alas, hard to come by. But let us take, as a reasonable alternate measure of culture whose brow does not get much higher, the number of full symphony orchestras good enough to have won recording contracts with Deutsche Grammophon. Only the Germans have a higher absolute number than the Americans.[28] And, as for the infrastructure required to produce high culture, only in Switzerland do more pianos (acoustic, of course, and counting both verticals and grands) change hands per capita than in the United States, with the Germans in hot pursuit for third place (figure 108). If we look at only grand pianos, twice as many are bought per capita by Americans as by the nearest European competitors, the Swiss, with the Germans a distant third.

I turn now to some—admittedly slapdash—indicators of high culture, but one has to look where the statistical light shines, and that is far from everywhere. Though the Michelin guides started rating New York only a couple of years ago, it already holds its own in terms of stars awarded its restaurants: fewer per capita than Paris, of course, but on a par with London (which fancies itself the current dining mecca) and above Rome and Munich. (Measuring Germany by impoverished Berlin would have been unfair) (figure 109). Much the same holds if we move from food to drink. Measured in proportion to output, there are more perfect American wines (Parker ratings of 100) than from any European country other than France (figure 110).

True, the American state spends less as a percentage of GDP than almost any European government on what the OECD defines as "recreation and culture," though not less than Greece and only a bit less than the UK and Ireland. These figures, it should be noted, include government payments to Europe's established churches. American households spend more on recreation and culture privately than any Europeans but the Icelanders, the Austrians, and the English. Add state and private money together, and total American outlays on the finer things in life fall in the upper half of the European middle ground.[29]

What do European state subsidies to high culture get the continent's citizens? Contemplate the cost of admission to the world's major opera houses (figure 111). If we look at how often poor but devoted opera buffs can pursue their passion, there appears to be no dramatic advantage to state subsidies.

108. Annual World Piano Sales

Per 10,000 population

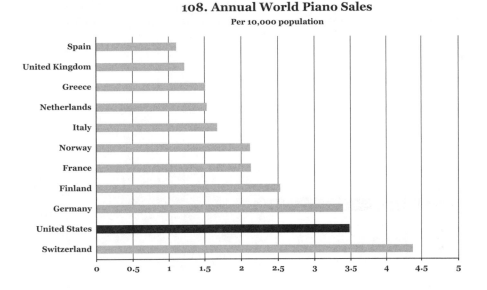

109. Total Michelin Restaurant Stars

Per 100,000 Population

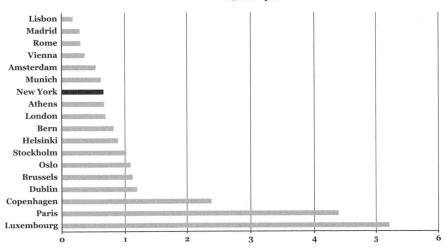

110. Perfect Wines

Wines with Perfect (100) Score from eRobertParker.com per Hundred Megaliters of Wine Produced

111. Ticket Prices in Major Opera Houses

US$ PPP, 2008

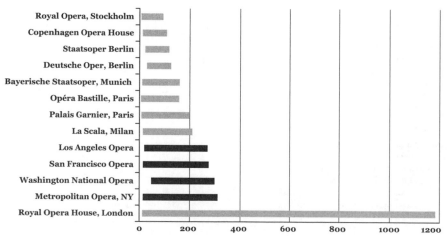

The Royal Opera in Stockholm, the Palais Garnier, and the Bastille Opera in Paris are the least expensive. Then comes a group of opera houses in the middle, where the cheapest tickets are priced between 11 and 20 dollars. This includes not only Covent Garden in London, the Copenhagen Opera House, La Scala, and the Bavarian State Opera, but also the Met in New York, and the San Francisco and Los Angeles operas. The most expensive lowest-price tickets are in Washington DC and in Berlin's two main opera houses. There is some differentiation, in other words, but no yawning chasms, nor any discernable distinctions between subsidized and market-driven institutions. In the boxes and grand tiers, however, prices vary quite a bit more. At the extreme, a seat can cost over a thousand dollars in London. In America, top prices cluster at about a quarter of that. In France and Italy, the best seats go for between 150 and 200 dollars. But the lucky Germans, outside of Munich at least, and the Scandinavians can get into the plush seats for less than a hundred dollars. (All these prices are, of course, in PPP dollar terms.) In other words, whether paid for by the state or the audience, all opera houses make the cheapest tickets relatively affordable, often less costly than the cinema. Bottom prices on the Continent are sometimes slightly lower than those in the English-speaking world, but not by much, and sometimes not at all. At the top end, in contrast, well-heeled opera lovers pay their own way in the English-speaking world. But on the Continent they enjoy discount prices, thanks to heavy subsidies from the average taxpayer. A reversed Robin Hood for *Rigoletto*.

Culture is not just what interests the aesthetes and connoisseurs; science must be considered as much a part of it. The United States also has a highly developed infrastructure of producing scientific knowledge, whether you measure it in terms of the number of researchers or in terms of expenditure on research (figure 112). Only Finland and Sweden spend a higher percentage of their GDP for such purposes. One outcome is a good record of patents— more per capita than any European nation for which we have figures, though Sweden is a close second (figure 113). Per capita, America also has reasonable success in winning Nobel prizes, falling at the center of the European scale, whether you measure it across the population, by the nationality of the winner, as graphed here, or by the nationality of the institution he or she worked at (figure 114).

Let us turn now to women and their rights and achievements. The power granted American women has been a leitmotif of European criticism from the beginning.[30] Even today, some European observers regard the emancipation of women as an unattractive American peculiarity. Emmanuel Todd is preoccupied

112. Research and Development

Expenditure as % of GDP

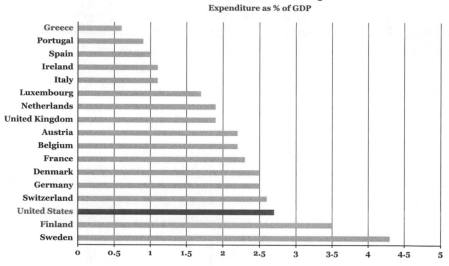

113. Patents

Per Million Population

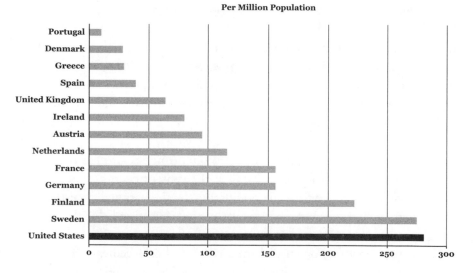

114. Nobel Prizes by Nationality

1950-2002 Prize Winners per 5 Million Population (2005 Population)

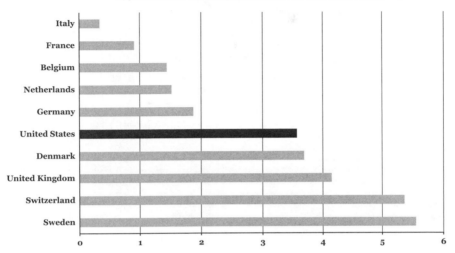

by what he considers the "gynocratization" of America, "the country of castrating women."[31] How do things stand today with women on both sides of the Atlantic? American women have no claims to paid maternity leave, though that does not seem to dampen their reproductive enthusiasm. Being on average younger, they have more babies than their sisters in any European nation.[32] Many of them work (figure 115). Only in Scandinavia is there a higher proportion of economically active women. And, by European standards, American female workers are paid reasonably well compared with men (figure 116). Only in Scandinavia and Switzerland are their wages higher in relation to their male peers. A larger proportion of American women have been to university than their sisters in Western Europe, outside of Scandinavia, Belgium, France, and Portugal.[33]

In politics, American women perform at the lower end of the European spectrum. As members of parliament or its equivalent, they are worse represented only in Ireland, Greece, France, and Italy (figure 117). There are proportionately fewer female ministers in Greece and Italy, and the same number in Luxembourg and Switzerland.[34] But in the economy, American women do well compared with Europeans. The proportion of female professional and technical workers is higher in the United States than in any European country except Iceland, where there are proportionately as many. So is the percentage of female legislators, senior officials, and managers, taken together (figure 118). American women are less likely to work in temporary positions than anywhere in Europe,

115. Women in the Work Force
Percent of Total

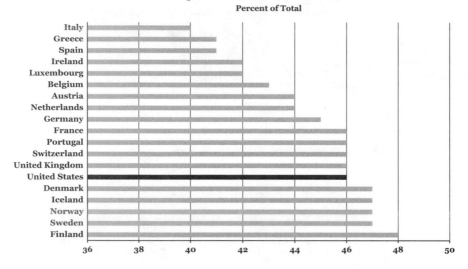

116. Women's Income
Ratio of Estimated Female to Male Earned Income

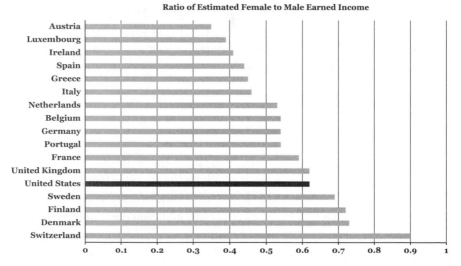

117. Women in Parliaments

Proportion of Seats Held by Women in National Parliaments (%)

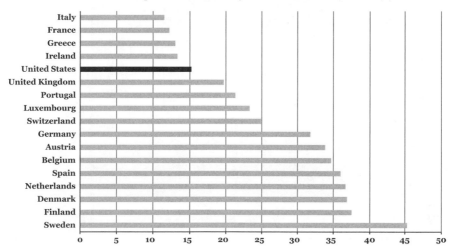

118. Women in Leading Positions

Female Legislators, Senior Officials, and Managers (% of Total)

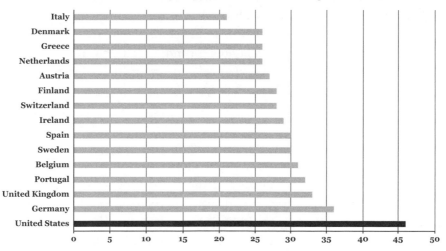

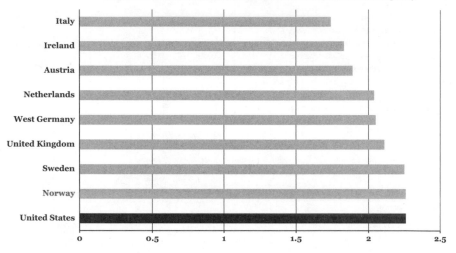

119. Gender Division of Housework
Gender Division of Labor Index, the Higher the Score, the Closer to Equality

and less likely to work part-time than anywhere other than Portugal, Greece, and Finland. Women in the United States are only half as likely as European women to work in pink-collar, traditionally female jobs. Danish women are most sexually ghettoized in the European labor market, Italians the least.[35] Perhaps part of American women's professional success is due to the support they receive at home. American husbands do more housework than most European men; only Scandinavian men are as helpful (figure 119).

Americans are often considered puritanical and squeamish when it comes to sex. But the available surveys on the relevant habits and attitudes do not bear this out, at least not compared to Europeans. Legal marriage-like unions for homosexuals are found among some U.S. states, as they are in some European nations (figure 120). Americans are equaled only by the Irish in the percentage that has experimented with homosexual relations (figure 121). They are middle of the European pack when it comes to affairs, one-night stands, the frequency of their lovemaking, and the number of their partners. The proportion of American respondents who admit to having participated in threesomes is bested only in Iceland, though the Norwegians are strong contenders in third place (figure 122). Americans are at the high end of the European scale in kinkiness (bondage, spanking, and other forms of S/M, role-play, dressing up, incorporating pornography in lovemaking, videoing or photographing during sex, and using sex toys). Only the British and the Finns are more likely to experiment (figure 123). The most unadventurous lovemakers are the Germans, followed by the Italians.

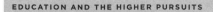

120. Gay Marriage–Like Unions

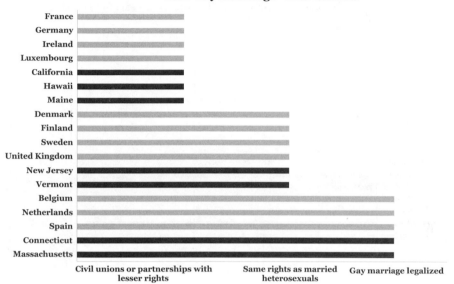

France
Germany
Ireland
Luxembourg
California
Hawaii
Maine
Denmark
Finland
Sweden
United Kingdom
New Jersey
Vermont
Belgium
Netherlands
Spain
Connecticut
Massachusetts

Civil unions or partnerships with lesser rights | Same rights as married heterosexuals | Gay marriage legalized

121. Homosexual Experiences

Percent of Respondents Claiming at Least 1 Homosexual Experience

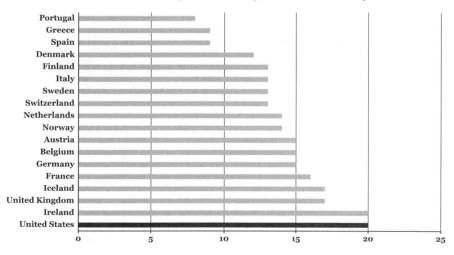

Portugal
Greece
Spain
Denmark
Finland
Italy
Sweden
Switzerland
Netherlands
Norway
Austria
Belgium
Germany
France
Iceland
United Kingdom
Ireland
United States

0   5   10   15   20   25

122. Three in a Bed during Sex

Percent of Respondents Who Claim to Have Had 3 in a Bed during Sex

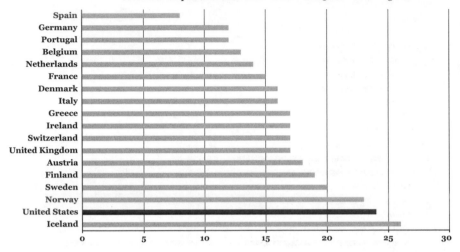

123. Non-Engagement in Sexual Indulgence

Percent of Respondents Who Claim No Sexual Indulgences

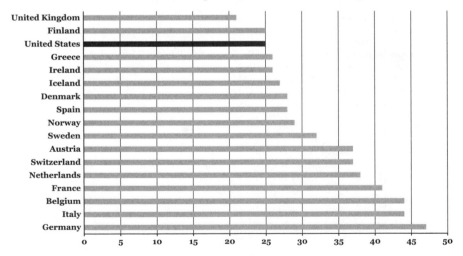

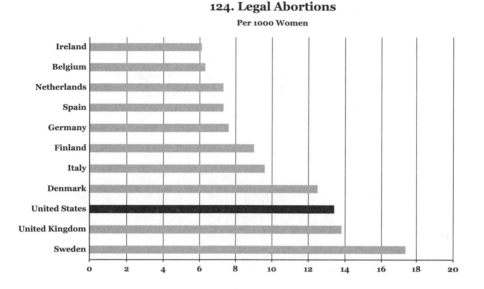

124. Legal Abortions

Per 1000 Women

As for the possible consequences of their lovemaking? Teenage births are very common in the United States by European standards, almost twice the highest European rate, in the UK. But out-of-wedlock births in America are in the middle range, below the UK, Austria, France, and all of Scandinavia.[36] That, in turn, is to some extent an outcome of the American marriage rate, which is slightly higher than Denmark, Europe's nuptial leader, and almost twice the Belgian rate, its laggard.[37] Though abortion remains controversial in the United States—as it does in Europe outside the Anglo-Scandinavian fringe—American women use it as much, or little, as Europeans (figure 124). Only in the UK and Sweden are legal abortions more frequent.

SEVEN
THE
ENVIRONMENT

IF WE TURN TO THE ENVIRONMENT and its protection, the contrasts between the United States and Europe are less stark than the debates over Kyoto and global warming suggest. Popular attitudes across the Atlantic appear to be quite comparable. A smaller percentage of Americans than any Europeans are fearful that current population trends are unsustainable. The percentage that fears strongly that modern life harms the environment is at the lower end of a very broad European spectrum. But a higher percentage of Americans than anyone other than the gloomy Portuguese are very worried about the environment. Already long before Al Gore and *An Inconvenient Truth*, proportionately more Americans considered global warming extremely dangerous than do the Dutch, Norwegians, Danes, and Finns. Relatively more Americans than anyone but the Swiss claim to be very willing to pay higher prices to protect the environment. Proportionately more Americans than any

Europeans are prepared to pay higher taxes for the sake of nature. Americans also claim willingness more than anyone other than the Swiss and the Swedes to accept a cut in living standards to achieve such ends.[1] A higher percentage of Americans think that government should pass laws to protect the environment than the British, Swiss, Dutch, Germans, and all Scandinavians other than the Danes.[2] American executives are more convinced that complying with government environmental standards helps their businesses' long-term competitiveness than their colleagues in Germany, Iceland, Austria, Luxembourg, Greece, Belgium, the Netherlands, Ireland, Italy, Spain, or Portugal.[3]

In a recent comparative ranking of environmental policy conducted by Yale and Columbia universities, the score assigned the United States was not impressive. But that of Belgium, the Netherlands, and Greece was worse.[4] The Achilles' heel of America's environmental policy is its energy inefficiency, which is partly related to the size of the country and the extremities of its weather. On most other measures, U.S. rankings are better. American spending (public and private) on pollution abatement and control as a percentage of GDP is bested only in Austria, Denmark, Italy, and the Netherlands.[5] The percentage of the government budget that goes to environmental research is low in the United States, but higher than in Sweden and Switzerland.[6]

Despite the myths of a hyper-motorized nation, Americans own fewer passenger cars per head than the French, Austrians, Swiss, Germans, Luxembourgois, and Italians (figure 125). Even if one takes the figures for all road motor vehicles, the U.S. figures are lower than the Portuguese and in the same league as the Luxembourgeois, Icelanders, and Italians.[7] The human damage cars wreak is average at worst (figure 126). Road fatalities, measured per vehicle, are higher in Austria, Spain, Ireland, and Belgium. Greece is by far the most dangerous place to drive, 50% worse than its nearest competitor, Belgium. Per capita, Americans drive much more than Europeans, some 70% more than the closest peers, the Italians (figure 127). Of course, they live in a large and (by the standards of Europe outside of Scandinavia) sparsely settled country. If we adjust for such factors, taking into account the size of the country, automobile usage is lower only in Finland, Sweden, and Greece (figure 128). And the ratio of car travel to the length of paved road is higher in Italy and the UK than America (figure 129). The same goes for the number of vehicles per kilometer of road: lower than all but Sweden, Norway, Iceland, and Ireland.[8]

American public transportation leaves much to be desired, but the country has more rail per head than all European nations except Finland, Sweden, and Ireland (figure 130). Railway per square kilometer is, of course, lower and largely a factor

125. Passenger Cars

Per 1000 Population

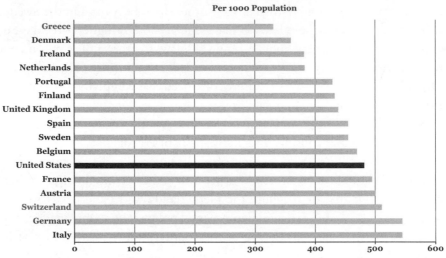

126. Road Fatalities

Per Million Vehicles

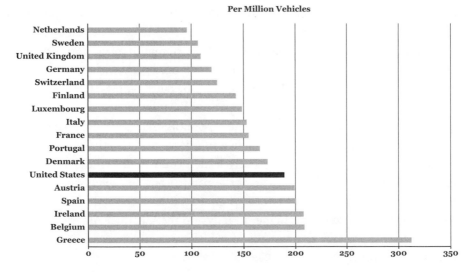

127. Passenger Transport by Car

Per Capita Passenger Transport in Private Cars (1,000 Passenger Kilometers)

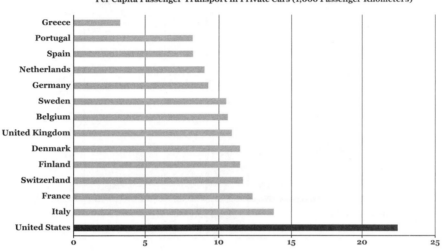

128. Car Passenger Kilometers per Size of Country

100,000 Passenger KM Traveled in Private Cars per Square KM of Country Size

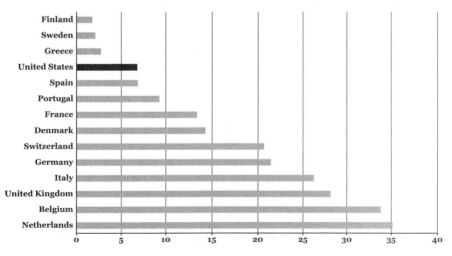

129. Car Passenger Kilometers per Km of Road

100,000 Passenger Kilometers Traveled in Private Cars per KM of Paved Roadways

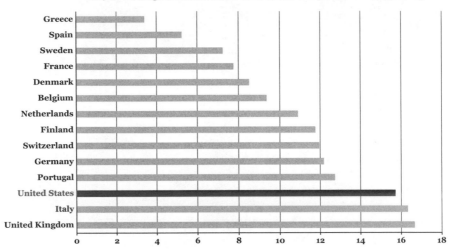

130. Length of Railways

Railways in Kilometers per 1,000,000 Population

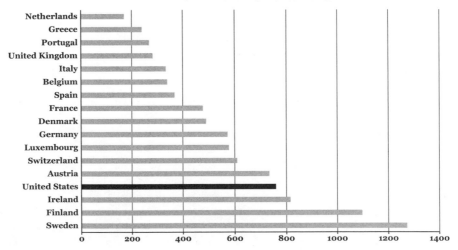

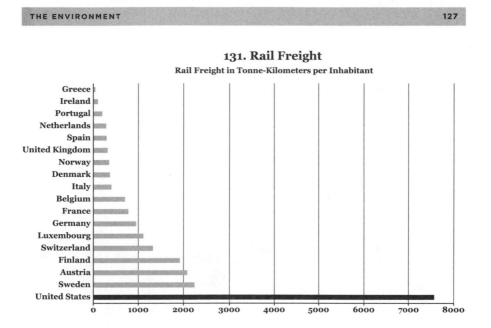

131. Rail Freight
Rail Freight in Tonne-Kilometers per Inhabitant

of the size and population density of the country. It is, in any case, higher than in Greece, Finland, Norway, and Iceland, and only a bit lower than in Sweden and Spain, all countries with similar population densities. Americans do not, it is true, themselves travel on this extensive rail network. In 2004, more passenger miles were racked up on American trains than in Italy or Britain.[9] With a bigger country, this still means proportionately far fewer riders. But the U.S. rail network transports Americans' freight (figure 131). Well over three times as much freight is carried by rail per capita in the United States than the closest European nation, Sweden. The American emphasis on rail over road for freight transport explains why a larger fraction of the nation's carbon dioxide output from transportation is produced by rail in the United States (2.2%) than in any European nation. And it is why a smaller percentage of transportation-related CO_2 is caused by road travel in the United States (83%) than anywhere other than Norway.[10]

Ecologically speaking, there is no advantage in sending passengers by rail if freight is sent by road. All European nations send a higher percentage of freight by road than America. In the nation with the highest rate (Ireland), the figure is close to four times the American (figure 132). As a result, the number of trucks (goods vehicles) per capita is lower in America than anywhere in Europe—one-third, for example, of the Norwegian, French, or Austrian levels (figure 133). And, contrary to popular belief, Americans do take buses much like Europeans—more so than the French, the English, and the Greeks.[11]

132. Road Freight

As % of Total Inland Freight

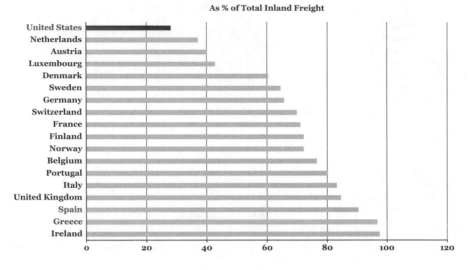

133. Goods Vehicles

In Use per 100 Population

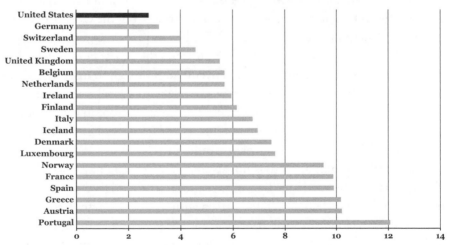

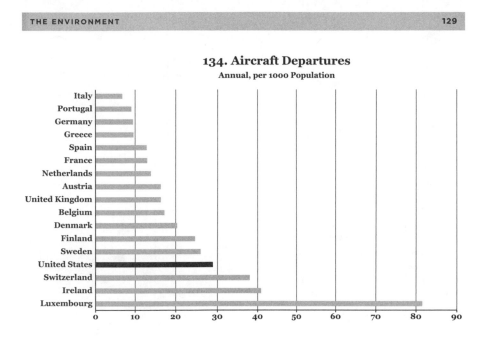

134. Aircraft Departures

Annual, per 1000 Population

Despite the size of the country and the importance of air travel for the domestic market, Americans take fewer plane trips per capita than the Swiss, the Irish, and the Luxembourgeois (figure 134). Subway usage in the largest cities puts the United States in the European middle ground. Per capita, New Yorkers travel by subway more often than Athenians, Berliners, and Londoners, as well as the residents of Oslo, Brussels, and Helsinki (figure 135). Looking beyond the singular transit system of New York, the Boston metro system has a higher annual ridership than that of Brussels. More San Franciscans ride the metro than do residents of Amsterdam, and more Philadelphians than those who live in Rotterdam. Chicago's metro has more passengers than Hamburg's. About two and a half times as many residents of Atlanta take the metro as do Glaswegians, which (depending on how the city is defined) is propor- tionately either a higher ridership in Atlanta or about the same. Ridership in Washington DC is only about 20% lower than in Rome.[12] The United States has a lower concentration of its vehicles in urban areas than anywhere else in the OECD, and a higher percentage of them is in rural areas than among any of our comparison countries other than Sweden and Austria.[13] In other words, Americans are more likely than most Europeans to use their cars where driving is required: in rural areas without mass transit.

Americans are not great walkers, clocking less than half as many kilometers per capita annually as the least ambulatory Europeans, the Portuguese. Nor

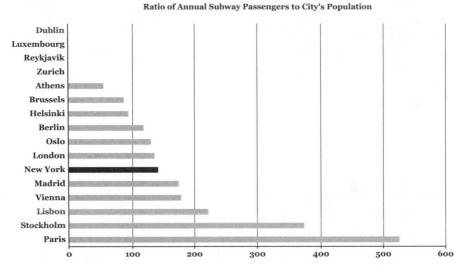

135. Subway Passengers

Ratio of Annual Subway Passengers to City's Population

are they avid bicyclists. But neither are the Spaniards, Greeks, Portuguese, or Luxembourgeois, who cycle equally little on an average daily basis, while the French and British cycle only one-tenth of a kilometer—one hundred meters—farther. If we look at the percentage of all trips taken by bicycle, the Americans are no worse than the British (1%). The Dutch cycle on average nine times as much as the Italians and French, and almost thrice as often as the Swedes and Germans. Bicycling can hardly be said to be a pan-European characteristic.[14]

We all know the stereotype: Americans sit alone in their outlandish SUVs while Europeans virtuously cram into trains. The opposite but more rarely conjured image is equally true: Americans parsimoniously take a local camping trip during their short vacations, while the Germans fly off to Phuket or Goa two or three times a year, and the British jet monthly to their holiday houses on the Costa del Sol.[15] If we try to measure the overall transportation footprint, we are faced with tricky business. American carbon dioxide output is, as we know, high to start with. But, of that output, only a moderate amount is produced by transportation, in the middle of the European range (figure 136). If we calculate energy used for transportation per capita, American figures are high, over twice the level of most European nations (except Luxembourg, where the numbers, in turn, are again twice as high).

Nations vary, however, in terms of population density, size, and consequently, the distances their citizens need to cover. The sparsely populated

136. CO2 Emissions from Transport
Percent of CO2 Emissions from Fuel Combustion Caused by Transport

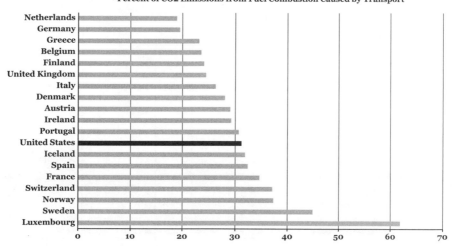

Scandinavian nations and Ireland rank higher in transport energy usage per capita than more densely settled countries like Denmark, the UK, Germany, and the Netherlands. Transport energy usage measured per square kilometer—in other words, divided over the size of the country—gives American figures that are higher than, but largely in the same league as, the Scandinavian nations, comparable to countries like Austria, Spain, France, Portugal, Greece, and Ireland, and significantly lower than in densely populated Belgium, Denmark, Germany, Italy, Luxembourg, the Netherlands, and the UK. If we combine these factors, taking account of both the consumers who use energy for travel and the distances that they have to surmount, and create a measure of energy (in million-tons-of-oil equivalents) per person per square kilometer, the results are as follows: France is the most efficient nation in Europe. The Scandinavian nations, except Denmark and Iceland, come next. They are joined by a series of more densely populated countries that nonetheless are frugal users: Italy, Spain, Germany, and the UK. Then come the heavily using nations: Belgium, Austria, Denmark, Iceland, Ireland, the Netherlands, and Switzerland. But the United States is lower than any European nation in this measure, using approximately one-sixth as much energy per person per square kilometer as the most efficient European nation (France). In other words, if we account for the demographic and topological circumstances faced by each nation, American transport energy usage compares reasonably well to European rates.[16]

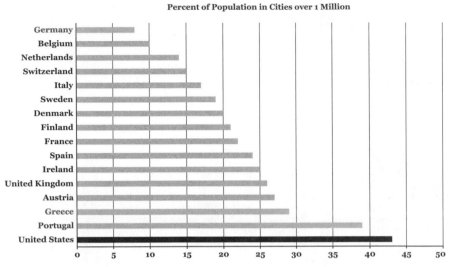

137. Urbanized Population

Percent of Population in Cities over 1 Million

Needless to say, calculations that take demography, geography, and topology into account work in both directions. Thus, if we look at energy used for household heating, in 1998 the citizens of Germany, France, Finland, Denmark, Norway, and Sweden used more than Americans per capita. But if we correct for the colder climate of Scandinavia, their consumption patterns fall to less wasteful levels, lower than the American. The Germans and French remain, however, more profligate users of heating energy than the Americans.[17]

By European standards, Americans are urbanized. A higher percent live in big cities than any Europeans (figure 137). Despite preconceptions of American suburbia, these cities are reasonably densely populated, falling in the lower half of the European scale, on par with those in Scandinavia. Indeed, the major surprise, sprung on us by the impartiality of statistics, is that Los Angeles is among the densest of America's cities, about a third more thickly settled on average than New York City (figure 138).

Americans produce a lot of waste per head, though the Norwegians are worse, and the Irish and Danes are close competitors (figure 139). But they recycle as well as the Finns and the French, and better than the British, the Greeks, and the Portuguese (figure 140). Since 1990, Americans' production of waste has scarcely gone up per capita, while in all European nations for which figures are available, there have been dramatic increases—over 70% in Spain,

138. Urban Density

Population Densities of Major Urban Areas in Inhabitants per Square Mile

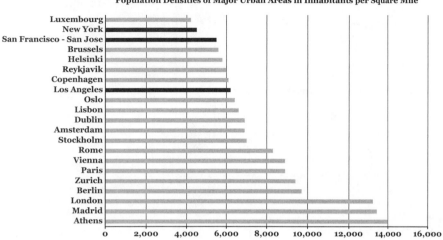

139. Municipal Waste

Municipal Waste Generation in Kg per Capita

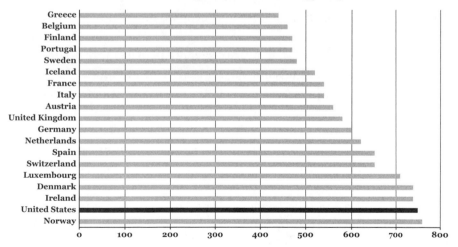

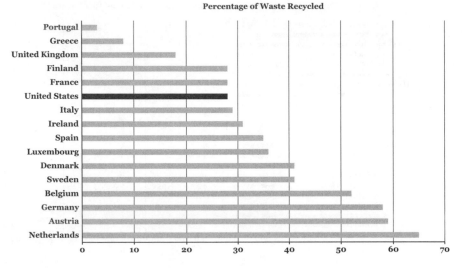

140. Recycling

Percentage of Waste Recycled

almost 60% in Italy, for example, over 40% in Norway, almost that much in Denmark and Austria, and well over 30% in Sweden.[18]

"The old world developed on the basis of a coalition—uneasy but understood—between humanity and its surroundings," the *Guardian* reassures its recycling readership. "The settlement of the United States was based on conquest, not just of the indigenous peoples, but also of the terrain."[19] Yet despite such common European conceptions, American conservation efforts are strong by European standards. Jeremy Rifkin insists that Europeans, unlike Americans, have "a love for the intrinsic value of nature. One can see it in Europeans' regard for the rural countryside and their determination to maintain natural landscapes."[20] Actually, the percentage of national territory protected in the United States is about double that of France, the UK, or even Sweden, despite its vast Arctic parks. Eleven European nations (out of 16) spare a smaller percent of their land than the United States (figure 141). A higher percentage of U.S. waters—marine territory—is set aside as nature reserves than in any European nation other than Denmark.[21]

The results can be seen by comparing how many species of animals are threatened by extinction in America with the numbers in Europe. Only in Ireland, the UK, Finland, Portugal, and the Netherlands are fewer mammals, measured as a percentage of species known, endangered than in the United States (figure 142). In Germany, which regards itself as in the ecological

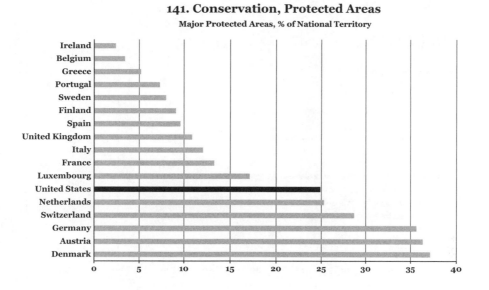

141. Conservation, Protected Areas
Major Protected Areas, % of National Territory

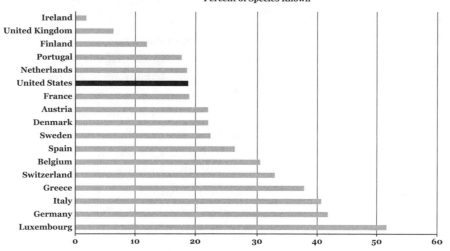

142. Threatened Mammals
Percent of Species Known

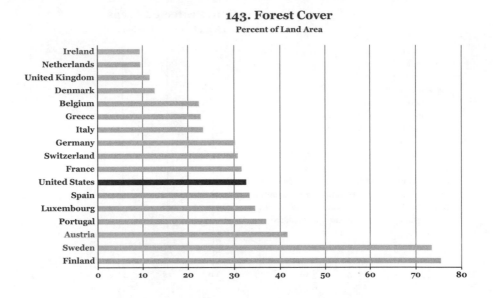

143. Forest Cover
Percent of Land Area

vanguard, over twice as great a percentage of species is at risk. Similar results hold for fish and birds. Obviously, some such disparities have to do with the length of settlement and population densities, both of which are less intrusive in the United States, though Scandinavia (outside Denmark) is even more lightly peopled. Nonetheless, there is more to the story than that. Why do densely populated nations like Denmark or the Netherlands set aside more of their land as nature reserves than sparsely occupied ones like Ireland and Sweden? Why are proportionately far more mammals threatened in Germany than in the UK, even though Britain is more densely settled? These are the outcomes of choices and policies, not just of geodemographic destiny.

Forest cover in the United States is also proportionately greater than in most European nations. Predictably, Sweden and Finland (countries with, respectively, two-thirds and one-half of the population density of the United States) are the European front-runners, joined by Spain, Austria, Portugal, and Luxembourg (figure 143). The intensity with which forest resources are exploited, measured as the percentage of annual growth harvested, is at the low end of the European spectrum, below that of Belgium, Portugal, Switzerland, the UK, Austria, Greece, Ireland, Finland, Sweden, and Denmark.[22]

Agricultural land devoted to organic farming in the United States, as a percentage of total cropland, is lower than anywhere in Europe.[23] But Americans'

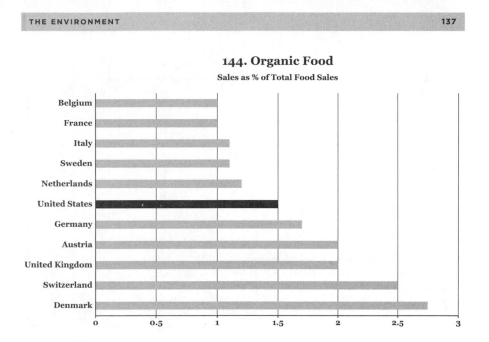

144. Organic Food

Sales as % of Total Food Sales

consumption of organic food is comparable to European levels and higher than in the Netherlands, Sweden, Italy, France, and Belgium (figure 144). And conventional American farmers are far less chemicalized than their European colleagues. Thanks partly to their use of genetically modified crops, they use pesticides sparingly (figure 145). Only Finnish, Swedish, and Irish farmers spray less per square kilometer of agricultural land. The Italians use over six times as much, the Belgians even more. Similarly, Dutch farmers use proportionately five times as much nitrogenous fertilizer as Americans. Only the Portuguese use less (figure 146). By European standards of agriculture, American farmers are practically organic to begin with. American water use, as a fraction of available resources, is middle of the pack (figure 147). Measured in relation to production, the results are much the same, with most of the Mediterranean nations coming in above the United States.[24]

Industrial emissions in the United States are highish, measured as a function of GDP, though off the European scale only for carbon monoxide. For volatile organic compounds, Norway, Portugal, and Greece are worse, Spain is the same, and Sweden a close competitor. For nitrogen oxides, Iceland is worse, while Spain and Greece, followed by Portugal, run close behind. For sulfur oxides, Greece, Portugal, and Spain emit proportionately more, while Iceland is almost as bad (figure 148). These pollutants have been coming down

145. Pesticide Use
Tonnes per Square Kilometer of Agricultural Land

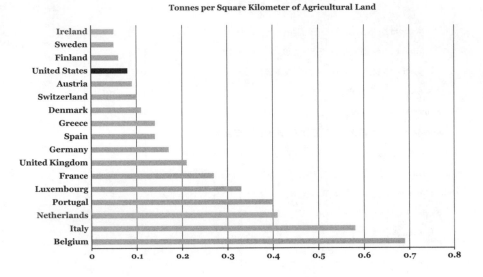

146. Nitrogenous Fertilizer Use
Tonnes per Square Kilometer of Agricultural Land

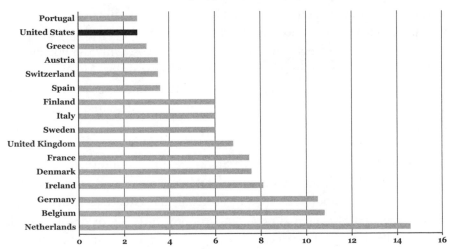

147. Intensity of Water Use

Abstractions as % of Renewable Resources

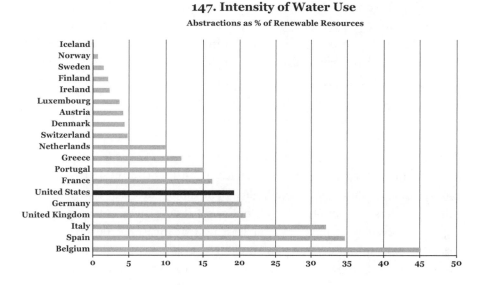

148. Sulfur Oxide Emissions

Kg per $1000 GDP

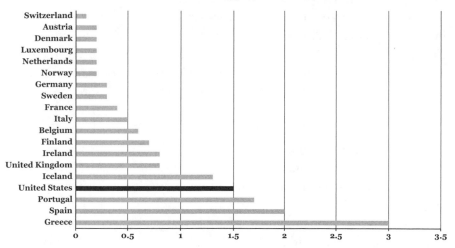

over the last decade or so as quickly in the United States as they have in several European nations. From 1990 to 2002, American sulfur oxide emissions dropped by 34%, a result that puts the United States in the European middle ground, better than Iceland, Greece, Portugal, and Spain. For nitrogen oxides, the improvement in the United States has been more rapid than in Austria, Greece, Iceland, Ireland, Portugal, Spain, and Norway.[25]

By European standards, America's city dwellers are exposed only moderately to particulate matter (figure 149). And these levels have been dropping faster than in Austria, Norway, Portugal, and Switzerland.[26] Take the American city most infamous for its bad air, Los Angeles: according to OECD figures from 1993, although ozone rates were higher than in all European cities, on most other measures of pollution LA was better off than its peers. Average carbon monoxide levels were lower than at least half of measured European cities, nitrogen dioxide rates were approximately the same as London's, lead rates lower than any European city other than Bergen and the same as Magdeburg, sulfur dioxide rates below any other than Trondheim, suspended particulate levels lower only in Oslo, Gothenburg, and Trondheim.[27] In other words, by these other measures, the only European cities with air as clean as LA (a metropolitan area of 13 million inhabitants) were small Scandinavian towns near the Atlantic coast.

By European standards, U.S. water pollution is moderate, at least in terms of organic pollutants emitted daily per worker (figure 150). Comparative data is hard to find. But in more specific measures, the Delaware River appears to be better off in terms of dissolved oxygen content than any river in Europe other than the Elbe, while the Mississippi holds its own above the Seine, the Arno, and the Mersey, and is at about the same level as the Adige and the Clyde. In terms of biochemical oxygen demand, another measure of water quality, the Mississippi is practically pristine, and unrivaled in Europe except by smaller rivers like the Skjern in Denmark and the Douro in Portugal. The Delaware, in turn, holds its position in the middle ground. When it comes to phosphorus content, these two American rivers hold a middle position. They shine in terms of ammonium content and have comparatively low lead, copper, and chromium levels.[28]

American electricity consumption per year and per capita is on the high end, but lower than all the Nordic nations except Denmark (figure 151). Energy efficiency in the United States, as measured in terms of energy use per unit of GDP, is not brilliant, but it is better than in Iceland, Luxembourg, and Finland and only a bit below the Swedish and Norwegian rates (figure 152). Oil use per capita

149. Airborne Particulate Matter

Particulate Matter 10 in Micrograms per Cubic Meter

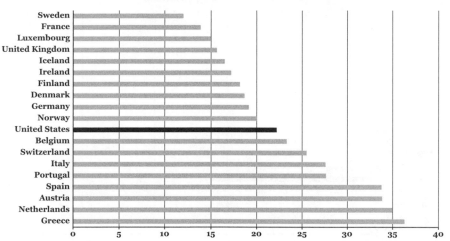

150. Organic Water Pollutant Emissions

Kg per Day per Worker

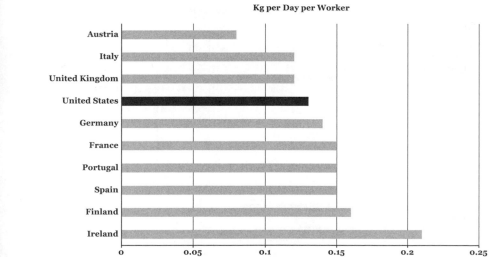

151. Electricity Consumption per Capita

Kilograms of Oil Equivalent

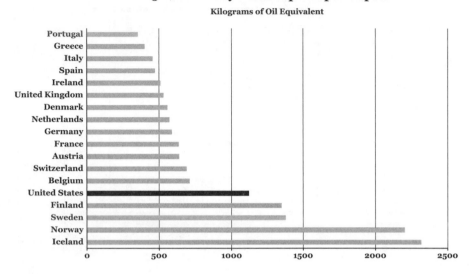

152. Energy Consumption per Unit of GDP

Tonnes of Oil Equivalent per 1000 US$

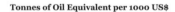

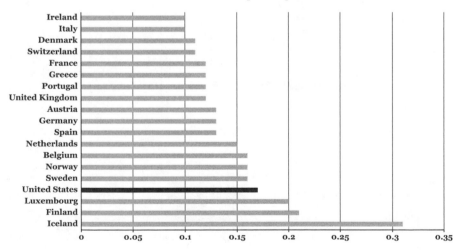

is high, though less than the Belgians and the Luxembourgeois (in this case, their figures are reported together), and only a drop higher than the Icelanders and the Dutch (figure 153). Measured as a function of economic output, American oil use remains within European norms, and indeed is lower than Portugal, Greece, Belgium, Luxembourg, the Netherlands, and Iceland (figure 154). Total American consumption of energy per capita is high, but less than in Iceland and Luxembourg and only a bit higher than Finland.

Over the last quarter century, energy consumption per unit of GDP has dropped dramatically in the United States, as it has in several European countries, such as Germany, Denmark, Sweden, the UK, and Ireland. Between 1973 and 2000, energy use per unit of GDP sank further in the United States (close to 50%) than in almost all of the OECD.[29] Similarly, American energy consumption measured per person has dropped, if more moderately (7%) since 1980. In the European countries we are looking at, this is true only for Denmark, Sweden, and Germany. In all other Western European nations, per capita energy consumption has risen, sometimes strongly—over 75% in Spain, 55% in Ireland and Greece, 40% in Iceland, 20% in Austria, Belgium, Italy, and Finland.[30]

As everyone knows, until China recently overtook it, the United States was the world's largest emitter of carbon dioxide. But if measured in relation to production, American output is not wholly off the European scale, though it is slightly higher than its immediate competitors, Luxembourg and Finland.[31] Measuring from 2003, the United States is middle of the pack in terms of how much more, or less, greenhouse gas has been emitted since 1990 (figure 155). Measured in terms of carbon dioxide output per unit of GDP (in PPP terms), the American figures have declined between 1990 and 2002 by 17%. That is a greater reduction of output per production than in nine Western European countries, and then there are two (Portugal and Spain) that have increased theirs. The same calculation done per capita shows a modest (1.5%) increase in American carbon dioxide output: a better performance than 12 of the nations we are examining.[32] American carbon dioxide output per unit of energy used (in other words, the carbon intensity of energy) is below that of Norway, Ireland, Denmark, and Greece.[33]

Rifkin claims that European culture's connectedness to nature means it has committed more firmly than the United States to shifting from fossil fuel to renewable energy sources.[34] Yet the facts speak otherwise. In its output of renewable energy, the United States is middle of the European spectrum on

153. Per Capita Oil Consumption

Barrels Consumed Daily per 1000 Population

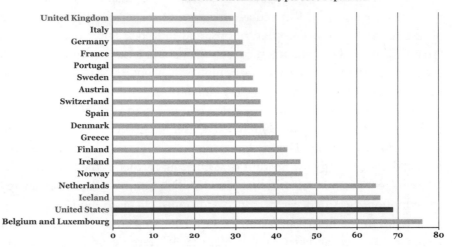

154. Oil Consumption per Unit of GDP

Tonnes per 100,000 US$ PPP GDP

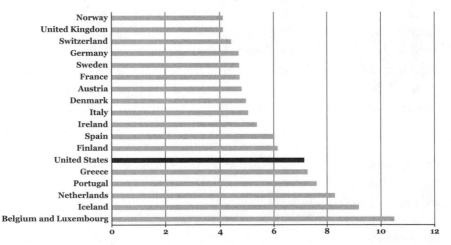

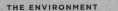

155. Rise or Decline of Greenhouse Gas Emissions, 1990-2003

Total Greenhouse Gas Emissions, 1990 = 100

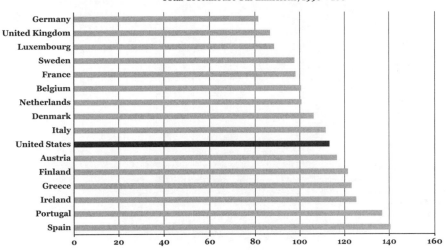

Germany
United Kingdom
Luxembourg
Sweden
France
Belgium
Netherlands
Denmark
Italy
United States
Austria
Finland
Greece
Ireland
Portugal
Spain

0   20   40   60   80   100   120   140   160

156. Solar Energy

Consumption as a % of Total Energy Consumption

Belgium
Finland
Iceland
Ireland
Norway
France
Italy
Netherlands
Sweden
United Kingdom
Spain
Denmark
Germany
United States
Portugal
Switzerland
Austria
Greece

0   0.05   0.1   0.15   0.2   0.25   0.3   0.35   0.4

157. Venture Capital Investment in Clean Technology Companies
Per Capita in US$

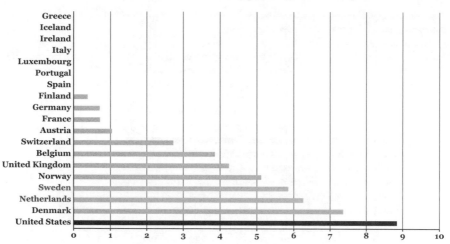

158. Nuclear Waste
Tonnes per One Million Tonnes of Oil Equivalent of Total Primary Energy Supply

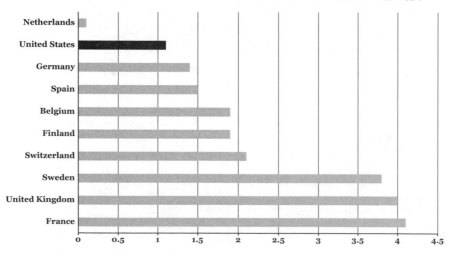

all counts, whether biogas, solid biomass energy, geothermal, or wind. Solar power as a percentage of total energy consumption, for example, is higher only in Portugal, Switzerland, Austria, and Greece (figure 156). The percentage of transport fuels from so-called biological sources (a misnomer, really, since oil in the usual sense is just very old biodiesel) used by Americans was topped only by Germans and Swedes.[35] American investors have ventured proportionately more capital in clean technologies than their European peers (figure 157). Proportional to total energy supply, the country's nuclear waste levels are moderate (figure 158).

EIGHT
CIVIL
SOCIETY

QUANTIFYING THE ATTRIBUTES of civil society, in turn, is complicated and slippery, but let us try. Americans are often thought to be unusually anti-government in their political ideology, practically anarchists by European standards. They are supposed to believe in individual reliance, be less inclined than Europeans to have the state help the worst-off, and more likely to regard the poor as having failed.[1] Surveys of attitudes do not, however, uniformly bear out such polarities. Proportionately more Americans than anyone but the Spaniards claim to obey the law without exception.[2] A higher percentage of Americans trusts their government a great deal than many Europeans, other than the Spaniards, the Swiss and the Finns (figure 159). A Pew Foundation survey in 2007 found that proportionately fewer Americans worried that the government had too much control than did Germans and Italians, with the French at the same level and the British just a percentage point lower.[3] A higher

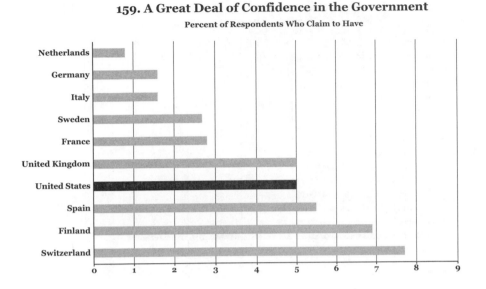

159. A Great Deal of Confidence in the Government
Percent of Respondents Who Claim to Have

percentage of Americans have a great deal of confidence in their civil service than any Europeans other than the Irish. Proportionately, almost five times as many Americans as Swedes say they trust their government bureaucracy (figure 160). But talk is cheap, and such findings may indicate desire as much as reality. The trust of Americans in their state apparatus can be measured more concretely by their willingness to pay taxes. Unlike many Europeans, Americans pay the taxes required of them. Only in Austria and Switzerland are the underground economies as small. In the Mediterranean, the rate of tax avoidance is much higher—over three times the American level in Greece and Italy (figure 161). The Montana survivalist—so beloved by the European media—holed up in his shack, provisioned for a siege, and determined to resist the government's impositions, is as uncharacteristic of the average American as the Basque or Corsican separatist, ready to kill and maim for his localist aspirations, is of the average European.

The simple polarities voiced by observers like Will Hutton, which place American individualism in binary opposition to European solidarity, have recently begun to give way to more sophisticated analyses.[4] The latest and most intriguing conceptual shift is proposed by Henrik Berggren and Lars Trägårdh. They argue not only that Swedes are more individualistic than Americans, but that the whole point of the Nordic welfare state is not so much to be solidaristic as it is to make citizens independent of each other—aging parents autonomous

160. A Great Deal of Confidence in the Civil Service
Percent of Respondents Who Claim to Have

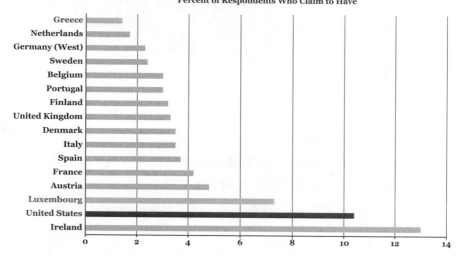

161. Shadow Economy
Size as % of Official GNP (Cash Approach)

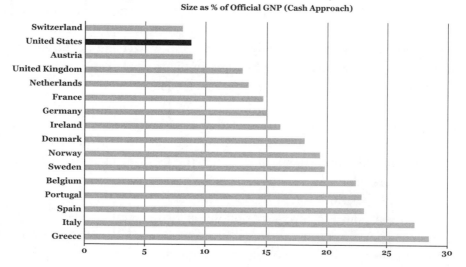

of their children, wives of their husbands, offspring of their parents. What the Swedes seek, in other words, is autonomy through the state.[5]

Robert Putnam and other social scientists have lamented the decline of civic cooperation and a cohesive civil society that they see as once having defined America.[6] Perhaps America has become more anomic in the age of TV and the Internet. But it still remains a society that, by European standards, is exceptionally based on trust, cooperation, and voluntary compliance with associational norms. Americans trust each other more than people in almost all European societies outside of Scandinavia (figure 162). They reject antisocial behavior more than all Europeans other than the Scandinavians, except the Danes, the Italians, the Austrians, and the Swiss.[7] They belong to civic associations more often than all Europeans except the 300,000 Icelanders (figure 163). Only in the Netherlands, Belgium, and Ireland is there a higher percentage of the workforce that is active in civil society organizations, whether paid or volunteer. The Italian level is only slightly more than one-third the U.S. rate; the Austrian is half.[8] It is sometimes pointed out that such civic participation in the United States is often linked to church membership. But even the most streamlined figures (stripping out church participation, union membership, which is often less than voluntary, and social movements) reveal that Americans are more eager joiners than anyone but the Dutch.[9]

The view of America as a balkanized stew of multicultural tribes, each arguing their right to separate identities, also turns out to be an exaggeration. While the hopes of wholly superannuating racial dilemmas in U.S. politics that have been encouraged by Obama's victory are unlikely all to be achieved, certainly the election of a mixed-race president with a background of different cultural experiences speaks of ambitions to transcend inherited polarizations. More mundanely, one attempt to quantify how far subcultural groups are given collective rights places the United States in the European middle ground, along with the UK, Germany, Denmark, and Norway. The United States is more willing to risk a fraying of the social fabric than those nations that aim to homogenize their foreigners, like France, Switzerland, Ireland, and Portugal. But it is less inclined to allow minorities to isolate and govern themselves than the Netherlands and Sweden, with their anything-goes policies.[10]

America is distinguished by the philanthropy and volunteerism of its citizens. Measured as a fraction of GDP, charitable giving in the United States is greater than in any European country (figure 164). Americans give

162. Trust in Others
Percent of Respondents Who Believe "Most People Can Be Trusted"

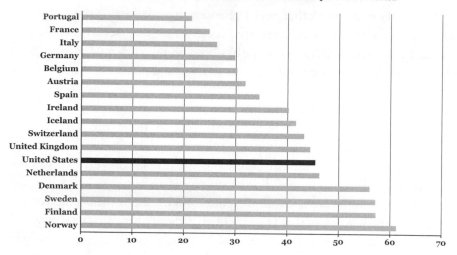

163. Civic Organizations
Density of Membership

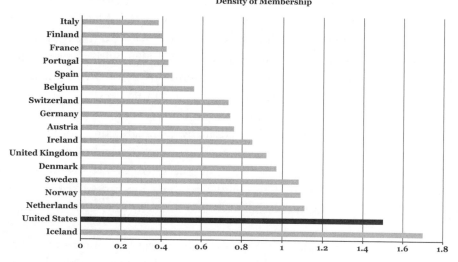

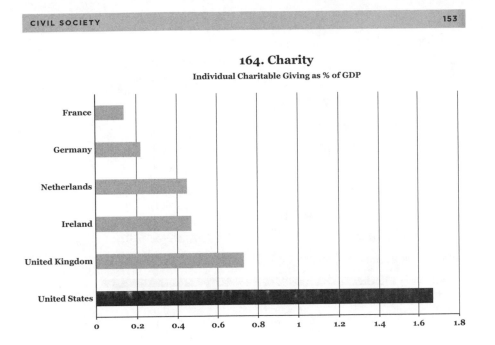

164. Charity
Individual Charitable Giving as % of GDP

proportionately over twice as much as their nearest competitors, the British, over seven times as much as the Germans, and almost a dozen times more than the French. No doubt the tax code, with credits for charitable donations, is partly responsible for this happy outcome, though the differences can be easily overstated. Other tax systems—those of the UK and Germany, for example—allow similar credits without prompting similar levels of giving.

Tax codes are unlikely to be implicated in another aspect of altruistic civil society: volunteering. Americans do volunteer work in greater numbers than anyone but the Swedes (figure 165). They donate blood more frequently than any Europeans, though the French are a close second (figure 166). Blood donated privately and voluntarily is safer, as Europeans learned tragically when their unwillingness to donate blood made them dependent on imported and infected plasma products during the early years of the AIDS epidemic.[11] In some accountings, Americans are not only more willing to donate organs than any Europeans other than the Swedes, their actual donation rates are topped only by the Spanish, Austrians, Portuguese, and Belgians. In others, they are more ready organ donors, both live and cadaveric, than any Europeans by far.[12]

A smaller percentage of Americans turn up for parliamentary elections, or their equivalent, than any Europeans other than the Swiss (figure 167). The

165. Volunteer Work
Percent of Adult Population Volunteering

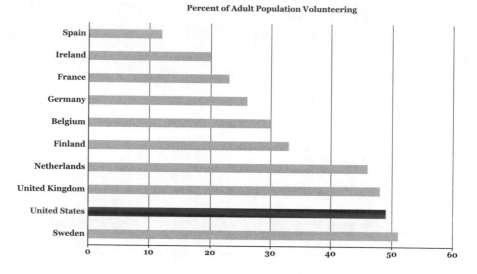

166. Blood Donation
Percent of Respondents Who Have Ever Given Blood

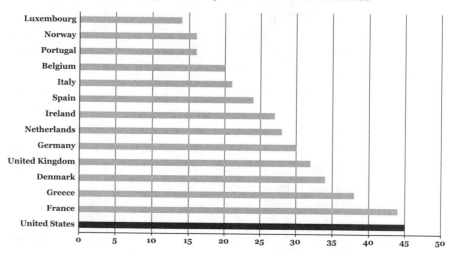

167. Voter Turnout

In Parliamentary Elections (%)

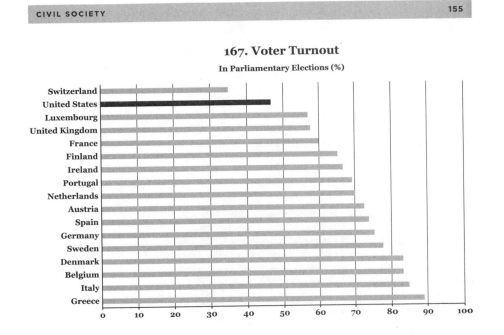

better off and more educated Americans are, the more like Europeans their voting behavior is. The poor and ill-educated are least likely to exercise their electoral power.[13] But Americans discuss politics much like anyone else (figure 168). Indeed, a higher fraction of them claims to be very interested in politics than anyone other than the Germans.[14] More claim to be active members of a political party than any Europeans.[15] Americans participate in other political activities more often than many Europeans. Proportionately more have recently contacted a politician or government official than anywhere other than Norway, Finland, and Ireland.[16] They sign petitions and join boycotts more often than anyone but the Swedes. They demonstrate more often than do citizens of seven of the countries we are examining. Americans even occupy buildings or factories more often than any Europeans except the Italians, Dutch, Belgians, French, and Greeks. But then, over a quarter of Greeks say they have occupied buildings in protest. If true, that indicates a chaotic country; if false, a lively imagination.[17]

Many Americans raise their children alone, more even than in the UK, where single parenthood is most prevalent in Europe (figure 169). By European standards, American families rarely eat together; only the Finns do so less frequently (figure 170).

But parents in the United States often talk with their offspring (figure 171). In only five European nations do families discuss things with each other

168. Frequent Discussion of Politics

Percent of Respondents Who Claim They Discuss Politics Frequently with Their Friends

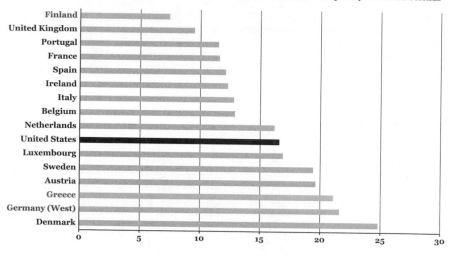

169. Single Parent Households

As a Percent of All Households with Children

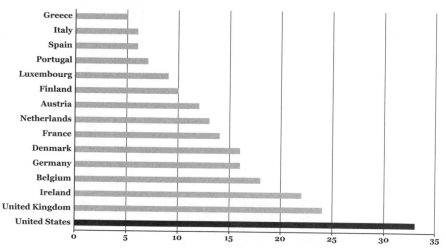

170. Eating with Parents
Percent of 15 Year-Olds Who Eat Main Meal with Parents Several Times per Week

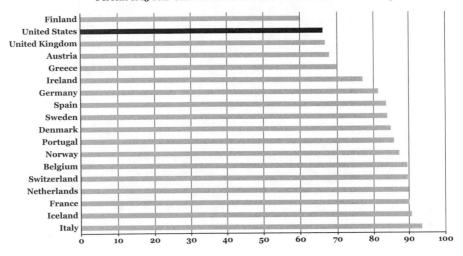

171. Talking with Parents
Percent of 15 Year-Olds Whose Parents Spend Time "Just Talking with Them" Several Times per Week

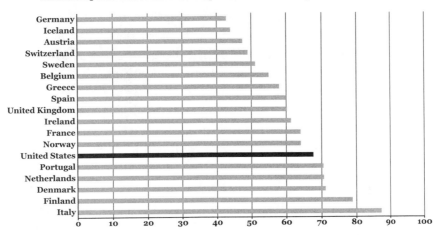

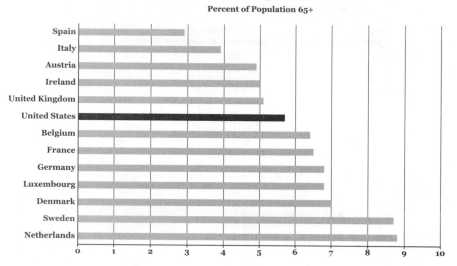

172. Elderly Living in Institutions
Percent of Population 65+

more often. By other measures, too, families are strong in the United States. Americans consider their parents worthy of unconditional respect more often than any Europeans other than the Spanish and the Portuguese, and at the same level as the Italians.[18] Many Americans keep their elderly parents at home, rather than bundling them off to an institution (figure 172). The Dutch and the Swedes, for example, are about 50% more likely to send their parents to an old-age home. The Spaniards and Italians do so much less. One would not want to read too much into such figures. It may well be that low use of retirement homes reflects their unaffordability and lack of subsidization by the state, rather than close family ties.

But American families do appear tightly knit. Siblings visit each other on a daily basis more often than anywhere in Europe outside family-oriented Italy and Spain. Adult children receive daily visits from their parents more often than in the UK, Denmark, Finland, Norway, and France, and much the same holds for children's visits to parents. Friendship circles also seem well-developed. Fewer Americans report having no close friends at their workplace than anyone other than the Italians and the Finns. Proportionately more Americans have at least 10 friends than do the Germans, Austrians, Italians, Spanish, French, Swiss, and Finns. More Americans say they have at least 10 close friends living near them than do the Austrians, Italians, Spanish, French,

Danes, Swiss, and Finns. And more visit these friends on a daily basis than the citizens of most of these countries, too.[19] Only in the Mediterranean, other than France, and in Ireland does a smaller percentage of people live alone than in the United States. Proportionately fewer Americans are socially isolated, with only rare contact to others, than in any European nation outside Ireland and the Netherlands.[20] Americans do not go out to eat or spend the night away as often as the Mediterraneans or the British, but they do so more than the Scandinavians, the Dutch, and the Germans.[21]

NINE
NATIONALISM

AMERICANS ARE PATRIOTIC AND NATIONALIST, but not more than some Europeans (figure 173). Unsurprisingly, Germans are least proud of their nation, and rather unexpectedly and cheerily, the Portuguese—not the Americans—are most proud, with the Irish tied for second place. A 2007 survey reveals that a larger proportion of Italians consider their culture superior than any other nationalities surveyed, including the Americans.[1] Another survey finds that only the Irish feel more uniformly proud to be of their nation. Proportionately more Austrians, Irish, French, and Danes claim they feel very close to their nation than do Americans. Americans are more likely than any Europeans to think that their country is better than most others. But proportionately more Portuguese, Danes, and Spaniards feel that the world would be improved if other people were like them. And any U.S. tendency to boosterism is tempered by the finding that a larger fraction of Americans admits that

173. Very Proud of Own Nationality

Percent of Respondents Who Claim to Be

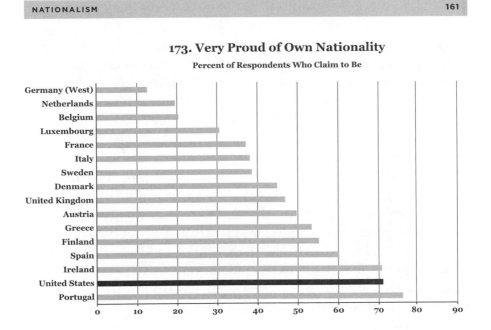

certain aspects of their country shame them than do the Germans, Austrians, Spanish, French, Danes, or Finns.[2]

No country more robustly projects its own nationalist aspirations in the products it sells abroad than the supposedly postnational Swedes. Swedish manufacturers, or at least their advertising agencies, seem convinced that the sheer fact of being Swedish is a selling point. Ikea's walls are adorned with musings on the preternaturally close relationship between Swedes and nature that allegedly sets them apart from the rest of humanity, as are packets of Wasa crispbread. Asko's slogan, "Made In Sweden," is festooned prominently on its products. Though it does not necessarily inspire confidence that the company's dishwashers are better than the competition, it certainly makes clear Asko's national origins. Absolut Vodka's tag—in uncharacteristically unidiomatic English—"Country of Sweden," does much the same. Saab hawks its cars as "Born from Jets," an unsubtle allusion to the company's standing as a pillar of the Swedish military-industrial complex.

"There is a surfeit of national symbols throughout the land," writes Josef Joffe, a sympathetic observer of America, "whereas no gas station in Europe would ever fly an oversized national flag."[3] That may be true for gas stations. Then again, Americans are not in the habit of painting their faces with the Stars and Stripes and drunkenly crossing the border northward, intent on beating up Canadian soccer fans. And consider the behavior of the supposedly postnationalist Danes. Their flag, Dannebro, is said to have floated down from heaven as a sign from God during the battle of Tallinn in 1219, part of the Danish Christian crusades against the heathen Estonians. Because of this mystic nationalist attachment to their banner, Danes think nothing of festooning their Christmas trees with flags. In America, only fire-breathing reactionaries would share such decorative instincts. But the Danes find this so unobjectionable that the Danish Cultural Institute cheerily explains to Germans on its Web site that this is a traditional ritual, much beloved by the locals. Indeed, during the nineteenth century, as Danes and Germans fought over the provinces Schleswig and Holstein, the national colors, red and white, became characteristic generally of Danish Christmas decorations.[4] Surveys reveal that the Finns (82%), Danes (83%), Norwegians (87%), and Swedes (85%) are all more willing to fight for their country than the Americans (71%).[5] Perhaps the postnationalism of at least the Scandinavians has been exaggerated. Located uncomfortably between the Russians and the Germans, they appreciate the value of a good army.

TEN
RELIGION
AND
SCIENCE

EVEN ON RELIGION, there is reason to question the usual stereotypes of an absolute polarity between the United States and Europe. Let us leave aside the extent to which secularizing Europe is the outlier in a religious world, not the United States. There are religious contrasts, to be sure, between America and Europe, but they are neither as stark nor undifferentiated as is often thought. It is frequently said that Americans are more religious than Europeans. These things are hard to quantify, but there is certainly data pointing in that direction. In 1999, a smaller percentage of Americans (1.4%) described themselves as atheists than did Europeans—by a small margin, with the Irish and the Austrians almost indistinguishably close to the Americans (figure 174). But then again, no European country except France (with 14.2%) has more than 8% avowed atheists. The Americans are closer (less than one standard deviation below) to the European mean than are the French, who are more than three standard deviations above it.[1]

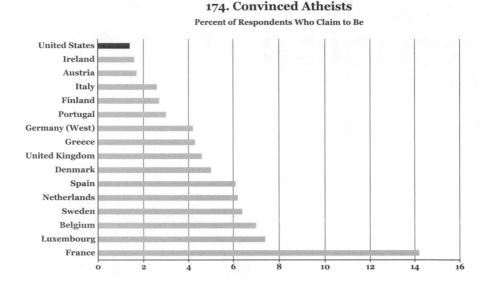

174. Convinced Atheists

Percent of Respondents Who Claim to Be

A smaller percentage of Americans consider themselves religious than the Portuguese and Italians.[2] Proportionately fewer Americans say they believe in God and always have than the Irish and Portuguese, and only a few more than the Italians.[3] A higher percentage of Americans firmly believes in God than northern Europeans, but the numbers are broadly comparable with the Catholic countries (figure 175). If the qualifier "firm" is removed, the American figures become much the same as the Mediterranean nations and, of course, Ireland (figure 176). Again, the United States is closer to the European mean (1.6 standard deviations above) than is the nonbelieving extreme, Sweden, at 1.9 standard deviations below it. Percentage-wise, more Americans (16.4%) attend church more than once a week than in any European nation (Ireland: 13.3%).[4] But fewer Americans, by far, attend church on a weekly basis than the Irish, and the Portuguese and Italians attend at the same rate. The American figure for weekly church attendance is only about as far above the European mean (1.2 standard deviations) as the Danish result (1.07 standard deviations) is below it (figure 177). Over a quarter of Americans report never attending church, the same as the Finns, compared to only 12% of Italians.[5]

Proportionately more Americans than Europeans believe in a life after death. But, excepting only Denmark, at least half the population of Western Europe believes in a life after death, and in some countries (Italy, Ireland, Portugal, Switzerland) it is well over two-thirds.[6] Proportionately more Americans than

175. Firm Belief in God

Percent of Respondents Who Have No Doubts That God Exists

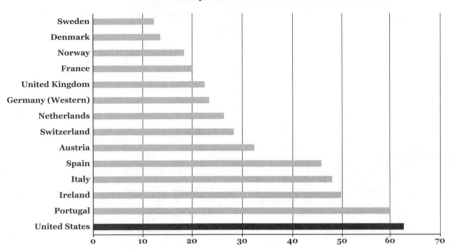

176. Belief in God

Percent of Respondents Who Claim to Believe in God

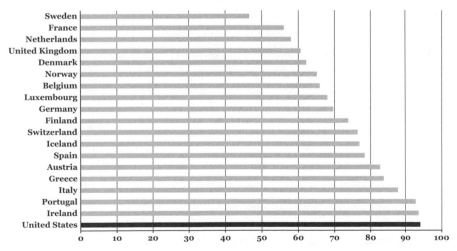

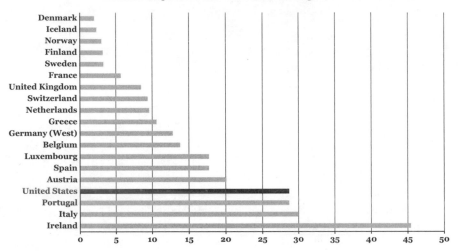

177. Weekly Church Attendance

Percent of Respondents Who Claim to Attend Religious Services Once a Week

any Europeans pray several times a day, but fewer Americans than Portuguese do so daily, and fewer Americans do so weekly than the British, the Italians, the Irish, the Spanish, the Portuguese, and the Swiss. The percentage of Americans who never pray is over twice that of Ireland.[7] More Italians than Americans sampled by the World Values Survey in 2005–2006 thought that the church provided answers to moral problems and more Italians and Finns that it did so for spiritual needs too. More Italians than Americans considered themselves religious.[8]

If we move from what people tell pollsters to what they do, the stark contrasts between American and European religiosity fade further. The number of Christian congregations per capita in the United States is within the European norm, with significantly lower numbers than in Greece and only somewhat higher than in the UK (figure 178). According to the World Values Survey, fewer Americans are members of religious denominations than is the case among the Swedes, Dutch. Luxembourgois, French, and Belgians (figure 179). American Catholics and their European coreligionists attend church in largely equal measure (figure 180). The Spanish and the Irish are there more often. American churches are not unusually well financed, whether per member or per capita, though only the latter is graphed here (figure 181). The churches of six European nations are better off.

Recent analyses claim that churches are more active in the United States than Europe for market-driven reasons: greater competition has led to a richer

178. Christian Congregations

Per Million Population

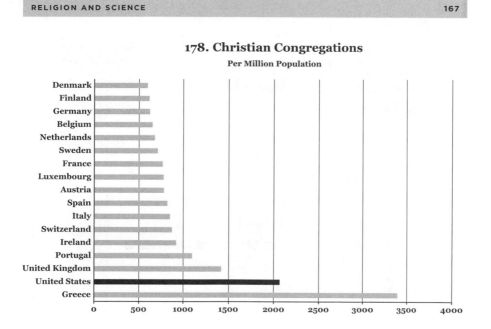

179. Membership in Religious Denominations

Percent of Respondents Who Claim to Belong to One

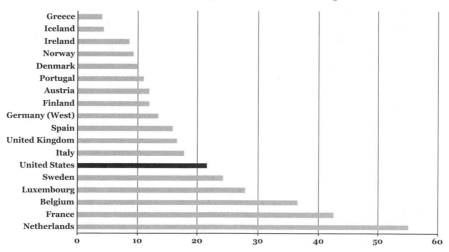

180. Catholic Church Attendance

Percent of Catholics over 35 Who Attend Church at Least Once a Month

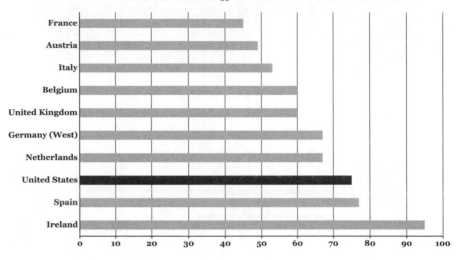

181. Church Income

Per Capita, US$

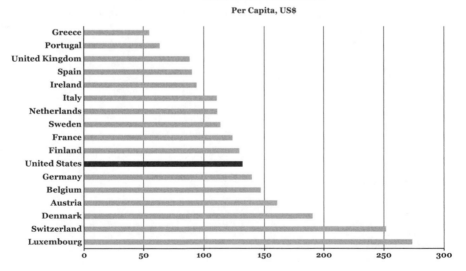

variety and higher quality of offerings, while Europe's state-monopoly religions have ceased providing for their citizens' spiritual needs.[9] Put succinctly,
European churches suffer from much the same problems as restaurants did
in the East Bloc. Indeed, there may be a parallel between spiritual and culinary satiation, perhaps even between religiosity and adiposity. It has often
been demonstrated that if a large variety of foods is available, more is eaten.
Is something similar true of religions? If Talleyrand could quip in the late
eighteenth century that America had thirty-two religions and only one sauce,
today the buffet table groans under bountiful offerings of both foods and religions. Americans display a distinct preference for more choice in food than do
Europeans, other than the British.[10] Something analogous seems to hold true
for religions.

   If the issue is thus one of supply and not demand, the implication is that
while spiritual longings do not differ much across the Atlantic, their satisfaction does. The only European nations where fewer people claim to think often
about the meaning of life than in America are Sweden, Germany, and Spain.
The others are pondering the big questions more.[11] The contrast, in other
words, is not so much between religious and secular mindsets, but between
how—if at all—largely equivalent spiritual needs are fulfilled. It follows that,
while spiritual requirements are satisfied by religious organizations in the
United States, they may find other expression in Europe. The World Values
Survey asks some questions of interest here.[12] For example, except for the
Danes and the Dutch, more Europeans say they believe in God than describe
themselves as religious (as do the Americans, too). This suggests a gulf between
inner belief and external behavior. Moreover, adding together those who
believe either in a personal God or in some sort of spirit or life force gives us
totals that are higher in some of the most secular nations than the respondents
who said merely that they believed in God. This holds for Iceland, Finland,
the Netherlands, and Sweden, but only moderately in Germany and not at all
in France and Denmark. In more conventionally religious European countries,
this gap does not exist. In other words, in the most secular nations there seems
to be belief in some higher power that is not captured by a simple question on
a survey about faith in God.

   Americans do differ religiously from Europeans on several important
points. A far higher proportion of them believe in both heaven and hell. That
adds grist to the usual mill. But consider the equally telling issue of the balance between the two—believers in heaven and believers in hell. In theory,
one might imagine that the two march in lockstep and that you cannot very

consistently believe in one without the other. But that would be to underestimate the human spirit's ability to accommodate itself comfortably in the world. The first conclusion to draw from a survey of attitudes toward heaven and hell is that modern humans are incurably optimistic. They may not put as much faith in an afterlife as their ancestors. But to the extent that they believe in a life after death, they are more likely to expect it to be heaven than hell.

More pertinent, however, is the relationship between those who believe in heaven and those who believe in hell and what this tells us about modern secularism. In the United States, the proportion between the two groups is most equal: five believers in heaven for each four believers in hell. The Italian ratio is about the same. Then follows a middle cluster of nations where the ratio between the two groups lies somewhere around 5:3: Germany, the UK, Spain, and France. Finally, the most secular countries are also those with the highest ratio of believers in heaven to believers in hell, with proportions around 2:1 in Denmark and Finland and almost 3:1 in Sweden and the Netherlands. The implication—as best it can be teased from the prosaic stuff of statistics—is that in the more secular nations, fewer, of course, are concerned with heaven and hell in the first place. But among those who do ponder such matters, the more secular the nation, the higher the relative emphasis on heaven over hell. Secularization may have dulled the fear of hell, but it has not entirely banished the hope of heaven.

None of this will stop people believing that there is a religious distinction across the Atlantic. Nor should it. But, as with so many aspects of the transatlantic gulf, this particular divide has been overstated. European observers who remark on the religiosity of Americans are often blind to the commonplace expressions of Christian sentiment in their own cultures. Indeed, the American observer of Europe is often puzzled at claims to secularism in the Old World, since displays of religion here are so frequent, so palpable, and so public, and yet—apparently—so taken for granted as to pass unnoticed. A tenth-century depiction of Christ's crucifixion is part of every Danish passport, regardless of whether its bearer is, as many nowadays are, a pious Muslim.[13] Crucifixes hang on the walls of Bavarian schools, greetings such as "Grüss Gott," or "God bless," are commonplace, Anglican morning prayers are held in English schools, and the flags of Denmark, Sweden, Norway, Iceland, Finland, Britain, and Greece all depict that central symbol of Christianity, the cross.

"Religion is palpable in U.S. schools, places of work, and public institutions," writes the Left-liberal English daily the *Guardian*. "God is invoked by soldiers and politicians in a way that would seem inappropriate in Britain."[14]

Really? Elizabeth II's title is Defender of the Faith. The Anglican church's 24 most senior bishops, known as the Lords Spiritual, sit in the House of Lords. In 2006, they helped block laws that would have legalized euthanasia.[15] And they have long influenced film censorship, abortion laws, rules for marriage, pornography licenses, and so forth. It is unimaginable that in Europe a president would begin his daily business with a prayer, claims Jürgen Habermas, the German philosopher. Yet that is precisely what is done in the British Parliament.[16] Jeremy Rifkin considers the fact that some 70% of Americans are said to favor school prayer evidence of their deep religiosity.[17] What, then, is it a sign of that pupils in British state schools are required by law to participate in a daily act of Christian worship?[18] Or that dinner at Oxford and Cambridge colleges starts with a Christian prayer as invariably as, for high table, it ends with port?

In Italy, the Catholic Church regularly meddles in politics, most recently gutting a law on fertility treatments and undermining hopes of extending legal rights to unwed couples, including gays.[19] The Vatican officially advises drivers to pray while behind the wheel.[20] In other countries, they are not even allowed to talk on their mobile phones. The Danish parliament is opened each year with a Christian service. In Holland, politicians from all parties make a point of giving their keynote speeches from church pulpits.[21] Article 139 of the German constitution enshrines Sunday as a day of rest and spiritual recuperation. Both Catholic and Protestant churches in Germany can and have had professors of theology whose opinions differed from official dogma (Hans Küng, Uta Ranke-Heinemann, Gerd Lüdemann, among others) removed from their positions at state universities. Out of the 18 European countries we are looking at, fully 10 have parties represented in parliament with the word "Christian" in their name.[22] The Christian Democrats are by far the largest grouping in the European parliament. For all of these parties, Christian faith helps shape their ideology and programs.

Even though he is now dead, one recent European head of state, John Paul II, is still considered able to cure the ill: a French nun of Parkinson's disease, a young man of lung cancer.[23] The Isle of Lewis (Outer Hebrides) enforces Sabbatarian legislation so strictly that the golf club and sports center are closed on Sundays, and playgrounds bear signs discouraging children from using them on the day of rest.[24] And let us not forget that Europe is a continent where people were, until a few years ago, still being killed in religious strife between Protestant and Catholic, Muslim and Orthodox. Serious debaters, a large body of public opinion, and several European countries

recently sought to have the EU constitution define Europe as a Christian culture. From their pulpits, Scandinavian pastors hint darkly that the 12 stars of
the EU flag are a symbol of covert Marian idolatry foisted on the Protestant
north by Brussels. In Greece, Orthodox religious instruction is mandatory
in state schools, with exemption possible only for the non-Orthodox, and
proselytizing by non-Orthodox religions is forbidden.[25] Battles are currently
being fought in Europe between Christians and Muslims over the permissi-
bility of building mosques.

The alleged theological divide across the Atlantic is only partly a contrast
between secularism and religiosity. As much, it is one between Catholicism and
high-church Protestantism on the European side, and low-church reformed
Christianity on the American. What often strikes Europeans as distinctive
in America is not the belief in something transcendent as such, but its personal, populist, and emotional expression. It is rarely American Catholics who
occupy Europeans' attention, since they are familiar from at home. Rather, it is
the evangelical and fundamentalist Protestants.

Take, by way of contrast, one theological dispute where the pie has been
sliced differently: the Anglican Church and its internal disaccord over the
ordination of gay bishops. American Episcopalians are as high-church as they
come in America. Episcopalianism is religion as Europeans understand it: the
province of tolerance, women, gays, minorities—a religion, in other words,
striving to make no claims on its adherents that would interfere with their secular lifestyles or embarrass them with the messy emotionality of low-church
enthusiasm. Meanwhile, desperate to prevent a schism, the Archbishop of
Canterbury, whose quotidian theological worries concern dilemmas like carbon footprints, recycling, and multicultural sensitivity, has vacillated, pander-
ing to the African and Asian congregations—for whom homosexuality is a
sin, hell and damnation mundane realities, and brimstone the elixir of their
sermons. The religious tail is wagging the dog of genteel Anglican religiosity in secular England, while in bible-thumping America, lifestyle issues have
trumped any serious discussion of actual theology in the Episcopal Church,
not to mention good and evil.

If Americans are, on the whole, more religious than most Europeans, it
does not follow that they have less overall faith in science. The choice between
rationality and religion does not seem to be zero-sum. The worldwide evidence suggests that societies with a strong faith in science also have strong
religious beliefs, and the transatlantic evidence confirms that.[26] It is true that
proportionately fewer Americans firmly agree with the Darwinian theory of

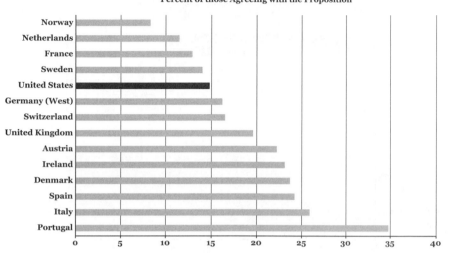

182. Science Does More Harm than Good
Percent of those Agreeing with the Proposition

evolution.[27] But, in other respects, Americans believe in the Enlightenment project of human reason's ability to understand and master nature. They fall in the European middle ground in approving animal testing to save human lives. They understand better than all Europeans (other than the Norwegians) the falsity of the proposition that all manmade chemicals cause cancer if you ingest enough of them, and better than anyone (other than the Norwegians and Swiss) that it is not true that anyone exposed to any degree of radioactivity will certainly die. They are more sanguine about the supposed dangers of genetically modified crops than any Europeans other than the Scandinavians (excluding Sweden).[28]

Proportionately fewer Americans agree with the proposition that science does more harm than good than any Europeans but the Dutch, Norwegians, Swedes, and French (figure 182). More American pupils agree with the statement that science helps them understand the world than students in any European nation other than Italy and Portugal. Confronted with the proposition that humanity depends too much on science and not enough on faith, the percentage of Americans who rejected it entirely in 2006 fell into the European middle ground, while more Italians than Americans embraced it wholeheartedly.[29] Relatively fewer Americans believe in astrology than in three major European countries for which figures are available: France, Germany, and the UK (figure 183). And fewer use homeopathic medicine (figure 184).

183. Belief in Astrology

Percent of People Who Take Astrology Seriously

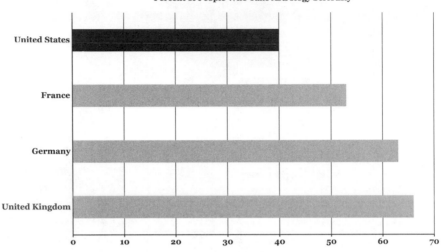

184. Homeopathy

Percent of Population Reporting Use of Homeopathy

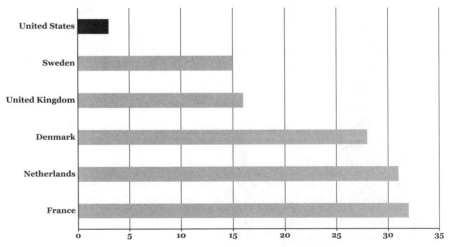

Although these questions were not asked of Americans by the International Social Survey Program, it is perhaps worth noting that close to half of Germans and Portuguese, and over a third of the Swiss and Austrians, believe that good luck charms do, in fact, bring good luck. Oddly enough, only a quarter of the Irish agree. About a third of Germans, Austrians, and Irish, and even more French and Swiss, believe that fortune-tellers can foresee the future. Over 40% of the Germans, Austrians, and Swiss (and almost that many French), as well as three quarters of the Irish, believe that faith healers have God-given powers. Over 40% of Germans, Swiss, and the French believe an individual's horoscope at birth affects his life. Finally, as a last fact to muddy the clarity of the alleged religious divide across the Atlantic: a higher proportion of the Portuguese believe in religious miracles than Americans (79%), followed closely by the Irish (71%), and at a slight remove by the Austrians (65%), Germans (62%), and Swiss (60%).[30]

ELEVEN
ASSIMILATION

LET US MOVE, NOW, from the otherworldly to the extraterritorial. Until recently, the assimilation of foreigners would not have been considered part of a comparison between Europe and America. America was a land of immigration; Europe was not. That is no longer the case. Overall levels of the foreign-born remain higher in the United States than in all European countries other than Switzerland and Luxembourg (figure 185). The difference is diminishing, however, as increasing numbers of foreigners make Europe their home. But the politics of counting foreigners is curious in Europe. In nations with virulent and powerful anti-foreigner political parties (Denmark, Austria, Norway, the Netherlands, France, and Switzerland) civil servants might wish to downplay the presence of those who could be regarded as an alien element. Bureaucracies in other countries might prefer to upscale the number of foreigners, perhaps to burnish their own multicultural qualifications.

185. Foreign-Born Population
Percent of Total

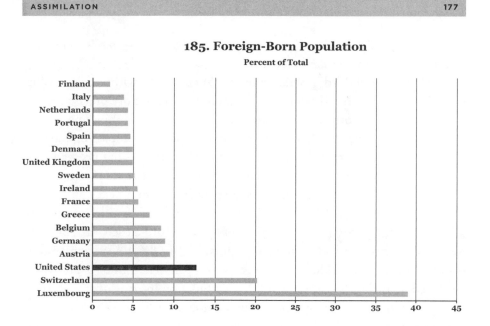

Consider the differences between two sets of OECD accounts of foreigners, from 2005 and 2007.[1] The figures in these reports come respectively from 2003 and 2005, though numbers for a decade earlier, i.e., 1993 and 1995, are given as comparisons. As might be expected, in all European countries the number of foreigners increased between 2003 and 2005. But in some nations, the reported number of foreigners grew so startlingly over a two-year period that it must be due to a rejiggering of the figures rather than to any actual inflow. In many cases, too, the numbers for 1995 given in the later publication are higher than those given for 2003 in the earlier one. For example, the Austrian figures for the foreign part of the population in 1995 presented in 2007 are 11.2%, while those for 2003 presented in 2005 are only 9.4%. Similar discrepancies hold for Belgium, France, Ireland, the Netherlands, Norway, and several other nations. The mystery only deepens if we look at what precisely the OECD claims to measure. In 2005, it was Europe's "foreign population." Of the nations we are looking at, only the numbers from the United States are for "foreign-born." In 2007, however, also the European figures are for "foreign-born," except those for Greece, Italy, and Spain, which are for "foreign." "Foreign-born" is, of course, a narrower and more precise category than "foreign." Excepting only lapses of record keeping, "foreign-born" can be determined by standard-issue statistics. Who counts as "foreign," however, is a more nebulous affair. Karl Lueger, the anti-Semitic mayor of Vienna in the late 1890s, once answered the question, "Who is Jewish," by saying, *das bestimme ich*—that is something I decide. Something similar holds true here.

Are second- and third-generation immigrants, with or without citizenship, considered foreigners? Though the later numbers use a more precise categorization ("foreign-born"), they tend to be larger, even for the same period, than the earlier, more nebulous, and presumably more encompassing category ("foreign"). That suggests that the inflation of the numbers has been particularly dramatic, though it does not identify the source of the confusion.

One of the most distinctive cases of reevaluated numbers comes from Sweden, a country with a liberal civil service and no significant populist anti-immigrant party. Let us examine its figures more closely. In 2005, the Swedes claim to have had a "foreign" population of 5.8% in 1993, which then dropped to 5.1% a decade later, in 2003. Two years later, in 2007, however, the Swedes say they had a "foreign-born" population in 2005 of 12.4%. These figures would imply that, ignoring other demographic events (births, deaths, emigration, and the like), during the years 2003 and 2004 an implausible number of some 650,000 foreigners—the equivalent of over 7% of Sweden's total 2005 population—immigrated to the country. To add to the confusion, the OECD claims that in 1995, foreigners made up 10.5% of the population— that is, almost twice the figure the Swedes had earlier, in 2003, themselves indicated for 1993.

If we instead examine the numbers used in a 2005 Swedish government report on the incidence of crime among foreigners, matters look different. A well-meaning account, this report reveals, but does not play up or exaggerate, the disproportional extent to which foreigners commit crimes in Sweden. The figures presented are for those residents registered in 1996 with the authorities (as are all people on Swedish soil) who were born abroad.[2] According to the report, of such foreigners, there were precisely 574,781, which, out of a population that year of 8,900,954, makes for 6.46%. Of these, in turn, over a quarter were Scandinavian, predominantly Finns, which is to say people about as culturally different from ethnic Swedes as the Welsh are from the English. If we count only non-Europeans but include the Turks, whom the report's authors have gallantly counted as Europeans, we get a percentage of salient, noticeable foreigners of 2.58%. This is nothing to sneeze at, of course, but nor is it the multicultural paradise that the well-meaning Swedish civil service might like to imagine.

The Swedes do not seem able to count their own foreigners. The French specifically refuse to do so, believing such knowledge to be discriminatory.

Remembering the old adage that what is not measured is not managed, should one worry that Europe is not facing up to the potentially weightiest issue of domestic politics? How successfully are such newcomers being integrated? On this huge topic, there is little reliable comparative data. It would be fascinating to have numbers giving us crucial insight into Europe's immigrant communities: poverty rates, home ownership, outmarriage, educational achievement, and the like. But such numbers are hard to come by.

We know that American attitudes to foreigners are generally more welcoming than in Europe. The percentage of Americans who believe that unless people share a country's customs and traditions, they cannot become fully part of it, is less than a third of equivalent figures in Austria, France, and Denmark (all nations with strong anti-foreigner parties), and half of what it is in Germany, the Netherlands, Norway, and Finland. On the other hand, all nations under the glass here broadly agree that immigrants improve a country by bringing in new ideas and cultures, with the United States in the European middle ground and low figures coming from the UK, France, and Norway.[3] America's foreigners appear to be a better-behaved lot, or at least they get into less trouble with the law than their peers in Europe. There are proportionately less than half as many foreigners in America's prisons as in the population as a whole. In contrast, in Sweden, Norway, and Germany, foreigners are over twice as likely to be in prison as the natives. In Switzerland and Denmark, the ratio is almost three times, and in Greece, no less than eight times.[4] True, many European nations grant citizenship only slowly and grudgingly, or else jailed foreigners might be natives behind bars. But even taking this into account, the contrast is striking.

In the absence of anything better, two comparative figures provide some tentative conclusions on how immigrants assimilate. The gap between the educational achievements of the children of immigrants and those of native-born parents has been measured. In math, this disparity for U.S. students is narrower than anywhere in Europe, and less than a quarter of the gap found in Germany and Belgium (figure 186). For reading, the results are similar, though in this case the Swedes have assimilated foreign pupils better than the Americans (figure 187). But on the whole, being the child of an immigrant, a second-generation citizen, means more of an educational handicap in almost all European nations than it does in the United States. The second measure quantifies the gap between unemployment rates among the native-born and foreign populations. Immigrant men in the United States actually do better than natives (figure 188). This is also true for Italy; and in Greece, being

186. Gap in Math Scores between Native-Born and Immigrants

Point Differences between Native-Born and Second-Generation Immigrant Children, PISA 2003

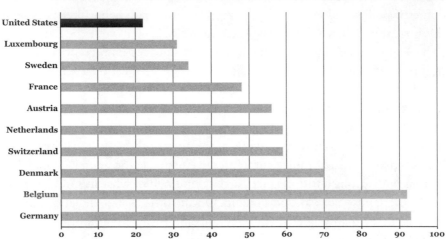

187. Gap in Reading Scores between Native-Born and Immigrants

Point Differences between Native-Born and Second-Generation Immigrant Children, PISA 2003

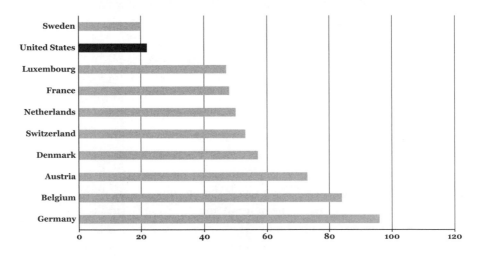

188. Increased Unemployment

Foreign-Born vs Native-Born Populations, Men, in % Points

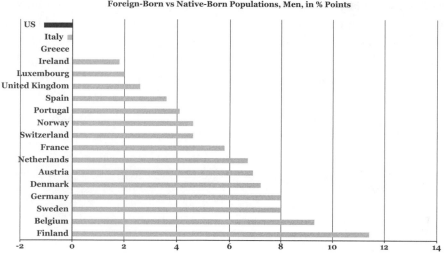

foreign is immaterial. But elsewhere in Europe, foreigners are far more likely to be unemployed than locals. In Finland in 2004, for example, while 10% of the indigenous male workforce was out of work, the unemployment rate among foreigners was over twice as high.

Perhaps such results are connected to immigration policies and the kind of immigrant who is admitted. If European nations allowed in only bona fide asylum seekers, while America welcomed the educated elite of the third world, then we could understand why the latter integrated easily and the former did not. But that is far from the case. The majority of immigrants to both America and Europe come in under the guise of family reunification. Only 13% of immigrants entering the United States in 2000 were admitted for economic or employment reasons. The UK alone grants admission to highly skilled foreigners in greater absolute—and therefore, of course, relative—numbers than does the United States.[5] The average immigrant to the United States is more likely to be a peasant from Guatemala than a software engineer from Bangalore. Moreover, in the absence of an economically based immigration policy in many European countries, asylum seekers here are in some measure a self-selected group. They are often economic immigrants who have to convince the authorities at the borders that they deserve asylum status. And it stands to reason that those who have managed to pay for and undertake the arduous and expensive trek to the Schengen borders are not always among the worst-off at home. To take one measure of this, immigrants to the United States are somewhat less likely than the native-born to have gone to university. In all European countries other than Belgium, Germany, and Finland, the reverse is the case: the new arrivals are better educated than the natives.[6] In Austria, for example, only Yugoslav and Turkish male immigrants are less likely to have university degrees than the natives. All other male foreigners, whether from Eastern Europe, the Middle East, Africa, or from elsewhere in the developed world, are over two and three times as likely to have been to university as native Austrians.[7]

TWELVE
LUMPING
AND
SPLITTING

IT IS OFTEN SAID THAT AMERICA is an economically more unequal society than Europe, with greater stratification between rich and poor. On average, the United States is a wealthier society than most European countries. The median American income—that earned by the recipient at the center of the income distribution—is higher than equivalent figures for all European nations other than Luxembourg (figure 189). Americans also earn higher per capita incomes, adjusted for purchasing power variations, than any Europeans other than the Norwegians.[1] That is, of course, easily compatible with widespread poverty and inequality. If incomes are distributed unequally, a high average could hide disproportionate wealth at the top and bitter poverty at the bottom. Americans do appear to tolerate a higher degree of inequality than Europeans. True, proportionately fewer Americans believe that income differences are necessary as an incentive than do Germans, Spaniards, or the

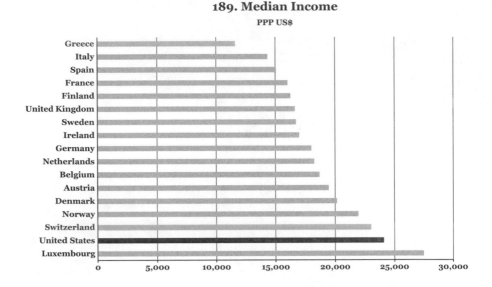

189. Median Income

PPP US$

Portuguese. Fewer Americans consider it fair that the rich buy better health care and education than do the British. But a smaller proportion of Americans than any Europeans rejects existing income differences as too large. And Americans do not agree, as many Europeans do, that the government should act to narrow income inequality.[2]

On a number of measures, high inequality does, in fact, appear to hold true for the United States—though rarely as starkly as is often presumed. For one thing, more billionaires per capita live in America than in any European country except Switzerland, with over twice that rate (figure 190). The American market is not inherently bloodier than the European. By itself, it does not produce more inequality than across the Atlantic. Pretax income inequalities in the United States lie within the European range.[3] But after taxes and transfers, American inequalities appear starker. One measure of this defines poverty as 60% of the national median income. By this standard, the United States has a larger percentage of poor citizens than any European country, though the figures are broadly comparable to those of the UK, Ireland, Spain, and Greece (figure 191).

If we look at the opposite end of the spectrum—among the wealthy, where the data are often better—things look much the same. Income concentration among the most prosperous has followed a similar development across western nations until the end of the twentieth century. In the early 1900s, the richest

190. Resident Billionaires
Per Million Population

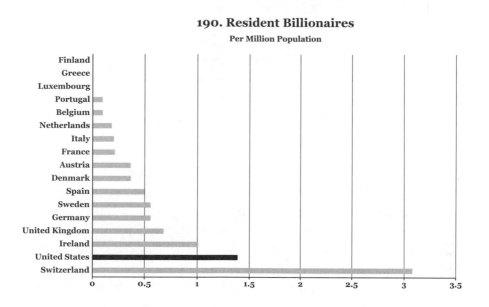

191. Overall Poverty
Percent of Total Population Under 60% of Median Income

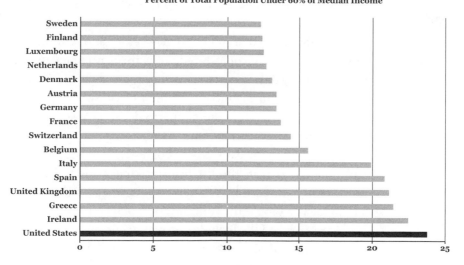

were very wealthy indeed. John Rockefeller counted for a larger proportion of America's total net worth in 1918 than the three richest Americans (Bill Gates, Lawrence Ellison, and Paul Allen) did in 2000.[4] Incomes, too, were disproportionately distributed. In 1928, the richest 1% of Americans received almost 20% of total income, and the richest one-tenth of a percent took home 8.2%. In the UK during the same year, the figure for the latter group was slightly higher (8.5%). It had come down from over 11% in 1913, whereas 1928 was the high point for wealthy Americans. The Great Depression and, above all, the Second World War, however, destroyed many great fortunes, drastically lowering the richest's share of total income and shifting the composition of their income from capital and dividends to wages. By the latter decades of the century in the English-speaking nations, it was no longer coupon clippers but well-paid managers who were the wealthiest, and they commanded a far smaller fraction of total income than their peers had earlier.

That was the situation until the 1980s. At that point, the West divided. The wealthiest citizens of the continental nations, among whom capital income continues to play a much larger role, stabilized their share at the comparatively low levels achieved during the 1970s. In the English-speaking world as well as in Sweden, concentration at the top once again began growing. By 1998, the wealthiest Americans took home over 14% of total income—still below their heyday 70 years earlier, but almost double their share in 1973. In the UK, the equivalent figure was much the same, some 12.6% in 1998, up from less than half that in 1978.[5]

Sweden, in turn, hovers between the Anglo-Saxon and continental extremes. If we look only at wage income, Sweden fits the continental model. If we add in realized capital gains, however, the story is another one. Capital gains figure more prominently in the income of the richest Swedes than for their peers elsewhere, in tandem with the twentyfold rise in prices on the Stockholm Stock Exchange between 1980 and 2007 (compared with five or six times in New York, London, or Paris). The progressivity of income taxes has also declined in Sweden, as in the English-speaking world.[6] Factoring this in, high-end incomes in Sweden began increasing again, as in the Anglo-American nations, in the late 1900s. The concentration of income remains less than in the United States or the UK. Including capital gains, the top Swedish percentile received over 10% of total income in 1999, compared to just over 16% for their American peers in 1998. Starting from a more egalitarian base, the tendency has been upward in Sweden, while among the larger continental nations, incomes of the wealthiest have remained flat.[7]

Incomes are one thing, total wealth another. The two are related, but not in a straightforward manner. Depending on whether they spend, save, or give away their money, those with high incomes, may—or may not—become rich. Wealth has different and arguably more socially significant effects than income. It can be inherited, helping create a class of the rich in a way that cannot necessarily be sustained by one cohort's windfall. The evidence for disparities of income suggests that the United States is at the high end of the European scale. But for inequalities of wealth, the results are less clear-cut. Wealth is generally more concentrated than income, because it can be saved up over a lifetime and—barring death duties and Napoleonic inheritance codes—transmitted to one heir. The share of total wealth owned by the very richest in America has come down substantially over the course of the twentieth century and, in distinction to incomes, has not risen again. For those in the top percentile, it peaked at just over 40% in 1930. It came down to a bit under 21% in 2000. For the top hundredth of a percent, the equivalent figures are 11% in 1919 and 3.9% in 2000.[8]

The difficulties come when trying to make international comparisons. Some European nations have lower wealth concentrations than the United States. In 1994, for example, those in the top percentile in France owned 21%, and the top tenth of that percentile owned 6% of total wealth. The comparable figures for the United States were 22% and 9%. The Spanish figures are even lower (16% and 5% for 1994).[9] Other nations, in contrast, have significantly higher concentrations of wealth. In Switzerland, net worth is concentrated at the top without compare. In 1997, the top 1% of the Swiss owned 35% of all wealth, some 14 percentage points higher than their American peers that year (21%). Only during the Roaring Twenties had the wealthiest Americans captured as large a share of the cake as their Swiss counterparts enjoy today.[10] These figures cover only those who actually reside in Switzerland. They ignore the vast fortunes parked in that country by wealthy Europeans who live elsewhere.[11] If that much is clear, other comparisons are murkier. In one recent accounting, the share of total wealth owned by the top 10% of Americans is high. But it is lower than in Switzerland as well as Denmark, and it is followed at no great remove by France and Sweden (Figure 192). A compilation of historical wealth distribution data by the UN University's World Institute for Development Economics Research puts the share of wealth held by the top 1% of Americans in 2000 as lower than the equivalent figures for the UK and Norway, and only slightly greater than Sweden.[12]

Let us take a closer look at Sweden, since that nation so often plays the foil to inegalitarian America. Wealth concentration at the pinnacle in Sweden,

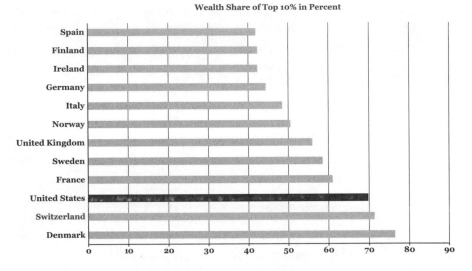

192. Richest

Wealth Share of Top 10% in Percent

measured by standard data, already puts that nation on par with American conditions. The top percentile of Swedes was worth 21.9% of total wealth in 2000 (United States: 20.8%) and those in the top one-hundredth of the top percentile had amassed for themselves as much as their American peers, namely 3.9%.[13] However, these numbers may be an underestimate. First, wealthy Swedish entrepreneurs have over the years taken themselves and their fortunes abroad and thus exited the Swedish tax net. Second, in hope of stemming tax hemorrhaging, the Swedish authorities began giving owners of closely held family firms (who might otherwise have gone into tax exile) significant fiscal exemptions to keep them residents of Sweden.

Here is a back-of-the-envelope calculation of the effects: the richest Swede (Ingvar Kamprad of IKEA, who lives abroad) has a fortune that, expressed as a fraction of Swedish GDP, is 20 times the equivalent fraction of the U.S. GDP enjoyed by Bill Gates. That, of course, is an artifact of being a rich man in a small country. But if we instead take the sum total of all Swedish billionaires, they have a net worth (85 billion dollars) that is twice as large a fraction of their nation's GDP (18.6%) as that enjoyed by their American peers (9.7%), who are worth 1.35 trillion dollars. Given that these figures do not include the Wallenberg family, whose assets—held in tax-exempt trusts—own controlling stakes in companies that account for 40% of the Swedish stock exchange, they still understate the wealth concentration at the pinnacle of Swedish society.

What do such figures testify to? Where billionaires live is in large measure determined by the tax system. Wealthy Americans have no fiscal incentive to move abroad, since their tax authorities consider them fair game regardless of where they live. Only 2% of the American billionaires listed by *Forbes* live outside the United States. Conversely, one-third of Swedish billionaires have gone into exile. Indeed, if we calculate the fraction of Swedish GDP owned by Swedish billionaires who live in Sweden, it is comparable to the relatively egalitarian American figure, namely 7%. One-third of Sweden's richest families, who own two-thirds of its largest fortunes, live abroad. In this manner, the Swedish tax authorities have arguably made their country more egalitarian. Not richer, of course, since the wealth has been exported, not redistributed, but more equal. In the European taxome, tax exiles disappear from national accounts into the Swiss, Liechtensteinian, or Caymanian fiscal havens. The percentage of wealth held offshore by wealthy Europeans is over two and a half times higher than by their American peers.[14] By going off the books, Europe's tax exiles lower wealth disparities for all European nations. They do not just shift fortunes from one country to another.

Given this, and returning to our Swedish example, if we add in the wealth moved from Sweden and factor in the tax breaks for closely held family firms granted by the Swedish tax authorities, the net worth of the richest percentile of Swedes increases by 50%. A similar calculation for the top percentile of Americans ups its net worth a mere 3% (figures for 2004). This brings the overall share of wealth held by those in the top Swedish percentile to 42% for 2000. That is twice as intense a concentration of wealth as is found in America for the same year.[15]

Having looked at the bottom and then the top of the income scales, we come to the relationship between the two, or the measure of inequality. The latest wave of figures from the Luxembourg Income Study, from between 1999 and 2004, marks out the United States as the most unequal of our countries, in this case as measured by Gini coefficients, a standard gauge of inequality (figure 193). As we have seen, inequalities have sharpened in the English-speaking world in recent years. It was not always so. Other comparisons based on aggregate data over several decades, from the 1970s through the mid-1990s, moderate this outlier status. One comparison—of the ratio of the richest quintile's income to the poorest fifth of the population's share—puts the United States within the European spectrum, lower than Ireland, and above Norway and Portugal.[16] Another, measuring average Gini coefficients, ranks the United States as more equal than France, Ireland, and Portugal (figure 194). A revised data set reveals

193. Income Inequality

Most Recent Gini Coefficients

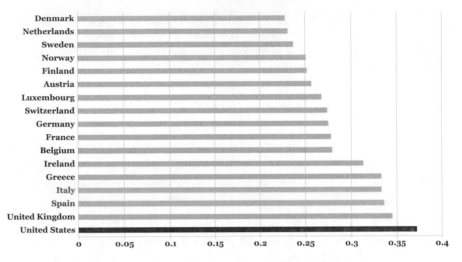

194. Income Inequality

Average Gini Coefficients, 1970s-1990s

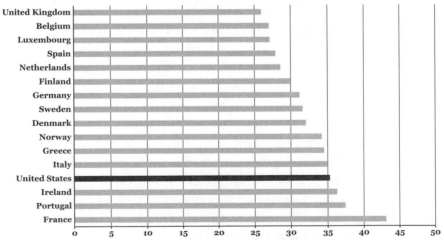

195. Distribution of Household Net Worth

Gini Index

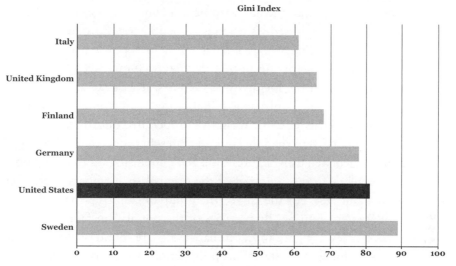

that those nations with higher Gini coefficients than the United States include all the Mediterranean countries other than France, as well as Ireland.[17] An even more recent measure of Gini coefficients for household net worth, using data from the new Luxembourg Wealth Study, ranks Sweden as less equal than the United States—in large measure because one-third of Swedes have a negative net worth and owe more than they own. Germany, in this accounting, is only slightly more egalitarian than the United States (figure 195).

Income and wealth disparities are certainly high in the United States compared with Europe, and have become more so in recent years, though the current crisis promises to temper that. Inequality and poverty are not, however, the same thing. Does a broad distribution of income mean that many Americans are poor? Since the United States has a median income ($24,119 PPP in 2000) that is over 40% higher than Europe's ($16,735 for the original six nations of the EU), and since incomes are more widely dispersed than in Europe, it is likely that proportionately more Americans fall below a relative definition of poverty—60% of median incomes, for example. But since the median is high in the first place, that does not necessarily mean that all those who do are destitute. If we compare the numbers of those who are actually, and not just relatively, poor on both sides of the Atlantic, results differ.

The definition of poverty used by most European governments is relative: half, or sometimes 60%, of median income is a common one. If the dispersion of incomes is compressed, as it tends to be in many European nations, the number of those falling below a relative standard of poverty will be lower. But that does not necessarily mean that they are well-off, except in relation to those above them in the hierarchy of incomes. If we take as an absolute poverty line the cash sum equivalent to half of median income for the original six nations of the EU (EU-6), Western Europe turns out to have a higher percentage of poor citizens than the United States. In the accounting graphed here, which is calculated using figures from 1993, about 10% of the U.S. population is poor, while in the countries of the original six members of the EU, the figure is about 12%. For the EU-15, the group of countries that comprise the bulk of Western Europe, almost 20% of the population falls under this absolute poverty level (figure 196). Similar results are found when we break out the numbers for each Western European nation, using more current data. Taking as an absolute poverty level a cash equivalent set at 60% of the median income of the EU-6 in 2000, not only do the Mediterranean countries have a higher percentage of poor citizens than the United States, but so do the UK and Ireland, as well as France, Belgium, the Netherlands, Finland, and Sweden (figure 197).

The other way around, things look much the same. In the United States, an absolute poverty measure is used, a certain amount of money per head. For various technical reasons, it is hard to compare these American and European figures. The European figures are recorded as disposable income (income plus transfers minus taxes), while the American figures are pretax and posttransfer income. If we take instead as a reasonable proxy of the absolute poverty level in the United States the equivalent sum we used above for Europe, but now from America, the results are comparable across the Atlantic. If poverty means to live on less than the cash equivalent of 60% of the median American income (for 2000), then the only countries that have proportionately fewer poor people than the United States are two Nordic nations (Norway and Denmark) and the wealthiest European countries, Luxembourg and Switzerland (figure 198).

It seems likely that if we could find comparable European figures for the official absolute poverty limits in America, the results would be analogous. When UNICEF measured child poverty, the results were similar. Using a relative definition of poverty, proportionately more American children were poor than European: 22%, compared to 21% in Italy and 20% in the UK, the

196. Low Income Population

Percent of Population that Is below 50% of EU-6 Median Income

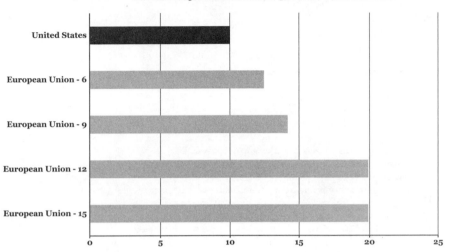

197. Absolute Poverty, European Scale

Percent of Population Below 60% of EU-6 Median Income, 2000

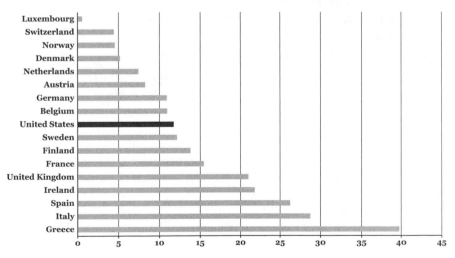

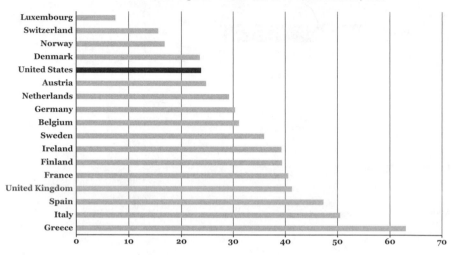

198. Absolute Poverty, US Scale

Percent of Population Below 60% of US Median Income, 2000

nearest comparisons. But applying the U.S. definition of poverty across the Atlantic revealed a higher percentage of poor children in Spain, Italy, the UK, and Ireland than in America. Germany and the Netherlands performed only slightly better.[18] In summary, whether you use an American or a European yardstick, the percentage of poor Americans (measured by an absolute level of poverty, and not just in relation to others within the same country) is within the European spectrum.

Needless to say, these figures are calculated in terms of purchasing power parity, which means that they account for cost-of-living differences, at least between the United States and the nations of Western Europe. They may not, however, account for them among the U.S. states. Even a look at the bleakest calculations of incomes, crunched on numbers from the mid-1990s, broadly corresponds with the point we are making here. The poorest 10% in America had higher incomes than the lowest decile in the UK, and almost the same as those in Sweden and Finland. Even poor American children, who fare perhaps worst of all social groups in America, did better than poor British children.[19] When Will Hutton assures us that "notwithstanding [America's] higher over-all per capita incomes, its poor are absolutely worse off than their counterparts in Europe," he is simply wrong.[20]

This raises a broader issue of comparability between Europe and the United States. The United States is not just a nation, but also a continent—or at least a large part of one. That is not the case for each European country. And yet, comparisons tend to be drawn between the United States as a nation and any individual European country, or set of them, and not the European continent as a whole. This, too, may affect the outcomes of comparisons across the Atlantic. A large area like North America encompasses a broad spectrum of living costs, and therefore wage levels, while a small country, like Denmark or the Netherlands, does not, or at least not to the same extent. In other words, the distribution of incomes within the United States is not just a measure of the socio-economic distance from Bill Gates to a single mother on welfare. It spans equally a geographical and cost-of-living differential between the average Manhattanite and the typical resident of Tupelo, Mississippi.

But income distributions in Europe are measured as the distance separating, say, the Oslo lawyer from the Bergen fisherman, not the Swiss pharmaceutical CEO from the Sicilian peasant (not to mention the Slovakian Roma). Given that the gross national income per capita of Luxembourg is over three times the Portuguese, or that the per capita GDP of central London is over five times that of northern Portugal, the pan-European income and wealth differentials are likely to be quite a bit wider than those within any given European nation.[21] Indeed, one team of economists has described Europe of today as being much like the United States in the 1930s, when it contained regions of extreme poverty, above all the Deep South, within a continent that was otherwise homogenizing in economic terms. The same team has shown that inequalities of manufacturing earnings are some 30% greater within the European continent (EU-15) than within the United States. Regional pay disparities are about 40% greater within Europe than across America.[22]

Regional disparities in GDP per capita are wide in the United States, as one might expect from a continent-sized country. They range from 65% to 332% of the national average. But in the UK alone, they are wider (a span between 60% and 446%) and in France they are almost as broad (77% to 316%). That means, of course, that within Western Europe as a whole, the span is at least as great as within the United States. The Gini index for regional GDP disparities is the same or higher than the American figures in the UK, Spain, Portugal, Italy, Germany, Denmark, Belgium, and Austria. On the other hand, regional disparities in labor productivity are larger in the United States than in most of Europe, while in unemployment, the United States ranks in the middle of the field.[23] Comparatively little work has been done on such trans-European differentials.[24] But two sociologists, Olli Kangas and Veli-Matti Ritakallio, have recently demonstrated the largely ignored but very wide geographical income differentials within Europe. Such differentials exist also within European countries. In Italy, the richest region (Milan) has a relative poverty line over twice as high as the poorest (Sicily). They are also found between the richest regions of Europe and the poorest. The national poverty line for Luxembourg is 2.7 times greater than that of Spain.[25]

Europe is not yet as integrated an economic unit as the United States. Cultural and linguistic barriers prevent workers from moving as freely among the EU states as they do within America. Indeed, mobility within the EU is surprisingly low. By far, the largest number of foreign residents in most European nations come from outside the EU, not from other nations within the Union.[26] With some Western European countries welcoming citizens of the former East Bloc, however, that may be changing. The migration of 600,000 Poles to the UK over the past couple of years may herald a new era, compressing wage differentials. Comparing the U.S.-as-continent to Europe-as-continent is still difficult. At the same time, it is no more distorting than to compare the United States to, say, Denmark.

The upshot is that, to compare like with like, one should differentiate the social from the geographic span of income and wealth differentials. Little if any work has been done on such comparisons. What is offered here is, at best, a preliminary and tentative step. If one interpolates the ratios of top to bottom quintiles of income between a sampling of U.S. states and most of the European nations we are examining, the results may surprise (figure 199). Income differentials appear much more nuanced than is revealed by a comparison between the U.S.-as-continent, on the one hand, with any one European country, on the other. The average income of the top quintile is a smaller multiple of the average of the bottom quintile in Wisconsin than in France and a smaller one in Utah than Spain. That is perhaps not surprising. But that this multiple is smaller in Alabama than the UK and smaller in Ohio than in Italy seems to be news worth reporting.

If we look at the percentages of the poor, measured in absolute terms, the results are similar. If we take the PPP cash figure for 60% of the EU-6 median income in 2000 as the top end of poverty, the outcomes are again unexpected (figure 200). No state in this sample, not even Arkansas, the poorest place in the United States by this measure, has proportionately as many absolutely poor citizens as Greece, Spain, Italy, and Ireland. Alabama, Tennessee, Texas, and Oklahoma have fewer poor than the UK. Mississippi has the same percentage of the impoverished as France. Idaho and South Carolina have fewer. New York and California, as well as half a dozen other states, including Georgia, have fewer

199. Mean Income Ratios of Top and Bottom Quintiles, 2000-2003

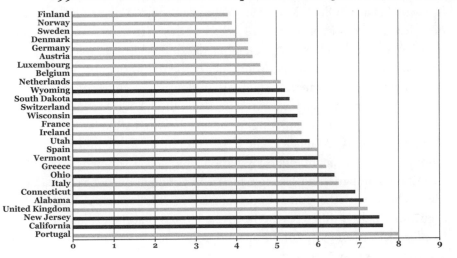

200. Population (%) under 60% of EU-6 Median Income, 2000

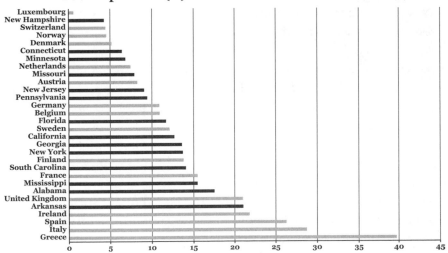

than Finland. Florida, Oregon, Kansas, and North Dakota have fewer poor than Sweden. Indiana, Ohio, Michigan, Nebraska, South Dakota, Pennsylvania, New Jersey, and Wisconsin, as well as eight other states, all have proportionately fewer poor than Germany. Iowa, Maryland, and Missouri have fewer poor than Austria. Connecticut and Minnesota are better off than the Netherlands. New Hampshire, the American state with the lowest percentage of the poor, has fewer than Denmark, Norway, and Switzerland, though not Luxembourg.

The complexity of comparing a continent with nations arises in other respects, as well. If one unpacks the U.S. figures by state and interpolates them among the European numbers by nation, one gets a different comparison than if one compares only averages for each continent, or if one compares the United States with the span of European nations. It follows that observers who argue for a radical difference between the United States and Europe do not, in effect, take the concept of Europe seriously. They cherry-pick the countries and the results they need to make their arguments. That is why, in transatlantic comparisons, Scandinavia, Germany, and sometimes the UK make consistent and regular appearances, while the major Mediterranean nations are routinely ignored, and the minor ones are almost never mentioned.

Jeremy Rifkin, for example, claims to have demonstrated a yawning secularity chasm spanning the Atlantic. He does so by selectively quoting the church-going statistics for Scandinavia alone, ignoring the Mediterranean.[27] Meanwhile, serious analysis shows that the United States is not obviously more exceptional in terms of its quantifiable religiosity than are Italy and Ireland.[28] Everyone is delighted to cite Finland as an exemplar of European achievement when it tops the education tables in the PISA studies, along with other outperformers like Korea, Hong Kong, Canada, and New Zealand. But, if so, then one has to take note of Finland's other—presumably equally European—characteristics that may help explain this, such as the exclusionary immigration policy that keeps the Finnish population (and thus its school children) more ethnically homogeneous than any industrialized nation outside Asia or the East Bloc. If Europe as a concept is to mean anything, then it has to include all its members, prosperous and poor, Protestant and Catholic, Nordic and Mediterranean. No one would allow the numbers from the United States to be similarly cherry-picked, including Connecticut but not Alabama, Minnesota but not Missouri, and so forth.

To demonstrate the effect of such a state-by-state unpacking, consider a graph that shows an undeniably stark difference: incarceration rates (figure 201). Even the lowest American figure (Maine) is slightly higher than the highest European

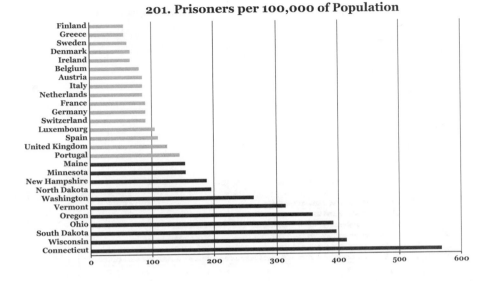

201. Prisoners per 100,000 of Population

figure (Portugal). But take the only other quantifiable set of figures that starkly differentiates the United States from Europe, namely murder rates. Even here, the outcome is not as polarized as usually thought, once we break out the local geographical units. If we unpack the numbers, localizing them geographically both in the United States and Europe, we see an unexpected juxtaposition of murder rates (figure 202). Of course, there are still dramatic differences. Most U.S. states continue to have higher murder rates than most European nations. But the picture is now more nuanced. Some U.S. states (North Dakota, New Hampshire, Maine, and Wisconsin are ones graphed here) are "European" in their murder rates. If to have a European murder rate means to come in below Switzerland then, in addition to the states already mentioned, the following states also qualify: Connecticut, Massachusetts, Rhode Island, Vermont, Iowa, Minnesota, Nebraska, South Dakota, Idaho, Utah, Wyoming, Hawaii, and Oregon.[29] Conversely, some European nations, like Switzerland and Finland, edge toward the "American" end of things.

An analysis of union membership gives similar results (figure 203). California is more unionized than Spain; New Hampshire and Wisconsin more than France, and Washington more than Switzerland. These results perhaps do not startle. But New York State turns out to have a higher union membership rate than those powerhouses of organized labor, Germany and the Netherlands. Given that New York State's economy is larger than all but five of Western Europe's countries, this is not a trivial result.

202. Murders per 100,000 Population

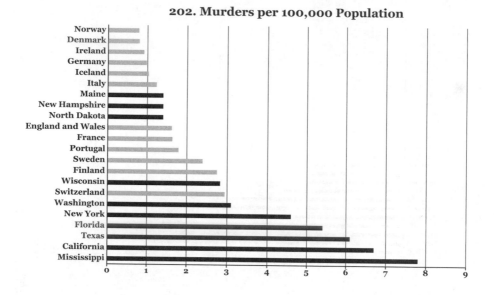

203. Percent of Workers Who Are Union Members

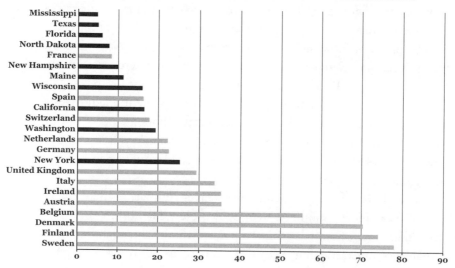

204. Life Expectancy at Birth in Years

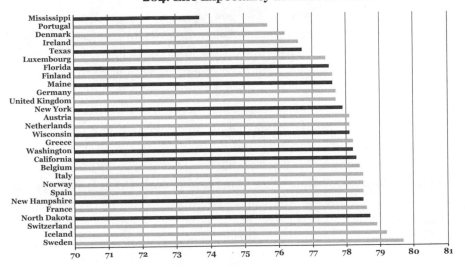

We get analogous results if we analyze life expectancies in the same fashion (figure 204). Only the lucky inhabitants of Hawaii live longer than the Swedes. But the residents of New Hampshire, Minnesota, Iowa, North Dakota, and Utah live as long, or longer, as the Norwegians. In Wisconsin, Vermont, Rhode Island, Massachusetts, Connecticut, Colorado, Nebraska, California, and Washington, they live at least as long as in Holland. In Oregon, Idaho, South Dakota, and New York, they live longer than in Germany. In Virginia, Maine, Texas, Pennsylvania, Ohio, New Mexico, New Jersey, Michigan, Illinois, Maryland, Wyoming, Kansas, Montana, Florida, Delaware, Arizona, and Alaska, life expectancies are longer than in Denmark, and in Missouri and Indiana, just as long. Generally speaking, it is only the residents of poor Southern states like Alabama, Arkansas, Georgia, Louisiana, Mississippi, and Oklahoma who live shorter lives than any Europeans, at least as measured at the national level.

Subnational figures would, no doubt, bring to light similar nuances in Europe. Thus, for example, Scotland's life expectancy at birth for men in 2000 (73.6) puts it in the same league as states like Illinois, Indiana, and Missouri. But the Clydeside conurbation (the greater Glasgow area, where men can expect only to become 71.3) is on par with Alabama, Louisiana, South Carolina, and Tennessee. Glasgow itself (69.2) is only the slightest notch above the statistically worst place in America, Washington DC (68.5), which is a capital with a huge ghetto and no hinterland.[30] Drilling down further, we discover that in the Calton neighborhood of Glasgow, men can hope to live only to the age of 54. The most ravaged group of American males, by comparison, are the residents of various South Dakota counties (Shannon, Bennett, and others) in and around the Pine Ridge Indian Reservation, who can hope to become 62. Black males in Washington DC make it on average to 63.[31]

If we look at amenable mortality rates (needless deaths that good health care would have prevented), we see that no American state bests the European winner, France. But Minnesota and Utah do better than the next-best nations, Spain and Italy. Sweden and the Netherlands are outpaced by Alaska, Colorado, Montana, Maine, New Hampshire, South Dakota, Washington, Vermont, and Wyoming. Germany is trumped by Connecticut, Hawaii, Idaho, Iowa, Massachusetts, Nebraska, New Mexico, North Dakota, Oregon, and Wisconsin. Denmark is outpaced by Arizona, California, Florida, Kansas, New Jersey, and Rhode Island. The UK and New York State run neck and neck.[32]

As we have seen earlier (figure 10) similarly interpolated results hold for minimum wages. Washington, Connecticut, Oregon, and Vermont have higher minimum wages than France, Ohio higher than the Netherlands, Maine higher than Belgium, Wisconsin higher than the UK, Minnesota higher than Ireland, and the Dakotas and New Hampshire higher than Portugal, Spain, and Greece. In other words, it is misleading to say that American minimum wages are lower than their European counterparts. Unpacking the statistics for a feature—unemployment—on which the United States, as a whole, has come off relatively well compared to Europe reveals a similar regional interpolation. Some European nations (mainly the Scandinavian and the English-speaking, along with the Netherlands) have "American" levels of unemployment, while some American states, like Mississippi, have "European" ones (figure 205).

Before leaving the issue of how to compare a continent-sized country to a continent of smaller nations, it is worth alluding to the proverbial oversized gorilla in the corner. That creature's name is Geopolitical Clout. The fact of the sheer size difference across the Atlantic influences all comparisons between the United States and Europe. In recent decades, America's military brawn has grown even more disproportional to Europe's. Its economic power is being equaled, but as a more seamlessly single market it remains a formidable competitor even to the EU, and in political and ideological terms, too, size matters. In other words, as societies these nations spanning the Atlantic may not be as different as often believed, but considered as states the disparity among

205. Unemployment Rate (%)

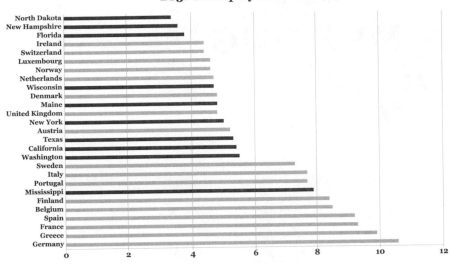

them remains glaring. This geopolitical imbalance colors the European view of America most obviously, but no doubt also has effects the other way around. In the twentieth century, Europe has both needed and resented, both sought and resisted, American intervention and influence. The humiliation suffered by Europe as a geopolitical supplicant to America as a state has influenced Europe's views of America as a society. Many of European anti-Americanism's tropes spring as much from this imbalanced relationship as they do from any actual empirical observations: big, pushy, brash, crude, violent, dangerous, and so forth. Hence the marked difference between the tempestuous passion that inflames Europeans both when they despise and when they adore America and the indifference with which they regard the other neo-Englands: kissing cousins, not the slatternly seductress.

THIRTEEN
A MEETING
OF THE
TWAIN?

SO WHERE DOES THIS LEAVE US? There are, of course, differences between America and Europe. But in almost all cases, they are no greater, and often smaller, than the differences among European nations. The span of European circumstance is such that the United States tends to fall comfortably within it. Therefore, either no coherent Europe exists, or the United States is a European nation. Formulated in a more sensible way, the similarities across the North Atlantic are at least as salient as the divergences. Yes, there are differences between Europe and America: murder and incarceration rates, as well as gun ownership and, more arguably, relative poverty rates on the one hand; the strength of civil society, assimilatory abilities, and some aspects of religious belief on the other. Other differences are ones of degree rather than kind: social policy, taxation, labor regulation, inequality, environmental policies.

Other much-remarked Atlantic divides can easily be exaggerated—the death penalty, for example. Popular opinion probably does not diverge across the Atlantic as much as official policy. A joint YouGov/*Economist* poll found almost identical responses between Americans and the British, with about one-fifth of respondents always in favor of death for murder and about the same number always opposed.[1] The United States still enforces the death penalty, and most Americans support it under some circumstances. Yet, 12 states do not have it, and another five have not carried it out for the last 30 years. If we add those states that have executed only five or fewer people since 1976, we find that over half the states, in effect, do not have capital punishment.[2] It could, in theory, be revoked tomorrow. Would America then be radically different? Did France change profoundly when it abolished the death penalty in 1981? Did the UK in 1998, Belgium in 1996, Spain in 1995, Italy in 1994, or Greece in 2004? Did they only then become truly European?[3]

For the large majority of social, economic, policy, and environmental indicators for which comparative data exists, the United States lies within the European spectrum. For a few, it lies slightly beyond its low or high end. But it tends to be closer to the nearest European outlier than to the other end of the spectrum. Often, too, the United States lies closer to the European mean than does the extreme European example at the other end of the spectrum. Labor regulation is light in the United States. But it is not that much lighter than in the UK or Denmark. The public sector is smallish in the United States. But the difference between America and Switzerland, Ireland, or Spain is less than between those nations and Sweden. Proportionately more Americans believe in God than do Europe's Protestants, but not many more than the Mediterranean's Catholics or the Irish, and—depending on the question—often no more at all. Doubtless, U.S. military might and spending is without compare. But even America's role as the only remaining superpower does not propel its military effort entirely out of the European spectrum. Military spending fits in, though admittedly just barely. (The Greeks spend a higher proportion of GNP on defense [figure 206].) Per capita spending on the military is about 44% higher in the United States ($1,275 in 2003) than its closest competitor, Norway ($884 in 2005), and about 70% above the French and British levels.[4] The size of the United States armed forces, however, is modest (figure 207). As a proportion of the population, it ranks below seven European nations, including Scandinavia, Greece, Switzerland, and Spain.

Would the snapshot picture presented here be different if we looked at change over time? Even if it is true, as I have argued here, that the United

206. Defense Spending

Military Spending as % of GDP

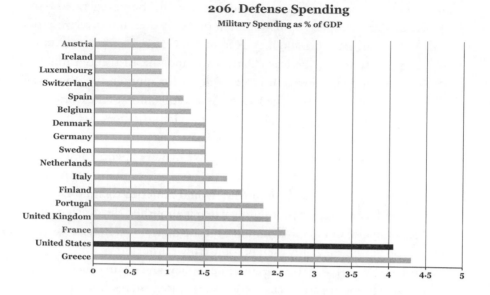

207. Armed Forces

Members of Active or Reserve Armed Forces per 1,000 Population

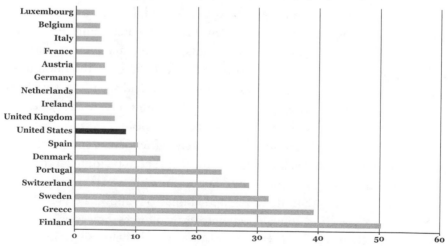

States and Europe are less different than is thought, might it be that they are growing apart? Or might Europe and the United States be approximating each other? It is difficult finding statistics that can be compared across the Atlantic, even for one moment in time. It is much harder to find viable series over a longer period. Only for some of the subjects covered here can we hope to answer such questions. Jens Alber, the distinguished scholar of social policy, has examined this question in detail. He concludes (his results apply to the expanded EU, not the narrower Western Europe used here) that over the last decade or so, divergences within Europe remain as large as, if not greater than, those between the United States and Europe. To the extent that there is convergence, it is not so much within Europe as between America and certain parts of Europe, above all the Anglo-Saxon nations and Scandinavia. One example concerns employment rates. At its meeting in 2000 in Lisbon, the European Council decided to increase the percentage of the working-age population employed in the EU to 70% by 2010. According to Alber's calculations, the United States has long surpassed this goal. Within Europe, the Anglo-Saxon countries, Luxembourg, the Netherlands, and Scandinavia have approximated the American rates. The larger Continental and Mediterranean nations have not.[5] We have convergence, in other words. But it is between part of Europe and the United States. (And possibly, if we decomposed the U.S. figures by state, we would find that the convergence was with some American regions and not others.) Convergence has taken place neither within Europe, nor between Europe as a whole and the United States.

A few more examples will illustrate the issues at stake in a comparison over time. The lack of universal health care in the United States is rightly seen as clearly signaling how different social policy systems are across the Atlantic. Of course, the divergence is not that European nations universally have public and state-financed health care on the model of the British NHS and that the United States does not. Some European nations do. Others have a mix of public and private, as does the United States. In the Netherlands, for example, 36% of the population (2005 figures) is covered by private health insurance, and 62% by public. (The equivalent figures in the United States are 59% and 27%.) Even 10% of Germans are covered privately, and in many European nations, private, supplemental top-up insurance helps fill lacks in public coverage: 28% of Danes, 9% of Germans, 64% of the Dutch, 86% of the French, a third of the Austrians and Swiss, and 10% of even the British buy add-on coverage.[6] Such supplemental insurance often meets the significant out-of-pocket expenses faced even by those covered by national insurance. Out-of-pocket expenses range from roughly 10%

208. Percent of Population with Health Care Coverage

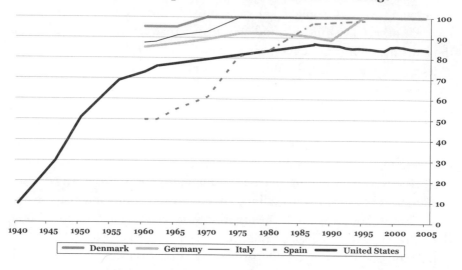

of total health expenditure in France and Germany through approximately 20% in countries like Finland, Austria, Italy, and Spain to over 30% in Switzerland. (By comparison, it is 15% in the United States.)[7]

The main transatlantic difference in health care is this: while even those European countries without a state-financed universal NHS-style system require their citizens to have coverage, the United States still allows its people to remain uninsured. Nonetheless, increasing numbers of Americans have either been insuring themselves privately or belong to groups (the poor and the elderly) that are covered by public programs. In 1940, 9% of Americans had health insurance. By 1960, that figure had risen to 73%. Two decades later, in 1987, it stood at 87%, lapsing slightly to 84% by 2005 (figure 208).

What does this say about convergence? First and foremost, much depends on the time frame. During the last two decades, the percentage of insured Americans has fluctuated moderately, with about 85% covered by one form of health insurance or another. Any downturn in insurance levels could, of course, be construed as the start of a divergence from Europe's largely universal coverage, just as any uptick could be seen as convergence. More plausibly, these fluctuations are minor variations in a system that has achieved what it can via voluntary membership and now needs to legislate to achieve universality. In a longer perspective, however, taking as the starting point any date between 1960 and 2005, the trend between the United States and Europe is

209. Enrollment in Tertiary-Level Education
Percent of University-Aged Population

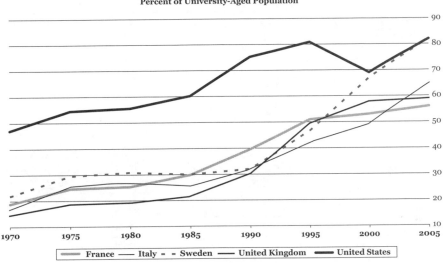

one of convergence, just as the trend has been convergent for those European nations that came more lately to universal coverage than the Scandinavian and British pioneers (Spain, Portugal, Switzerland, Greece, Austria, Belgium, France, and so forth).

Or take an example of a policy where convergence runs the other way across the Atlantic. The number of young people who attend postsecondary education rose to high levels earlier in the United States than in most European nations. But all developed nations have tended in this direction during the postwar period. Enrollment rates in tertiary education in America grew from 47% in 1970 to 81% in 1995 (figure 209). In Scandinavia, which began from a much lower position, the approximate 1970 U.S. rate was reached by 1995. In Sweden, which we have graphed here, enrollments increased from 22% to 48% between 1970 and 1995. In Denmark, Britain, and France, the increases were very similar. The Mediterranean nations followed closely. Italy and Greece rose to 42% by 1995, Spain made it to 48%, and Portugal to 39%. Between 1995 and 2005, the gap across the Atlantic narrowed, but more so in some European nations than others. If we take UNESCO's figures, by 2005, 82% of young Americans went on to postsecondary schooling. The Scandinavian countries approximated the U.S. level: Iceland at 70%, Sweden at 82%, Norway at 78%, and Denmark at 81%. The European continent, in contrast, stabilized at a lower level. France was at 56%, and though we do not have figures for Germany, it

210. Annual Hours Worked per Person Employed

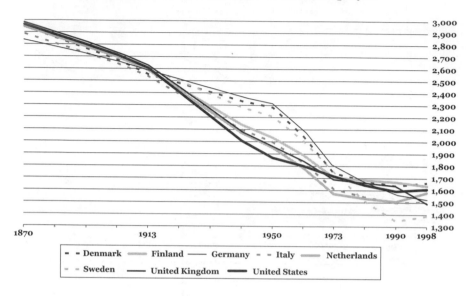

is likely to have been similar to Austria at 49% or Switzerland at 45%. The Anglo-Saxon, the small continental nations, and the Mediterranean countries held a middle position (the UK and Netherlands at 59%, Spain and Italy at 65%). Much as we saw with employment rates, some parts of Europe and the United States almost completely converged (Scandinavia). Others (Central Europe, the English-speaking nations, parts of the Mediterranean) did not.

As a final example, take working hours. If we look at the long sweep from the late nineteenth century to the present, we see that average working times have fallen overall in the countries graphed here, from very high levels in 1870 to about half that today (figure 210). This time series does not shake our confidence in the conclusion we came to earlier, from looking only at the figures for one moment in time. The hours put in by Americans, though highish in the scale, are within the European spectrum. Danes and Finns work even harder on average. The convergence, in other words, does not separate the United States from Europe. The same goes for the slight recent variation from the overall trend toward shorter working hours. Between 1990 and 1998, the average worker in some nations began putting in longer hours: not just Americans, but also the Swedes, the Dutch, the Danes, and the Italians. This may, of course, be a statistical blip, given the short interval from the previous data point in 1990. Or it may be a new trend encouraged by globalization and its attendant competition. Either way, the conclusion about convergence remains broadly the same as for working hours overall.

Time-series statistics mostly do not exist for the many and diverse variables we have looked at. But if they did, would they add much to the snapshot image presented here? It would be difficult, if not impossible, to say anything that would hold true for all of Europe. Trends—convergent or otherwise—describe only particular fields of activity, whether social policy, education, health outcomes, employment, or the growth of government. Convergence or divergence has generally taken place not between the United States and an abstract Europe as a whole, but with parts of it: Scandinavia, the English-speaking fringe, the Continentals, the Low Countries, or the Mediterranean. Each of these, in turn, stands in similarly vacillating relationships to the other parts of Europe and also, of course, to the various regions of the United States. There is often as much difference within Europe as between various parts of it and America. And that, of course, is one of the central points we have been making. Our snapshot picture of the relationship between Europe and America of the late 1990s and early 2000s is not significantly altered, but only complicated, by looking also at time-series statistics.

The direction of movement in any convergence or divergence depends largely on the time frame chosen. In some respects, the United States and Europe are diverging. In others, they—or parts of them—are converging. Economic inequality, for example, has been increasing in the United States during the past decade, as it has in English-speaking Europe and Sweden. For the other continental nations, inequality appears to have leveled off. But during the 1980s, inequality in the UK grew at a more rapid pace than in the United States. The same holds true for Sweden from about 1983 to 1991, and for the Netherlands from about 1985 to 1990.[8] And if one looks at a really long time series, in this case, measuring wealth shares of the top ventile (5%) of the population from 1740 to 2003, what impresses above all is the congruence of the seven countries studied (the United States and six European nations). Indeed, according to one compilation of long-term historical data, the wealth share of those in the bottom four percentage points of the top ventile of Americans was lower well into the 1990s than the equivalent figures for Switzerland, Sweden, France, and Denmark, and approximately equal to Norway.[9] The longer the time span, the greater the appearance of convergence. In any case, by shifting the time frame, one can easily alter the import of the figures and thus the argument. For the point we are making here, there is no virtue to using time-series statistics instead of a snapshot. Just as one could, if one wanted, cook the books for a snapshot, the same could be done for a time series. A time series (at least one of five or ten years, which is usually the best on offer) is, in that sense, just a bigger snapshot.

This brings us to a final methodological issue. Some scholars believe that even developed and otherwise similar nations are qualitatively different from each other and can be sorted into political and institutional categories that are distinct in kind and not just degree. Of course, the United States and Europe systematically differ organizationally and institutionally on many counts. America has a presidential and two-party political system with majority voting. It is highly federalized and decentralized. It has no European-style system of national collective bargaining and has never brought forth a successful or influential labor party. On the other hand, Europe is politically hugely diverse: it has the last remaining theocracy in the world, the Vatican, and the only absolute monarchy, Liechtenstein, outside of Swaziland. Even Bhutan has become a constitutional monarchy, although one could argue about North Korea's god ruler.

Consider Italy's hyperparliamentarianism, with its endless carousel of governments. It is surely as different from Sweden's 75-year Social Democratic all-but-monopoly (or Bavaria's half-century rule by the Christian Socialists) as the more-or-less two-party systems of Britain, Ireland, France, Greece, and Spain are from America. France has a powerful, directly elected president, much like America. So does Finland and to a lesser extent Iceland, though parliamentary supremacy reigns elsewhere in Europe. The Germans, Belgians, Spanish, and Austrians, not to mention the Swiss, know as much about federalism as the Americans. The English and French have majority voting systems. Collective bargaining covers 98% of all workers in Austria, but only 34% in the UK. Harold Wilensky, whose magisterial comparison of developed nations stresses the crucial role of institutional differences, points out that the United States shares many of its supposed peculiarities with the English, Irish, and the Swiss.[10]

The United States has never had a successful labor party. This absence was the core of the first sustained formulation of American exceptionalism, Werner Sombart's classic query from 1906: *Why Is there No Socialism in the United States?* The latest attempt to answer that question casts its comparative wing not over Europe, but rather Australia, another neo-England which, unlike the United States, did develop a labor party.[11] But this comparison raises the question of how important major structural differences are. Australia has had more socialism than the United States. Yet for all the statistical indicators we have looked at here, excepting universal health insurance, there is scarcely any (least of all those related to social policy) on which Australia is not closer to the United States than it is to Europe. The question, then, is whether even political institutions ultimately separate Europe from other developed nations. Does the important dividing line run down the Atlantic? Or do the distinctions of politics crosscut Europe as much as they unite it?

A look at the historiography of the welfare state will demonstrate what I mean. The "welfare state" used to be a classic concept illustrating the gap that separated the United States from Europe. Early accounts divided the world into a small elect of the solidaristic welfare states, of the sort found in Beveridge's Britain and in Scandinavia, and a large mass of what were then called residual welfare states.[12] Gøsta Esping-Andersen's *Politics Against Markets*, from 1985, was perhaps the classic formulation of this binary typology.[13] Already in his next book, however, Esping-Andersen moved from a Manichaean duality to a New Testament trinity. Rather than envisioning a single axis with two end poles along which welfare states were positioned at different removes from the ideal, he came to conceive of three separate routes of welfare state development: Social Democratic (Scandinavia), liberal (the United States, UK, Australia, New Zealand, Japan), or conservative (Germany, France, Italy, and Belgium).[14] These forms of welfare state were qualitatively different, corresponding to different social, political, and historical circumstances—not simply different points along the same path. Important from our point of view is that, in Esping-Andersen's tripartite typology, European countries ended up spread across all three categories. There was no one group into which all European nations fell.

Once the possibility of opening up the inherited dualistic typology had been broached, difficulties arose. In the first, dualistic, model, nations were either among the solidaristic elect or they were consigned to the portmanteau of the residual category. There was little argument about which countries fit where. But as soon as more subtle categorizations were elaborated, typological disagreement arose. The Australians were aghast at being consigned to the outer darkness, placed as they were in the same liberal category as the United States.[15] Unable to argue that Australia was a Social Democratic welfare state and unwilling to fit it into the conservative model, they invented a new category: the radical welfare state.[16]

Over time, ever more categorizations of welfare states arose. Richard Rose compared their spending and wealth and classified welfare states into four categories. He included two European nations, Finland and Switzerland, in the same group (rich, not-so-big government) as the United States, Canada, Japan, and Australia. He, too, mixed European and other developed nations together.[17] More recently, the idea of a Christian Democratic welfare state, long broached by adherents of such parties in Germany, France, and the Low Countries, but not taken very seriously by welfare state theorists, has begun to command more respect.[18] Maurizio Ferrera has proposed the concept of a Mediterranean or south European welfare state model to describe the (unsustainable) high-spend, low-tax systems of social provision that have evolved in Italy, Spain, and Portugal.[19] The radical welfare state has come to include not only Australia, New Zealand, and Great Britain (who at least are kissing cousins), but also (in an act of heroic conceptual exogamy) Finland.[20]

Other recent scholarship also uses four categories, with the European welfare states spread over at least three.[21] One reexamination of Esping-Anderson's work argues for five rather than three categories.[22] Another recent study, Timothy Smith's book on French social policy, shows how, in terms of labor market policies, Scandinavia and the Low Countries share as much with Canada and the United States as they do with France.[23] Francis Castles and his collaborators have helped break up the early categories in a series of studies where each country is treated in a remarkably untypologizing fashion. No one nation is typecast as representative or emblematic of any broader category. Each is treated according to its own peculiarities.[24] Increasingly, the act of typologizing welfare states seems ever more cumbersome and at odds with empirical reality. Fritz Scharpf's conclusions on the ability of certain nations (Denmark, the Netherlands, Switzerland, and Australia: together at last!) to preserve labor market and social policy protections in the face of economic globalization, sit uncomfortably with his invocation of Esping-Andersen's classic trinity of liberal, conservative, and Social Democratic welfare states, since his countries are obviously spread across all three.[25] Most dramatically, Esping-Andersen has thrown in the typologizing towel altogether, predicting no less than 18 distinct worlds of welfare capitalism.[26]

We could doubtless find as many different welfare states as the Americans have religions or the French sauces. But at least scholars agree that the European states do not fit together in one. Welfare state typologizing has fallen victim to its own success. As categories became increasingly numerous, supple, and sophisticated, they began to approximate the individual historical reality of each national development. They become more truthful, but also less useful as ideal types. In the most recent and sophisticated work, any categories still in use do not neatly box together all European, or even only European, nations.

A similar crosscutting can be found in scholarly typologies of capitalism. A very influential study of the subject, by Peter Hall and David Soskice, groups various types of capitalist systems so as to span the Atlantic: Germany, Scandinavia, and the Netherlands are coordinated market economies; the Mediterranean countries are possibly another type of capitalism altogether, and Britain, Ireland, and the United States are liberal market economies.[27] Jonas Pontusson's book on liberal and social market economies has the suggestive subtitle "Social Europe vs. Liberal America." But, in fact, his typology categorizes in a way that does not cut down the middle of the Atlantic: Ireland and the UK join the United States as liberal market economies, while only northern European countries qualify as social market economies, and the Mediterranean nations are relegated to their own separate typological purgatory.[28] So much for the transatlantic divide.

But enough typologizing! Our point has been made. Once typologies are extended to cover the developed world and not just Europe, they begin to package non-European nations—whether Australia, Canada, New Zealand, Japan, or the United States—together with various regions of Europe. Rarely, if ever, do important categories distinguish between Europe as a whole on the one hand, and other nations, including the United States, on the other. As I have been arguing in this book, the main line of distinction almost never runs down the North Atlantic.[29]

FOURTEEN
SEPARATED
AT BIRTH?

TO RETURN TO THE BULK of our material in this book, what absolute differences separate the United States from Europe? The United States is a nation where proportionately more people are murdered each year, more are jailed, and more own guns than anywhere in Europe. The death penalty is still law. Religious belief is more fervent and widespread. A smaller percentage of citizens vote. Collective bargaining covers relatively fewer workers, and the state's tax take is lower. Inequality is somewhat more pronounced. That is about it. In almost every other respect, differences are ones of degree, rather than kind. Often, they do not exist, or if they do, no more so than the same disparities hold true within Western Europe itself. At the very least, this suggests that far-reaching claims to radical differences across the Atlantic have been overstated.

Even on violence—a salient difference that leaps unprompted from the evidence, both statistical and anecdotal—the contrast depends on how it is framed.

211. Catastrophic Death

Murder, Fatal Injury and Suicide Rates per 100,000

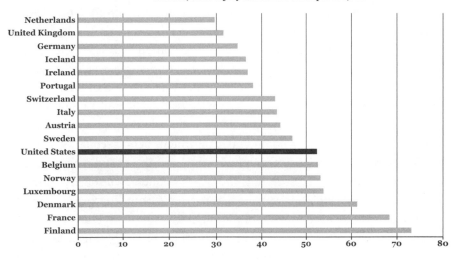

Without question, murder rates are dramatically different across the Atlantic. And, of course, murder is the most shocking form of sudden, unexpected death, unsettling communities, leaving survivors bereaved and mourning. But consider a wider definition of unanticipated, immediate, and profoundly disrupting death. Suicide is often thought of as the exit option for old, sick men anticipating the inevitable, and therefore not something that changes the world around them. But, in fact, the distribution of suicide over the lifespan is broadly uniform. In Iceland, Ireland, the UK, and the United States, more young men (below forty-five) than old do themselves in. In Finland, Luxembourg, the Netherlands, and Norway, the figures are almost equal. Elsewhere, the older have a slight edge. But overall, the ratio between young and old suicides approximates 1:1.[1] Broadly speaking, and sticking with the sex that most often kills itself, men do away with themselves as often when they are younger and possibly still husbands, fathers, and sons as they do when they are older and when their actions are perhaps fraught with less consequence for others. Suicide is as unsettling, and often even more so, for survivors as murder. Equally, fatal accidents are self-evidently life-altering, shattering events of a similar magnitude. All three—murder, suicide, and fatal accidents—are unpredictable, unexpected, and avoidable deaths. Their shock is profound. If we measure their combined incidence, the results place the United States in the European middle ground, below Belgium, Denmark, Finland, France, Norway, and Luxembourg (figure 211).

Yes, there are differences between Europe and America. The United States has more guns, more jails, more religion, fewer taxes, less of a state. But equally, you could formulate an exceptionalist argument for almost any Western European nation, depending on the subject. Each graph presented here has extremes. But those extremes are not always the United States. Sometimes they are the English-speaking fringe (on the low end of many aspects of social policy, on the high in terms of poverty, inequality, and crimes other than murder). Often, they are from the Mediterranean nations (on the high end of religion, energy use, tax avoidance, voter turnout, family cohesion; on the low end of foreign aid, educational spending and attainment, gender equality, environmental affairs, civil society). Sometimes, they are the Scandinavian nations (on the high end of social spending and gender issues, civil society cohesion, and volunteering). But despite many disparities within Europe, no one gets embroiled in principled discussions of whether there is Dutch, Swedish, Greek, or Irish exceptionalism—except all the Dutch, Swedish, Greek, or Irish tub-thumpers at home, who, by definition, are unknown elsewhere. No one formulates an argument about the exceptionalism of any single European nation intended for broader consumption because no one cares enough to bother. The case for American exceptionalism does not spring spontaneously from the evidence. Instead, the evidence is laboriously marshaled to support a position adopted for other reasons. Something more than mere difference is at work.

In quantitative comparisons, America often lands toward the Mediterranean end of the European spectrum. That comes as a surprise mainly to northern Europeans. Americans know that their country is as influenced by the Mediterranean as by northern Europe. It could be argued that the Mediterranean nations are the poorest in Western Europe, that some have been dictatorships until recently, and that all are striving to become more prosperous and more like their northern brethren. Consequently, so the argument proceeds, it is illegitimate to consider the Mediterranean as representative of Europe, or at least of Europe's aspirations, and it is argumentative sleight of hand to suggest that an American placement at this end of the table somehow positions it, too, within a European framework.

There are two answers to this view. First, perhaps Italy aspires to become like Sweden, but surely no more than Mississippi hopes to be like Massachusetts. As the area south of the butter/oil divide grows wealthier and more like the north, so, too, does the region south of the Mason-Dixon line. Secondly, the evidence of convergence to a northern European norm is inconclusive and, if anything, points in the opposite direction. GDP per head does not determine political culture. Despite both being wealthy democracies, America and Sweden remain different—just as Japan, too, is a prosperous, developed nation yet has not developed a European-style welfare state.[2] But if this is true, then it holds within Europe as well. There is no reason to suspect that Italy, even as it grows richer, will become more like Sweden either. As we have seen, a veritable garden of flowers blooms in the scholarly literature on models of social policy. Since they differ so markedly from what is found in northern Europe, the welfare states and the economies of the Mediterranean are safely quarantined in typologies of their own. The convergences, if any, occur as often between America and parts of northern Europe as they do between north and south within Europe itself.

America is often seen by Europeans as a land of extremes: sometimes the smallest this, but most often the biggest that. Bernard-Henri Lévy, who considers himself a sympathetic observer, pronounces gargantuism of everything from parking lots and airports to campaign budgets and public deficits as one of America's essential characteristics.[3] Such perceptions are governed by relative sizes: a badger marveling at the sheer incoherence of an animal so large and ungainly as an elephant. A nation that is also a continent will likely embrace more extremes than any one part of another continent. As this book has suggested, however, the spread is often as wide within Europe as it is within America. The span of per capita income, for example, is slightly wider between the poorest European country (Portugal) and the richest (Norway) than between the most impoverished U.S. state (Mississippi) and the wealthiest (Connecticut).[4] Life expectancies for men are wider (6.7 years) between the longest living state (Hawaii) and the shortest (Mississippi) than the 4.8 years that separate the best-performing European nation (Iceland) and the worst (Portugal). Add any one of the new EU arrivals, however, other than Slovenia, and the balance tips the other way.[5] Or take as basic an indicator of modern economies as the rate of female participation in the labor force. The United States spans less of an extreme than Europe: a difference of 20 percentage points between West Virginia and South Dakota, compared to one of 31 percentage points between Italy and Iceland.[6]

Perhaps the only consistent rule of transatlantic difference might be that the American state is, on the whole, less interventionist than its European counterparts and that Americans want and expect it to play a lesser role in their lives. And yet, is even that true? By European standards, the American state is laissez-faire in some respects, like employment law and the overall rate of taxation. But, even by European standards, it is quite meddlesome in others. True, state spending is low. But the state's activities are not exhausted just by redistribution, nor are they measured only by the level of its outlays. Many state activities are highly interventionist even though they are largely cost-free, compared to redistributive measures. (Or, rather, the costs they impose are not paid directly by taxes.)

The American state has long micromanaged its citizens' bad habits, regulating alcohol and smoking, for example, in ways more similar to Scandinavia than the Mediterranean. Here, Europe has followed the American lead, with even the Germans, Italians, and French outlawing smoking in bars and restaurants. In *On Liberty* (1859), John Stuart Mill drew his examples of governmental policing of morality from America, not from Europe: laws enforcing the Sabbath, liquor regulation, and persecution of the Mormons. Though widely assumed, the idea that the American state has always been laissez-faire in inclination and vestigial in construction has been undermined by recent historical work. Even in the nineteenth century, as we now know, the American state was strong, ambitious, and interventionist.[7] A sophisticated future history of the American state will reveal not that it was weak or small across the board. Instead, it will examine why it chose to dig into some aspects of its citizens' lives rather than others. European states, too, have varied widely in what they have focused on, as well as in how much their subjects have tolerated their intrusions. The notion that one single style of European state covers everything between the anarchic Mediterranean and Germanic *Kadavergehorsamkeit* is simply a myth.

America has long mandated extraordinary rights and protections for the handicapped, in excess of what has been attempted in most European countries. The 1990 Americans with Disabilities Act remains the international standard. In Europe, the handicapped occasionally still have to make do with quaintly corporatist measures, like those reserving—at least until recently—certain professions: elevator and parking lot attendant positions for the disabled in the UK, jobs as switchboard operators for the blind in Greece, and as masseurs in Italy.[8]

In public health, the United States has been draconian compared to many European nations, imposing harsh sanctions on the contagiously ill. In combating the AIDS epidemic, America employed similarly stringent measures as the Swedes, Austrians, and Bavarians, while other European nations were more laissez-faire.[9] U.S. authorities enforce vaccination of children more rigorously than many European nations, and they insist on fluoridating water and pasteurizing milk and cheese in a way that is without compare among at least the

Mediterranean nations. No fiscal authorities are more powerful and persever-
ant than America's Internal Revenue Service, which taxes its citizens regardless
of where in the world they live and on everything they earn throughout it.
Indeed, the IRS makes it almost impossible ever to cease being an American
citizen from a tax point of view. Antitrust or anticompetition regulations were
implemented earlier and are stricter and more punctiliously enforced in the
United States than the EU. On testing and regulating medicines, the United
States has long been more stringent than many other developed nations. The
federal aviation authorities in America enforce the most effective safety strictures in the world. As the banking and credit crisis has shown, the U.S. government does not shy away from intervening in the economy when it seems
necessary. Generally, white-collar crime is more harshly controlled and pun-
ished in the United States than elsewhere in the world.

U.S. courts mete out heavy punishments to producers and providers
of services, holding them to strict standards of liability. Europeans often
regard American consumer protection laws as burdensome evidence of a
nanny state—not a concept one hears often applied to the United States.
"To European eyes," John Micklethwait and Adrian Wooldridge report, "it
sometimes looks as if Americans are determined to criminalize, pathologize,
regulate or legislate out of existence almost every hazard."[10] In environmental legislation, the United States was an early and strict intervener.[11] Having
once itself been a copyright rogue state, the United States is now among the
most ferocious enforcers of intellectual property rights. Americans may be
allowed to buy guns in a way that surprises many Europeans. But they meekly
drive at prescribed speeds that would infuriate the Italians, not to mention
the Germans. In Germany, speed limits on the highways are considered a
restriction of citizen's rights, and no political party has supported a proposed
curb of 80 miles per hour. *Freie Fahrt für mündige Bürger*—freely translated
as "Pedal to the metal: Every citizen's right!"—is as bizarrely incomprehen-
sible a slogan to Americans as the citizen's right to bear arms is to Germans.
And, of course, a far higher percentage of Americans than Europeans suffer
the state's most direct impositions, as prisoners in its jails. Incarceration is the
ultimate interventionism. Indeed, if we take account of the very high percentage of European inmates who are foreigners, the contrast across the Atlantic
is even more startling: America locks up its young and especially its black and
Hispanic men; Europe jails its foreigners.

The American state is low-spending on some things—unemployment benefits, or the statutory part of pensions. But on others, and not just the military,

it is more generous: on research and development or education. The American state's and U.S. businesses' vast spending on biomedical research, reflected also in the large fraction of GDP spent on health care, allows significant free riding by the rest of the world.[12] On public-financed health care for those Americans lucky enough to receive it, the United States is positively profligate. Not all Americans are generously covered, of course. But so much is spent on the comparatively few who are that the per-recipient sums are almost 50% greater than those of the next highest country (Luxembourg), twice or thrice most of the rest of Europe, and six times the Greek level.[13] Needless to say, that is not desirable—any more than are large amounts spent on unemployment benefits, whether because many are out of work or because so much is given to those who are without jobs that they become insulated from the labor market. Not necessarily high but effective spending is what the welfare state seeks. If the authorities can convince their citizens to eat lots of fish, they can save on installing defibrillators in public places. Public spending alone does not guarantee ideal results. Sometimes, the same (or an equivalent) result can be had by other means. Outcomes should concern us more than process.

That is what this book has been looking at: outcomes, more than how they are achieved. Full employment is better than having many out of work, even if the redundant are treated generously. Health and safety regulations, sensibly enforced, are better than disability pensions. Prevention beats cure. Usually, a similar result can be arrived at by various routes, but outcomes cannot be the only thing. One cannot reach them by any means possible. A Ministry of Happiness that puts LSD in the drinking water, as in *Wild in the Streets*, the 1968 film depiction of the American counterculture, would generally be thought to have cut one corner too many. Nor is sending the out-of-work into exile in order to spruce up unemployment figures the done thing, though enrolling them as students or pensioning them off as disabled are standard tactics. But in many respects, similar goals can be achieved by different means. Sometimes, certain means may be better than alternatives. At other times, the choice among them may not matter much.[14] Nowhere is it inscribed that there is only one way of solving the problems of modern society, or that the optimal solution of one era will remain so forever.

Consider the problem of providing communications outside the home: pay phones are a public solution, mobile phones a private one. In this case, the public solution has largely been eclipsed by the private one. In the developed world, mobile phone penetration is almost total, and the use of public pay phones has steadily declined. In the third world, mobile phones are a classic instance of the advantages of backwardness, as they allow skipping landline technology with its massive infrastructure. In poor and rich countries alike, the private solution has trumped the public one. Ever fewer people are excluded from using mobile phones. Public pay phones will eventually disappear altogether, possibly with a residual network, propped up by public subsidies, remaining in rich countries for emergencies and for the destitute.

One canonical answer does not solve a problem once and for all. Nor is there an argument to be made *sub specie aeternitatis* for either a public or private solution. The best feasible answer at one moment may change under different technological and social circumstances. Computers can be made accessible, both via public stations or in private Internet cafes, as well as by developing cheap laptops even the poor can afford. Analogously, if the goal is to have a well-educated population, must that be achieved by state-financed and state-run educational systems at every level? Or can it be done in myriad ways, some of which are private? Does it matter so long as the outcomes are similar? Does a nation have to achieve a goal in a certain way? Or is it enough that it has achieved the goal? If our aim is education for all up to the level they are able to benefit from, and if we agree that it does not have to be achieved in one particular way, then surely Europe and the United States are fundamentally similar.

What about the other outcomes we have been looking at? If different routes to the same goal are legitimate, then the contrasts usually drawn across the Atlantic in terms of social policy are moderated. Old age and disability are dealt with in a largely comparable fashion in the United States and in Europe. American unemployment benefits are what the Grimm brothers would have called stepmotherly. But proportionally fewer Americans in recent years have been unemployed than Europeans, in some measure thanks to flexible labor regulation. Is this an allowable trade-off, where labor-market and social policy in the United States provides a total package that can be compared to Europe's more exclusively social-policy solution? That is ultimately a political question that cannot be answered here. But would we want to make this the litmus test that separates the United States from Europe? Or are we willing to let more than one flower bloom?

There is an obvious gap in health policies across the Atlantic: 100% coverage versus 85% coverage. In this instance, we would not want to be blinded by outcomes only. As already noted, infant mortality in the United States is off the European scale. No one would want to come into the world as a poor American child if he could instead be born in Europe. Being uninsured in the

United States does not mean that one is also untreated. There are medical opportunities (not least hospital emergency rooms) even for those without insurance. But it certainly means that one is not treated to the state of the art. The uninsured in America are more likely, for example, to be diagnosed for cancer at an advanced, and less curable, stage than those who are covered.[15] But does getting a raw deal in a technologically sophisticated system make you worse off than getting a fair deal in a less effective health care system? To judge by health outcomes alone, the answer is not so obvious, though receiving worse care than your fellow citizens must be at once humiliating, saddening, and infuriating.

We do not have five-year cancer survival rates for the uninsured, but we do have them for black Americans. Of course, being black and being uninsured are not the same thing. While some 12% of white Americans have no coverage, 20% of African Americans do not. There are social and genetic reasons why disease profiles vary between blacks and whites. Access to high-quality medical care is far from the only factor that explains why blacks die younger than whites. Indeed, given that amenable mortality is over twice as high for blacks as for whites, it may well be that being white and uninsured is a better fate than black and covered.[16] With all these caveats in mind, let us assume that, for the purpose of discussion, being black is a reasonably accurate proxy for being maltreated by the American health care system.

If so, then the brutal fact remains that for the four main cancer killers, only an African American woman with breast cancer is worse off than most Europeans, and even she is as likely to survive for five years as her Welsh and Portuguese sisters. African Americans with lung cancer have a better chance of surviving five years than Danes, the English, Finns, Norwegians and Swedes, and the same chance as Icelanders and Italians. African Americans with colon cancer have better chances than the Danes, English, Welsh, Scots, and Portuguese, and are one percentage point off the same rates as Icelanders, Italians, Norwegians, and Swedes. Black American men with prostate cancer are better off than any Europeans other than the Austrians.[17] In other words, a rational actor deciding behind a Rawlsian veil of ignorance whether it is preferable to risk being afflicted with cancer in America or Europe would not have a clear and persuasive reason to choose against America, even given a 10% chance of being born an African American and belonging to one of the least fairly treated groups for whom we have numbers. After all, you also risk being born a Dane. Of the 24 cancers for which we have five-year survival rates for both Danes and African Americans, for 13 the Danes die proportionately earlier, for 3 the results are equal or within 3 percentage points of each other, leaving only 8 for which you would rather have ended up in Denmark.

Please don't let me be misunderstood: this is not an argument against universal health care, a reform that America desperately needs for both moral and practical reasons. Here, obviously, outcomes are not all that matters. The individual's chance of being uninsured in America is profoundly unfair, however functionally inconsequential the actual result may be on a macro level of population well-being. It is, however, to suggest that fairness is not the only thing that counts. Ensuring equal access to less than brilliant results—a commonplace in Europe—may be fair, but it is not optimal.

This takes us close to the heart of where an Atlantic divide may exist, namely fairness. Is America a less fair society than Europe? Some observers admit that this is true, adding that Americans believe in the market and competition and embrace incentives that encourage self-help. In this logic, inequality of incomes spurs workers to greater efforts. Make things too equal, and lethargy results. With this argument, America's less-regulated labor market helps explain its higher per capita GDP. Americans choose liberty and the chance of prosperity over equality; European preferences are reversed. Rich people show what one can aim for. Hence America's love affair with ostentatious display.

America's preference for inequality is coupled to the belief that the United States is more socially mobile than Europe and in that sense more fair. Present inequality, in this logic, is unimportant since people can better themselves in the long run. Unequal at any given moment, American society offers chances to its citizens over their lifespans. Those born poor have a fair chance to rise. Perhaps this is the moment to correct this widespread American misperception. Evidence is mounting that social mobility in America is not higher than in Europe. It is lower than in Scandinavia especially, though it remains above that in the UK.[18]

Other observers also admit that America is a less fair society than Europe, but explain this as a historical imperative, not as a conscious choice. One of the tragic legacies of slavery has been to divide the nation by race. Add to that the hard work of assimilating successive waves of immigrants. The resulting ethnic, religious, and social lumpiness of American society has hampered the putting in place of the mechanisms of social solidarity that were easier to achieve in the more homogeneous societies of Western Europe.[19] It is no secret that the welfare state began earlier and flourished more luxuriantly in those nations that were most ethnically, religiously, and socially uniform—in agrarian, Protestant Scandinavia.[20]

In America, the continuing presence of an ethnically distinct underclass, even as other outsiders have successfully assimilated, has limited the ability of reformers to strive for universalist social policy that includes all citizens. As we have seen, take out black homicide and the American murder rate falls to European levels. Child poverty rates, which are scandalously high in the United States, fall to below British, Italian, and Spanish levels if we look at the figures for whites only.[21] Look only at the white population and the amenable mortality rate in the United States rises from worst place among our nations to the same level as Finland's and better than Portugal, the UK, Denmark and Ireland.[22] PISA scores for American whites (for combined science literacy, 2006) rank above every European nation other than Finland and the Netherlands, rather than—as is otherwise the case—two-thirds of the way down the hierarchy.[23]

If we could strip out the urban underclass from the numbers, it seems a fair bet that the United States would be even less statistically distinguishable from Western Europe than I have shown that it already is. It might not be Sweden. But it would be like the Netherlands, France, or Germany, and more than hold its own vis-à-vis the Mediterranean or the UK and Ireland. This is not in any sense to excuse the atrocious negligence with which the problems of racism have been dealt. It is to point out how much of the divergence between the United States and Europe, to the extent it exists, can be pinpointed as the outcome of specific and changeable causes. If anything significant does distinguish America from Europe, it is not a grand opposition of worldviews or ideologies of the sort espoused by the mouthpieces of transatlantic difference, whichever side of the ocean they hail from. It is the still unresolved legacy of slavery and its tragic modern consequence of a ghettoized and racially identifiable underclass. Whether Obama's election will mark a turning point in this respect remains to be seen.

The question of ethnic heterogeneity and social isolation in ghettos should interest Europeans since their societies are rapidly becoming more like America's in this respect. Europe's birthrates have plummeted, and immigration continues unabated. It is a demographic certainty that an ethnically and religiously distinct lower class in Europe will grow in decades to come. Perhaps Europe will turn out to have been lucky. Having instituted universalist social measures, highly regulated labor markets, and redistributive fiscal policy at a time when such choices could still be made in the belief that it was all being kept in the family, so to speak, Europe may weather the expansion of its social community to include distinct outsiders. On the other hand, it may be that the social fabric will fray in Europe as it grows more ethnically and religiously plural. The jury is still out.

FIFTEEN
THE
POST FACTO
STATE

SOME CRITICS OF AMERICA turn out to be bean counters. They admit that the American outcomes in certain fields are comparable to what is found in Europe, only to point out that the cost has been higher. The fundamental premise of the recently published *American Human Development Report* is not so much that the United States is doing poorly in comparison with other nations, though of course some outcomes are nothing short of shameful. More annoying to the authors is that the United States is being inefficient and has not been able to parlay its front-running GDP status into an equivalently primary position in other respects.[1] Tony Judt argues that, "for every dollar the United States spends on education it gets worse results than any other industrial nation."[2] Indeed, the United States spends more per pupil than anyone else, but gets results that are only in the middle of the European spectrum. From a cost-benefit analysis, America should be getting better value for its money. The same is often said of health care, where the United States spends disproportionately even more, yet gets only moderately good results.

On three out of four of the fundamental activities of modern government—education, health, social insurance, and defense—America turns out to be a big spender. For education and health, the U.S. state spends as much as any country in Europe, for defense much more so, but for social insurance, it is at the bottom of the European scale. If we look at how American society as a whole—privately and publicly—allocates its resources, however, by European standards it spends lavishly on health, education, and defense, and at about the European average for social insurance. Perhaps there is a pattern here.

Consider high spending for a moment, not from the bookkeeper's vantage, but from the political theorist's. A nation with a high GDP per head has more wiggle room than poorer countries. It may be that America's choice to spend freely is in fact a tactical political decision rather than a slothful financial one—to be generous, rather than profligate. For one thing, as James Galbraith has argued, high levels of American spending on education, health care, the military, and even domestic security translate ultimately into high employment.[3] What may seem inefficient from the circumscribed vantage of education or health care looks more defensible from a broader view, as refracted through a concern for labor markets.

The high levels of spending in the United States also benefit humanity at large. America's massive health care outlays admittedly pay for a bureaucracy that is more deadweight than even the French or German. They also fund a biomedical research machine without compare. When, for ideological reasons, the U.S. federal government under the Bush administration clamped down on stem cell research, the voters of California mortgaged their children's future to foot the bill for research for all mankind. Proposition 71 in 2004 set aside three billion dollars of taxpayers' money over 10 years, making the California Institute for Regenerative Medicine the largest source of funding for embryonic and pluripotent stem cell research in the world. By comparison, the UK, which is considered liberal in its approach to stem cell research and keen to be a contender in the field, was projected in 2005 to be spending about thirty million pounds sterling (or a bit over fifty million dollars at the PPP exchange rate) annually over the upcoming decade. The British government subsequently agreed to double its share for two years. But that still leaves the UK—a country almost twice the size of California—far behind that state.[4] Other European nations, like Germany, heavily restrict research and funding into such topics. In the same fashion, America's generous educational outlays go not only to urban sink schools, but also to superlative institutions of higher education whose research ranks highest in the world and whose students come from around the globe. In other words, America's combined private- and public-sector spending fuels global research in medicine, technology, and science.

More broadly, the ability of America to spend disproportionately on crucial policy areas lubricates the gears of choice, whose grinding would otherwise signal the engagement of difficult political choices. Generally, there is a trade-off between pre facto and post facto approaches to solving problems. If you have a population thoroughly imbued with a Protestant work ethic, perhaps you do not have to worry as much about the moral hazard of unemployment insurance as you would with a variety of cultural traditions coloring attitudes to the workplace. If your citizens have an internalized belief in the sanctity of the state and a common attitude of deference toward authority, perhaps you can get away with skeleton-crew policing. If your country's children are taught at home to respect both their parents and schools, you could well make do without an entire infrastructure of remediation.

Heading a problem off at the pass is more efficient and certainly more effective than patching up the consequences after the fact. But taking a pre facto approach assumes that everyone is agreed on what the problems are and how they should be dealt with since, by definition, the issue does not yet exist. You need a high degree of social cohesion and a consensus on social values. Pre facto interventions work when you can take harmony and agreement for granted. In contrast, a post facto approach has the problem thrust upon it. It requires much less discussion of whether something must be done. Humpty Dumpty must now be put back together again. But the act of returning an omelet to its pristine ovumnal state is harder than making sure in the first place that Humpty does not sit on walls, tempting gravity.

A society with a reasonable degree of social, ethnic, and religious homogeneity can more easily head off coming problems than one bereft of such communalities. Lacking the informal socialization of a broadly unified civil society, a fragmented and heterogeneous nation is obliged to fall back on the overt and after-the-fact exertions of formal authority.[5] Europeans often consider officious user instructions on consumer products and overly literal health-and-safety warnings as an American bad habit that is slowly spreading across the Atlantic. Smirks greet the warnings on packages of peanuts that declare "May contain traces of nut products." We feel our intelligence insulted by Kit Kat wrappers instructing us to "Open here," as though we could not figure that out.[6] But such punctiliousness is perhaps motivated as much by a decreasing ability to take for granted much common knowledge of any sort and the consequent need to spell things out. How many youngsters from modest backgrounds have not been shamed by making a false move when first encountering an artichoke at a fancy dinner party? How much more humane if artichokes came with preprinted instructions. Every intersection in America without a light brandishes stop signs to indicate who has the right of way. In Germany, there are no stop signs, because drivers know that the car approaching from the right has priority. One system spells it out, assuming nothing; the other relies on implicit knowledge.

If the informal habits of civil society still dictate what is eaten and when, if mother still prepares the nightly dinner and children are not yet allowed to indulge in the independence of the culinary Noah's ark at the mall food court, then obesity may take longer to gain a hold. Absent such consensual and informal regulation, the authorities could—as they have in America—instead legislate to ban trans fats from restaurants and soda from schools, regulate the number of fast-food outlets in poor neighborhoods, and require restaurants to post the caloric counts of their meals on the menus. Can this be the supposedly laissez-faire American state in fact micromanaging the bad habits of its citizens, much as absolutist Prussia banned smoking in the eighteenth century? Or should this be understood as the post facto state drawing the truest arrows it has in its quiver?

In Germany and Scandinavia, access to mass transit, especially subways, is controlled informally, by voluntary compliance, enforced occasionally by spot-checks of tickets. Elsewhere in the world, even in allegedly groupthink Japan, access is gained by passing a ticket barrier, after which the passenger need fear no control. Those who have experienced the nerve-jangling surprise controls in Germany or the Nordic nations—as fellow passengers morph into ID-flashing transit police, demanding tickets and hauling off miscreants while a smug sense of communal recognition settles over the dutiful—know how powerful an enforcement mechanism this system of honor-cum-surprise-checks is. In comparison, the control-at-entrance (and sometimes exit) mechanism bares its fangs up front, but leaves the transit network itself blessedly free. The honor system is based on communal groupthink, a mass transit superego that avoids the free-rider problem in its most literal sense by keeping passengers in line with an unspoken but firmly ingrained cultural ethos.

As the first nation of immigrants in the West, the United States was also the first forced to deal with the trade-offs between informal socialization, on which its systems of authority could stake very little, and the more overt controls required of its motley citizenry. The American state has relied more on a post facto system of authority than has, until recently, proved necessary in Europe. Post facto controls have suited American circumstances in that they take no knowledge or behavior for granted and require few commonly shared and implicit assumptions. It is, however, likely that they are less efficient, since they cannot rely much on prevention. Steering a Noah's ark of a society is more costly, complicated, and circuitous than herding a flock of merinos.

Ethnic fragmentation may have left Americans unwilling to support explicit public spending whose benefits were reaped by others of a different skin color.[7] But that has not eliminated the need to spend to solve problems. In fact, it may lead to even more spending, or at least inefficient spending. An obvious example of a highly dysfunctional post facto approach is the way emergency rooms are used in the United States for routine but otherwise unavailable medical care, rather than treating illnesses as they first arise. With their many uninsured patients, Americans are more likely than Europeans to seek care at emergency rooms.[8] The uninsured are treated, but they receive too little care too late, and at a high cost: a bad outcome for all. A study of homeless alcoholics in San Diego, for example, found that they consumed an inordinate amount of medical resources (over $8,000 worth per person annually). By enrolling them in a program of regular health care, the costs generated by these formerly uninsured patients were cut in half.[9]

In other instances, the dysfunctionality of a post facto approach is less blatant, and its advantages as a means of dealing with the hybridity of U.S. society more evident. Why the American preoccupation with biomedical research and its potential spin-offs? It would be nice to think that it was just altruism, or even national prestige, that inspired America to lead the world in biomedicine. That may be part of the story. But there are political benefits as well. At its borders and in its immigrant neighborhoods, the American state has deployed the full armamentarium of overt disease control: quarantines, sequestration, fumigation, vaccination, and the like. For American citizens, in contrast, such drastic interventions have been harder to impose.

During the early years of the AIDS epidemic, for example, the Swedish authorities happily assumed the power to lock up those whose behavior threatened to spread the disease, whether prostitutes, gays, or just average seropositive citizens who refused to obey official strictures. To Swedes, the good of the community, without question, trumped the rights of the individual. The American authorities, in contrast, had been issued no equivalent ideological blank check. Instead, they had to tread delicately around the prickly sensibilities of sexual and ethnic minorities who feared being the first victims of any drastic impositions. A technological breakthrough (a vaccine or a cure) thus promised much greater political payoffs in America than in Sweden, where old-fashioned public health tactics—however draconian they seemed to the outside world—were considered both necessary and sufficient to deal with the epidemic. By intervening in nature, the American authorities hoped to be able to avoid imposing on society. It was no coincidence that the American state poured vastly greater sums into research on HIV than all other nations put together, some 90% of global government research funding.[10] "Medical research," as then-congressman Melvin Laird put it in 1960, extrapolating the argument made here to its most general level, "is the best kind of health insurance" the American people could have.[11]

Take education as another example of a problem that can be dealt with via different approaches. A good schoolwork ethic, inculcated by parents intent on getting their children into the best universities and insistent on the normality of hours of nightly homework, does wonders. Asian Americans made up 12% of California's population in 2006; they supplied 36% of all students at the University of California the following year. Ponder what it is that unites the five top scorers in the 2006 PISA science study (Finland, Hong Kong, Canada, Taiwan, and Estonia). It cannot be educational philosophy or approach. Finland's is a product of the 1960s. Children of all abilities are put together in the same classes. No marks are given until ninth grade, and lots of work is done in small groups. Taiwan, in contrast, has a strictly structured system, with school uniforms and rigorous, lengthy classroom work. Teaching is geared to a set of national exams in ninth grade. More notable is how the top scorers—apart from Canada—are homogeneous societies with few foreigners, modest social stratification, and therefore little need to bring cultural and social outsiders into the mainstream. Finland has a lower proportion of foreigners, by far, than any Western European nation, barely half as many as the next most homogeneous nation, Italy. There is, admittedly, a large (5.5%) Swedish-speaking minority, but it settled in the Middle Ages and constitutes a prosperous bourgeoisie. These are countries where the informal socialization of civil society can do the heavy lifting, and little post facto intervention is required from the state. Canada is admittedly an exception to this distinctive trend. Can the high percentage of Asians (almost 9% in 2001, compared with 4% in the United States) be part of the explanation?

To gauge the educational effect of an only moderately undulating social landscape of this nature, consider a study that compares school performance of the federal states in America with other nations. As we have seen above, in the 2003 TIMMS study of math and science performance, the United States as a whole cut quite a smart figure in international comparison. The TIMMS results for eighth graders have been rendered statistically comparable with the National Assessment of Educational Progress results achieved within each American state. Barring the unlikely possibility that the various federal states have quite differing educational philosophies and practices, we are led to conclude that the moderation of extreme social stratification and the paucity of ethnic minorities that characterizes some American states, but holds less true in others, is impressively correlated with higher scores. Thus, in a complicated and heterogeneous place like California, eighth-grade science pupils scored above their peers in Italy and Norway, but below England, Sweden, the Netherlands, and Flemish Belgium. But a state like Minnesota, with an ethnic makeup and a civic spirit akin to that of its Scandinavian roots, beat out every West European nation, bar none.

The same holds (again for science) for Montana, New Hampshire, North and South Dakota, Massachusetts, Vermont, and Wisconsin. In turn, Colorado, Connecticut, New Jersey, Ohio, Virginia, Idaho, Maine, Oregon, Utah, Washington, Wyoming, and, perhaps somewhat surprisingly, Michigan and Missouri, were beaten only by England, the top West European scorer. When the 2007 TIMMS tests included Massachusetts and Minnesota separately as benchmarks, both fourth and eighth graders in each state ranked higher in math than their peers in any West European nation. For science, the results were the same for fourth graders, though eighth graders in Minnesota ranked just a tad below their English peers. As the West sinks collectively into educational mediocrity, it is worth remembering that all American states, and all European nations studied (Finland was not part of this particular project), were roundly bested by a collection of Asian entities, including Singapore, Taiwan, South Korea, Hong Kong, and Japan.[12]

The main point here is that the relationship between civil society and the state that governs it is a reciprocal one. The authorities of the state do not act on civil society in the abstract. States face dilemmas and issues that vary according to the civil societies they rule. A state like that of unfortunate Albania, which has to keep grips on a society where blood feuds are fought out over generations, will have different tasks set for it than one faced with a citizenry that is content to stand in the pouring rain on a dark night, waiting for the traffic light to turn green. Enver Hoxha, Albania's former Communist dictator, sought to stamp out blood feuding by punishing those who fought vendettas by burying them alive in their victims' coffins.[13] Jaywalkers rarely require quite as much arm-twisting to be brought to heel.

The contrast between pre facto and post facto approaches, as well as how much they are embodied in the policy styles of European and American governments, should not be exaggerated. On the American side, the strength of civil society in even an ethnically mixed and stratified nation has been one of its surprising successes. Informal socialization of arriving immigrants helped turn them into Americans, lessening the need for authorities to crack the whip of official stricture. That, in the spirit of the title of one book, is *How the Irish Became White*. On the European side, the assimilation of outsiders has been a long and continuous process for all the continent's nations. Turning regional minorities into national citizens and *Peasants into Frenchmen*, as the title of another classic work puts it, has been part of the endeavor.[14] Europe has also digested waves of immigrants before, whether Poles into France or Jews into every nation. However big these differences across the Atlantic may have been in the past, they are rapidly diminishing.

If America was the first post facto state in the developed world, it is no longer alone in facing such trade-offs between informal socialization and overt control. In the era of globalization and mass peregrinations, things are changing in Europe, as well. To return to the example of mass transit, in Berlin, *Schwarzfahrer* caught without a ticket nowadays give false identities and cause fines to be levied on innocents (usually friends or family, whose names and addresses the culprits know offhand). In a time when communalities have eroded, the failure of informal processes of control leads to major problems of formal authority. The era of the turnstile awaits a culture that can no longer take for granted the ethos of voluntarily paying the price of admission. Municipal regulations in large German cities now limit the size of the animals that may be grilled on sunny weekend afternoons in pits dug into the otherwise manicured lawns of public parks. Needless to say, these stipulations would not have been necessary 30 years ago. Multiculturalism brings with it the need to spell out what once was taken for granted.

Of course, it is not just immigrants who bring different standards. Standards can and do change by themselves, and informal socialization may be eroded, for example, by economic incentives at odds with commonly held values. What if you are rewarded over and above your take-home pay for calling in sick? Generous sick leave with no waiting days and no stipulated doctor's note assumes that the healthy will not abuse the system by shirking. But pain thresholds, a sense of what is required and reasonable, as well as a notion of what one is entitled to from the state, and, most generally, the prevalent work ethic—these all vary, both among cultures and over time within one. Sweden's rate of sick days is now one of the highest in the world and about four times the Dutch. This is not, we hope, due to a chronic weakening of the Swedes' constitutions. In all seriousness, the Swedes themselves attribute it to the massive stress they are subjected to. More likely, it reflects a changing sense of what is tolerable and expected—as well, of course, as what the system permits in the way of abuse. However strong it remains in Holland, the informal socialization that discourages malingering appears to be evaporating in Sweden. It will be interesting to see how long the conscientious and dutiful will continue to allow such massive, if unspoken, redistribution to the lazy and feckless before more formalized post facto controls are imposed. When Italy recently introduced stricter controls for sick leave on civil servants, absences from work dropped 37%. As a *Financial Times* headline tartly commented: "New labour laws greatly improve health of Italy's state workers."[15]

SIXTEEN
HOW
THE WEST
WAS ONE

WHEN AMERICANS COMPARE THEIR COUNTRY to others, it is almost invariably to find fault with it. Of course, there are tub-thumpers on the right wing, for whom the United States is the greatest nation and comparisons are drawn merely to underline that preeminence. But they are a predictable lot, and intellectually of no consequence. Comparisons with abroad are of little use when preaching to the choir if the choir does not care. Most conservative Americans are too uninterested in Europe to sit still for comparative explanations of U.S. superiority. Mitt Romney got very little traction from attacking French health care and other things Gallic during his abortive run for the Republican nomination in 2007. The vast majority of Americans' comparisons are undertaken by social scientists with liberal leanings who hope that the United States will some day approximate Europe when it comes to family allowances, universal health insurance, parental leave, and the like. For them,

Europe means northern Europe. They either ignore the south or see it too as aspiring to north European status. Stockholm is the mecca toward which the social science faithful pray. Because of their political reform agenda—fervent but unfulfilled—the tone they strike is wistful.

Take as a recent example the *American Human Development Report*, published by a preeminent institution, the Social Science Research Council, and prefaced by multiple well-wishes from the great and the good. It is modeled on the UN's attempt to sum up economic and human well-being in a single number, to compare nations and progress over time.[1] Its wealth of information lays bare the sometimes dramatic disparities within the United States and shows where it is lagging in relation to peer comparison countries. That is all well and good, and who could fault it? It is when sight is lost of the larger picture that worries begin. Thus, the report presents a chart (Figure 1.2) showing an apparently precipitous decline in America's human development ranking. The United States stood in second place, after Switzerland, in 1980. This held steady until 1995, when it plummeted over the next 15 years to land at the 12th spot in 2005. America's numerical score has increased steadily, we are reassured. But the scores of other countries have risen even faster. As a result, the United States has fallen behind its more efficient competitors. What this ignores, however, is that in 1975, the earliest year for which the Human Development Index was calculated, the United States ranked sixth among developed nations, behind Denmark, Canada, Sweden, Switzerland, and the Netherlands, and on par with Norway. Only after this did it rise to the second position. In 2000, it had fallen to the ninth spot. It revived briefly in 2004, moving to the eighth, only to fall four places the following year.[2] There may, of course, be a larger secular decline here. But it may equally be a question of the inevitable oscillations of finely calibrated measurements.

Let us look more exactly at the range of differentiation. The UN's Human Development Index ranks 177 countries, from poor Sierra Leone in last place at 0.336 up through happy Iceland (and Norway) at the peak, clocking in at 0.968. Among those nations the UN classifies as having high human development, the spectrum bottoms out with Brazil at 0.800. America and Western Europe cluster in the top 10% range. Only Portugal (0.897) falls below that. The United States (0.951) is at the bottom of the top 5% range, with seven of our countries above it. Between the United States and Iceland lies a span of 17 points on a scale of 1,000. In other words, the jockeying for position takes place at the very pinnacle of the totem pole, within a section that is less than 2% of its overall length.

My point is not that Americans should break out the champagne to congratulate themselves. Of course, there is room for improvement, and serious deficiencies can be revealed by such comparisons. But there is a curiously hubristic quality to American social scientists' self-flagellation. If America is not number one, or very close to it, then—so seems to be the attitude—it is nothing. The idea that the United States might be just another country, muddling through somewhere along the bulge of the bell curve, is rarely entertained as an acceptable possibility. In this sense, liberal American social scientists pay an inverted homage to the idea of American exceptionalism. They are disappointed when the United States is not, in fact, exceptional, and indeed refuse to accept it as just one of the pack. Godfrey Hodgson has recently argued that the idea of American exceptionalism is a myth and that the United States has always been much more like the nations of its European roots than many patriotic Americans and their historians will admit.[3] I agree entirely and have sought to hold the mirror to his story, hoping to convince European skeptics that the similarities are greater than they too may think.

From this vantage of American exceptionalism, the rise of other nations—whether Europe in the postwar era, Russia during the cold war, now China, and perhaps India—appears as a threat that scales back America's relative preeminence, demoting the nation from its self-anointed position at the pinnacle of everything. This is the zero-sum mentality of Olympic medal ratings. When swimmers win gold by reaching the end of the pool one-hundredth of a second sooner than their closest competitor, we are not, of course, calculating any practical payoff—shorter aquatic commutes, speedier lifeguards, zippier pearl divers. We are in a world where the law of diminishing returns exacts an excruciating price. The jockeying for position and the acclaim that goes to the top few competitors hinges on microscopic differences discernable only with the help of highly specialized technology. Insofar as comparisons with our competitors spur us to greater efforts, they are welcome. But if they prompt us to lose sight of the larger picture while obsessing over ever-finer distinctions among those at the top, then we are again dangerously close to parsing minor differences narcissistically.

What do Americans lose by not being number one? The answer depends on whom they are competing with. If laggards are overtaking them and they are no longer improving, or not improving as fast as others, there may be a problem. If, however, their peers are inching past them in an ever-tighter race where the distinctions among competitors are rapidly diminishing, then in practical terms it may not matter. Like the Olympic swimmers, they are

212. Human Development Index Trends

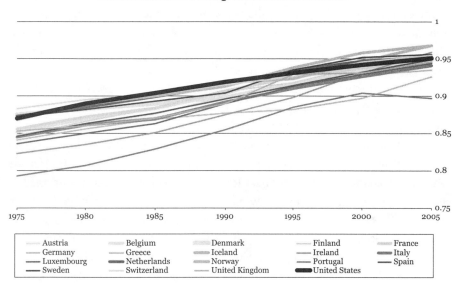

Austria	Belgium	Denmark	Finland	France
Germany	Greece	Iceland	Ireland	Italy
Luxembourg	Netherlands	Norway	Portugal	Spain
Sweden	Switzerland	United Kingdom	United States	

jockeying for position in an ever more crowded and splendidly endowed field. In 1975, the span in the Human Development Index between the lowest of our nations (Portugal) and highest (Switzerland) was 0.09. In 2005, the equivalent figure, now with Iceland at the top, was 0.071. In other words, the playing field on which our countries compete has shrunk by over a fifth, and the average score has risen almost a full 10 percentage points, from 0.852 to 0.947. The competition is fiercer, the game has improved, the distinctions are diminishing. In sum, there is ever tighter clustering ever further toward the top. That is, of course, precisely what we would hope for. But it should also serve to shift our attention away from the relative rankings of the nations competing within this ever smaller sphere of excellence, which become less and less meaningful. Instead, we should look at the increasing concentration of these nations around the top of the scale. What we see here is not a picture of relative loss of position, but of convergence at the top (figure 212).

In other words, Americans should welcome, not fret about, the relative slippage (if such it is) that the United States has suffered. Better to be but one in a field of thoroughbreds than top dog of a pack of mongrels. The United States does not become poorer in a tangible sense just because China is now growing faster than America is—any more than the British were impoverished by the Italian *sorpasso*, that brief moment in 1987 when the Italian economy appeared (the black market was suddenly factored into the statistics) to be larger than the British, or the Italians are now by the Spanish *sobrepaso*. The only quality being discounted is *amour propre*. Nor has America's educational system been gutted because other nations now send almost as many, and in some cases more, of their eighteen-year-olds to university.

Yes, there are some disparities—revealed by such comparisons—that should worry Americans. Life expectancies, and what they divulge about health care, lifestyles, and social conditions, may be one. When I was born, in 1956, an American male could hope statistically speaking to make it to about 66. My son, were he to be born this year, could expect to live almost a full decade longer. My Japanese peer would have looked forward at birth to about one less year of life than me. But his son would expect to live four years longer than my baby. Those are four years that I would wish my son to have, too, of course. But is it possible, even if Americans adopt universal health care, eat more fish, slim down, and so forth? In Japan, females can expect to live to become 86. In America, Asian females live almost three years longer than that (88.8).[4] Latino females in the United States, who are unlikely to be among the best treated by America's health care system, live more than four years longer than white females, Latino males three and a half years longer than their white peers. These statistical snippets suggest that there are issues beyond health care, and even lifestyle, that may influence longevity. Short of turning Japanese, there may be little my son can do to achieve a Japanese lifespan.

My point is not that Americans should ignore the warning signals that comparative surveys send out. It is that the message is not one of unrelieved gloom. Thus, to stick with the *American Human Development Report* as the state of the art, we are told that homicide and suicide "are significant contributors to premature death nationwide." For homicide, that is undeniably the case. But it is surely worth pointing out that, comparatively, of all the problems the United States has to worry about, suicide is not one of them. The United States ranks either eleventh or eighth (the report cannot quite make up its mind), well below most European nations outside the Mediterranean.[5] We are told that the differentiation of income levels between the richest and poorest congressional districts is three to one (Table 2.4). But to evaluate the significance of that fact surely we need to know that comparable disparities within Western Europe as a whole are similarly great. The disparities between New York's 14th and 16th congressional districts are recounted: the Upper East Side and the South Bronx. Only two miles apart, they are yet so different that average life expectancies vary by four years. We are not told that between the Calton and Lenzie neighborhoods of Glasgow, eight miles apart, the mortality differential for men is 28 years. Or that in Hampstead in north London, men live on average 11 years longer than in St Pancras, five stops down the Northern Line tube.[6]

We are told that American public schools segregate pupils into two systems, for whites and for minorities. But we are not told that in test outcomes, American public schools are less stratified than in most of Europe, outside Scandinavia (figure 99, above). A graph is presented in the Report (Figure 3.8) as though it shows that in Germany, 99% of 18-year-olds graduate from high school, while in the United States only 75% do. But we are not told that the United States (along with New Zealand, which also has a 75% graduation rate) uniquely does not differentiate between general and vocational streams of secondary education. In Germany, only 38% of pupils attend an academic, university-preparatory secondary school. The remaining 62% are in vocational tracks that generally end in 10th grade. The 25% of U.S. pupils who do not finish high school leave for manual jobs between 15 and 18, depending on when they are legally allowed to end their schooling. Their peers in Germany exit at around the same age for the same goal. The only difference is that they take with them a 10th-grade completion certificate that registers them—however misleadingly—in the OECD's statistics as having completed secondary education.

The reality is that more 18-year-old Americans than Germans earn the qualification that, in theory at least, allows them to attend university (73% in the United States, 35% in Germany). In tandem, more of them actually enter higher education (64% in the United States, 35% in Germany).[7] As we have seen (figure 101, above), twice as many young Germans as their American peers are neither in education nor gainfully employed. In other words, the chart purporting to show the comparative failure of U.S. secondary education does nothing of the sort. In effect, it manufactures a problem that—for all the difficulties of American public high schools—is equally shared by much of Europe.

We need to know that America has problems, of course. But to understand how big and pressing those issues are, we also need to put them into perspective. Which of America's problems are off the scale compared to its peers and which are common—if regrettable—parts of being a modern nation? When one is used to being the biggest and best at everything, even the problems have to be jumbo-size. And when one compares a continent-size country to the rarefied, dollhouse atmosphere of, say, a Norway, or even a Netherlands, obviously many issues—above all, of disparities and divergence—will seem larger. Take Western Europe as a whole, rather than salami-slicing it, and the range and scope of problems appear much more comparable to those faced by the United States. To point this out is not to minimize anything. It is, however, to insist that comparisons have to put things into context and perspective.

It is instructive, for example, to discover that the income differential within New York City is starker than within London. There is a ratio of 2.7 in median incomes between the 16th and 14th New York congressional districts. The most abrupt median income disparity between London parliamentary constituencies, in contrast, is 1.7, the span separating West Ham from Richmond Park.[8] It is less illuminating to be told that the maximum span of median U.S. incomes varies threefold from California's 20th congressional district (Fresno) to New York's 14th (Upper East Side). In the UK, a much smaller country, the span is smaller but still significant, at 2.5 between Blackpool South and Richmond Park.[9] I have been unable to find figures on median incomes by unit of political representation elsewhere in Europe. But the range of median annual income between Luxembourg and the Greek mainland (in equivalent currency terms) is three and a half. The range of disposable income (in Euro terms) between Hamburg and northern Portugal is three (and would be larger if we could statistically isolate Blankenese or another of Hamburg's tony neighborhoods). And the range between central London and Greece's Ionian Islands is close to four.[10] We now begin to get a comparable sense of the disparities. Stark income differentials within one city are a disgrace. Large variances within a huge continent are more to be expected. Not all differences are fractal.

SEVENTEEN
ACORN
AND OAK

TO PARSE THE SUBTLE DISTINCTIONS between Europe and America must strike observers from other parts of the globe as an exercise in the narcissism of minor differences. Like twins keen to differentiate themselves, some nations eagerly distinguish among countries that are, seen globally, much of a muchness.

During the cold war, the unity of the North Atlantic nations against the Soviet empire was obvious. But after the fall of the Berlin Wall, new antagonisms emerged. Iraq, Iran, North Korea, Afghanistan, Israel: these are the immediate bones of contention. The larger issue has been the role of the United States, the one remaining superpower, as its regnum is tested by Middle Eastern wars, Russian saber rattling, and Chinese aspirations to great power status. Perhaps, as some Europeans argue, the United States has become a rogue state, unilaterally exempting itself from the strictures of mutual dependence in an increasingly interwoven world. Perhaps, as some Americans reply, Europeans live in a cloud-cuckoo land where conflict is considered ultimately to be based on misunderstandings, not real differences, and talk can therefore replace guns. These are geopolitical debates we need not enter into here.[1]

We are concerned, however, with the geopoliticians' frequent and facile elisions between internal and external politics. Because Americans own guns, they like to go to war. Because they drive big cars, they need to secure oil supplies in the Middle East. Because they are religious, they see themselves as crusaders. Because continental Europeans do not have functioning armies and refuse to pay for any, they turn foreign policy into a talking shop. Because they spend their money on social benefits, they cannot afford to defend themselves and must therefore appease the aggressors. Because of their own traumatic past, they refuse to acknowledge the continuing reality of evil in the world.

In this book, I have shown that, in almost every quantifiable respect, the United States and Western Europe approximate each other. Earlier, I have accounted for some of the ways that social scientists have tried, and failed, to typologize differences between Europe and America. Here, in contrast, I am interested in another question. Not how is America different, but why would one ask this question in the first place? Why assume that America is different? Is it the sheer fact of novelty? Of starting at a historically definable moment? Of geographical distance? Of the geopolitical patrimony of cheap and plentiful land and scarce and well-rewarded labor? Or is it that America's political culture defined itself from the start as a reaction to its European origins?

Look at the other neo-Europes. They reveal that the notion of American exceptionalism cannot stem simply from the United States being a new society. European visitors to New Zealand nostalgically enthuse: "It's just like England was 30 years ago." Canada is considered to be more "European" than the United States. And the French recognize the Québecois as closer soul mates than *les anglo-saxons*. All the other neo-Europes enjoyed the peculiarities that were America's: cheap land, expensive labor, few or comprehensively defeated first nations, the absence of feudal elites, vast distances from the mother continent. And yet, they are not regarded as inherently different from Europe. That was the implicit conclusion of Seymour Martin Lipset's ingenious thought experiment, when he compared Canada and the United States to show that, despite similar geographical circumstances, they possessed distinct political cultures.[2]

If the United States and Europe are perceived as different, the reasons should be sought in political culture, not geopolitics. Perhaps it is because the United States was founded as a reaction to its European past that it seems more different from its origin than it really is. We do not have to be Hegelians or psychoanalysts to appreciate that reactions to something depend on that against which they react, and that they are symbiotically related to it. The narcissism of small differences has worked both ways across the Atlantic. American exceptionalists claim that the United States is more different from its European origins than is in fact the case; European exceptionalists insist on having found more novel circumstances in the New World than their anecdotes actually sustain.

Most of the American literature on American exceptionalism focuses on themes like how the United States avoided Europe's battles with the old regime, how liberalism became the entrenched and dominant ideology, how socialism never took hold, how the middle-class ethos of America's founders set the tone for centuries thereafter, how disestablished religion became more important than in Europe, and so forth. American exceptionalists do not argue that America is radically different from Europe. Rather, they examine how the United States picked and chose from its many European legacies, fortuitously sidestepping some of the nastier ones. The United States was the lucky heir, not the rebel that threw it all over. *Amerika, du hast es besser,* "you are better off," as the German national poet Goethe put it in 1827, not, *Amerika, du bist ganz anders,* "you are totally different."

More recently, the historiography of the American past has begun to deemphasize the idea of exceptionalism. Historians today portray the American state and social policy as heavily influenced by European examples, and often quite akin to the Old World.[3] Even the welfare state, which used to be a *locus classicus* of American exceptionalism, is increasingly written through a broad North Atlantic focus that sees as many commonalities as differences.[4] Thus, Matthieu Leimgruber's recent history of the Swiss welfare state analyzes this under-studied European system through the historiography of U.S. social policy precisely because it is more comprehensible in American than in European terms.[5] The onset of world history also works to diminish differences within the industrialized world. It has relativized, if not vanquished, a sense of historical difference across the Atlantic.[6]

If one takes a pan-European view, even some of the classic differences so often alleged between Europe and America become effaced. Immigration no longer distinguishes the two in any binary sense.[7] Norway never had an aristocracy, nor did Iceland or the northern half of Sweden. But arguably, the American South did. Even open frontiers and supposedly sparsely settled circumstances—commonly taken to be constituent elements of America's founding myth—existed also in the Germanizing east. Breslau is arguably the mirror pendant to Milwaukee: each a Germanized town with breweries, a *Rathaus*, and beclocked church steeples. Its nightmarish variant was Hitler's vision—long after the closing of the American frontier—of a Germanic yeomanry settled across the depopulated steppes. The closing of the eastern frontier came only with Stalingrad, in the winter of 1942–1943. And did the European colonies not play much the same role as the American West?

The arguments for radical differences across the Atlantic are mainly of European origin. America did not break with its European past nearly as sharply as Europeans often claim. The French revolutionaries, as later their Russian comrades, were far more radical than the American founding fathers: beheading their masters, murdering real and imagined opponents, attempting to refashion human nature, even rejiggering time itself. Compare that to the glorified tax revolt of the prudent and bourgeois American colonists. European observers have a penchant for portraying America as far more "other" than it actually is. Tocqueville, Weber, Adorno, and Heidegger, as well as their more excitable epigones, Jean Baudrillard, Emmanuel Todd, and the like: these are the writers who have informed the ideas of radical American exceptionalism that are now *bien pensant* thinking across Europe. As Josef Joffe has rightly noted, Europeans treat the United States less as a country, considered soberly in its own right, than as a canvas—a continent-sized Rorschach blot—on which to project their own preoccupations.[8] *Winnetou lässt grüssen.*

Of course, there are differences. Las Vegas is not Baden-Baden. But neither is Bergen Bergamo. Are differences across the Atlantic any greater than those between Spitzbergen and Sardinia? Yes, Paris and London are more alike than Paris, France and Paris, Texas. But Oslo and Palermo are much more different than Santa Monica and Notting Hill. To take another example: Swedish expats in London (of whom there are some 50,000, an impressive number that corresponds proportionately to a million and a half Americans living in the city) like sending their children to American-style schools in the UK, rather than to English public schools. They find the informal egalitarianism of U.S. education so like the schools of their own social democracy and more culturally familiar than the British system, with its sex segregation, religious instruction, compulsory Latin, frequent testing, Saturday classes, and obligatory uniforms.

Of course, regions, nations, and continents invariably differ. But why assume that variations across the Atlantic are of kind and not just degree? Surely, the

founding of the United States as an offshoot of Europe implies that its culture
was transplanted. The acorn never falls far from the oak. Louis Hartz once
proposed that the new societies emanating from Europe each continued the
course of the mother society as it was at the moment of their birth.[9] Thus,
South America became feudal, America capitalist, and Australia socialist.
Whatever gripe one may have with the specifics of this theory, Hartz's main
point stands: a new society arises by asexual reproduction, becoming first a
copy, then an extension of the parent. And indeed, recent social science work
indicates that the political and social attitudes of immigrants' native land tend
to remain with them, coloring their behavior in the new home country.[10] Who
would dare explain the politics of Minnesota (or Saskatchewan) without reference to Scandinavia, of New York City or Boston without mention of Ireland
or Italy, of Cincinnati without Germany, of Appalachia without Scotland?

But unlike New Zealand, for example, where the seeds were fairly few and
from the same highly specialized subspecies (Victorian missionaries and civil
servants), America was seeded not by just one original acorn, the *Ur-Eichel*,
but by many. Europeans often find it hard to grasp America's unexpected mul-
tiplicity of facets and local cultures, masked as they are by the apparent gloss of
a unified nation and a single language. But what a European reads as American
exoticism is often only a transplanted aspect of another part of Europe that he
encounters with fresh eyes, or possibly for the first time, when in the United
States. Hans Magnus Enzensberger provided a brilliant riff on such internal European exoticism when he transposed perfectly true news items from
Italian newspapers into the rather more sober milieus of Bonn, Amsterdam,
and Scandinavia. Imagine thirty thousand Dutch pensioners storming and
destroying the main office of the state retirement fund. Or the German president involved in an international alcohol smuggling ring. Or the Swedes running out of postage stamps because the printing presses had rusted. Or over
a hundred thousand Danes drawing disability pensions for alleged blindness
while also possessing drivers' licenses and cars.[11]

In a sense, America does something similar, holding up the mirror for visiting Europeans to unfamiliar facets of their own continent. Thus, northern
Europeans assume that America's mechanisms of public authority will be
much like what they are accustomed to from home. They are then horrified
to discover that American habits of public order are at least as Mediterranean
as they are northern European. As has often been remarked about traffic in
Boston: what do you expect from a city populated by Italians and the Irish?
Hannover it is not. But what a Hannoverian finds charming and exotic when

on vacation in Rome, he considers anarchic and unexpected when navigating his way out of the tunnel from Logan Airport.

Conversely, what Mediterraneans mock as American puritanism is often a variant of regulatory styles that the United States has learned from, or at least shares with, Scandinavians and other northern Europeans. Prohibition, for example, was imposed in the United States during the early years of the twentieth century, as it was in Norway, Iceland, and Finland, not to mention the Soviet Union. The state-run alcohol monopolies of Pennsylvania, New Hampshire, and 16 other U.S. states mimic those still found in all Scandinavian countries other than Denmark. Prohibition and the strict control of alcohol sales is, in other words, as European a phenomenon as it is American, however unaware of this Mediterranean visitors may be.

Nor is controlling drugs by bans and jail more of an American peculiarity than it is a Scandinavian one. The same goes for the regulation of commercial sex work. Prohibition and police enforcement are used as much in Sweden and Finland (where prostitution—going against the grain elsewhere in Europe—has recently been recriminalized) as in some American states. Or take those American gender discrimination policies that Mediterraneans or, for that matter, many British, love to mock: quotas in the workplace and in politics, the policing of official language, the regulation of behavior in schools, factories, and offices, and the attendant and heavy-handed apparatus to enforce all of this. All these aspects of modern gender relations, laughed at by many Europeans as another example of the gynocratization of American society and its politically correct excesses, have been, of course, practiced earlier and more vigorously in Scandinavia, the heartland of modern feminism.

But then, well-educated Frenchmen or Italians—and surprisingly many Germans and British—know a great deal more about America than they do about their northern neighbors, and are therefore innocently unaware of what they are up to. The reverse is less true, since northern Europeans enjoy comparing themselves favorably to the supposedly less orderly and productive southerners. Indeed, one of the dirty little secrets of the EU is the vast and pervasive contempt the Protestant north feels for the Catholic south—rarely acknowledged, except perhaps in discussions of corruption in Brussels, and scarcely registered in the Mediterranean.[12] America's foreignness to Europeans is often the exoticism of one part of Europe itself to another.

As we have seen, there are few quantifiable measures of socioeconomic reality where the span within Europe is not as great as the divergence between Europe and the United States. Hand on heart, which cities more resemble each other: Stockholm and Minneapolis or Helsinki and Thessaloniki? And as the European Union widens eastward—possibly even to the point of taking in Turkey, a Muslim country mostly in Asia—the most recent newcomers (many from regions once called European Turkey and part of the Ottoman Empire) efface many of the issues that do distinguish the United States from Europe. These new arrivals, as indeed Europe's many recent immigrants from Asia and Africa, are very religious, skeptical of a strong state, unenthusiastic about voting, and allergic to high taxes. From the vantage of old Europe, they are, in other words, more like Americans. How odd, really, that Europeans seek to identify an enemy in a culture with which they have so much in common, just at the moment they are being joined by ones with whom they actually share even less. How odd of them to turn their backs on a country which, like their own continent, espouses the Reformation, the Scientific Revolution, the Enlightenment, democracy, liberalism, free but appropriately regulated markets, and religious toleration.

Even a few minutes watching the Eurovision Song Contest strengthens both a belief in the continued vitality of relations that span the Atlantic and one in a hugely variegated Europe, diverse to the point of incoherence. This must be the nightmare that keeps the empire-builders in Brussels awake at night: a vastly expanded Europe, stretching from Kamchatka to the Azores, from the North Pole (now festooned with Danish flags and Russian submarines) to the Dead Sea, with its pidgin English lingua franca and droning, generic Europop, ritually incanting "Hello Europe" even as the voting descends into unabashed tribalism. Imagine now that Europe's voters were given a choice also between the Australians and the Serbs. With whom will, say, the Norwegians cast their lot? Place your bets, ladies and gentlemen.

Of course, this choice will never be on offer. The world is too complicated a place for the binary blimpishness of all-or-nothing alternatives between America and Europe. Both sides of this particular divide would do well to consider how proximate and similar the two slopes of their supposed conceptual chasm in fact are. Whether American conservatives or Europeans across the board, each enamored of their own reflection, unless we break this spell of self-enchantment, we risk suffering the fate of Narcissus. Readers will recall that Ovid's ill-fated hero dies of thirst, for fear that kissing the water's surface will disrupt the image that has so enthralled him.

A NOTE ON SOURCES

WORKING WITH INTERNET SOURCES is to enter a Borgesian universe of ever-shifting reality. A URL that works one day delivers you to a blank screen the next, or—almost more frustrating—to a new version of the Web site that you had earlier worked with for hours without problem, but which now, its administrators cheerily announce, is new and improved and therefore—from your point of view—unnavigable, at least without starting from scratch.

The usual conventions of scholarly footnoting, which presume a stable referent, are largely undone. I have attempted to be as precise about where I have found data as I could without turning this book into a vast mass of footnotes preceded by a smidgen of text. Often I have supplied URLs. They may work. Some URLs are so long and complicated that you are unlikely to transfer them accurately from these pages to your browser. That frustration will then be compounded when—even when correctly transcribed—the Web site they lead to turns out to have changed in the meantime. In such cases, you are better off following the instructions I also supply on how to find the information, detailed below. Or you may find it easier simply to Google the name or description of the document in question.

Some Web sites have ever-changing URLs, depending on how they are accessed. Source-OECD is one such. Some Web sites are freely accessible from anywhere. Some require a subscription that is often available to those who have institutional affiliations with major research universities, but which can also often be gotten at through terminals at public libraries. Some require various formalities of registration. And some, but almost none used here, require money to be paid for access.

Some Web sites are ones that must be navigated once you are in. In those and similar cases, I have tried to supply a thread to follow. Thus, for example, a reference such as "Eurostat. Statistics, Regions and Cities, Main Tables, Regional Statistics, Regional Economic Accounts—ESA95, Disposable Income of Private Households" means that, from the Eurostat home page, you should click on the subsequent links indicated and will—with luck—eventually make it to the table that gives Disposable Income of Private Households.

The information used here was consulted mainly in 2008. It may well have changed several times in the interim. I have foresworn the usual pseudo-scholarly piety of indicating in each case the precise date on which I last consulted an Internet source. That would be merely another bit of information you would have to take on faith, and what is the point of knowing when the URL worked if it no longer does? I have thought it more useful to supply explanations of how to find the information, as mentioned above.

OECD materials are, except in the few cases otherwise noted, available through SourceOECD.

ABBREVIATIONS

CDACS: Center for Democracy and Civil Society, Georgetown University,

IARC: International Agency for Research on Cancer

ISSP: International Social Survey Programme. From the GESIS—Leibniz-Institut für Sozialwissenschaften Web page (http://zacat.gesis.org/webview/index.jsp), select ISSP, By Module Topic, then topic and study. Having chosen the study, click Variable Description, Archive and ID variables, click on the Table tab, select Country, select Add to column, enter your ID and password. Select Substantial Variables, select variable in question, select Add to row.

WDI Online: World Bank, World Development Indicators Online

WHOSIS: World Health Organization, Statistical Information System

WRI: World Resources Institute

WVS: World Values Survey. There are two sets of WVS surveys, the Four Wave Aggregate and the 2005 survey. If not otherwise noted, the data comes from the most recent results of the Four Wave surveys, which for our countries means from between 1996 and 2001. When data comes from the 2005 Wave that is noted as WVS 2005. Available at: http://www.worldvalues-survey.com/

NOTES

INTRODUCTION

1. Robin Cook, "A Strong Europe—or Bush's Feral US Capitalism," *Guardian,* October 29, 2004.

2. Timothy Garton Ash, *Free World: Why a Crisis of the West Reveals the Opportunity of Our Time* (London, 2005), chapter 1. Much of what follows here fleshes out in greater detail suggestions put forth in his very interesting chapter 2.

3. Robert Kagan, *Of Paradise and Power: America and Europe in the New World Order* (New York, 2006).

4. Jean-Marie Colombani and Walter Wells, *Dangerous De-Liaisons: What's Really Behind the War Between France and the U.S.* (Hoboken, NJ, 2004), p. 114.

5. Russell A. Berman, *Anti-Americanism in Europe: A Cultural Problem* (Stanford, 2004), p. 59.

6. Ziauddin Sardar and Merryl Wyn Davies, *Why do People Hate America?* (Duxford, UK, 2002), p. 103.

7. Margaret Drabble, "I Loathe America, and What It Has Done to the Rest of the World," *Daily Telegraph,* May 8, 2003.

8. British Council, *Talking Trans-Atlantic* (2008), Figure 0.1, p. 12. Data from January 2008. Available at http://www.worldpublicopinion.org/pipa/pdf/mar08/BritCouncil_Mar08_rpt.pdf.

9. Quoted in Philippe Roger, *The American Enemy: A Story of French Anti-Americanism* (Chicago, 2005), p. 272.

10. The numbers were run on whatever period each site allows, unclear in the case of Limbaugh's. Compared to some 3,500 references to America and the United States, Limbaugh makes only 261 to Europe, and only 162 to the supposed archenemy of U.S. conservatives, France.

11. Anders Åslund, *Building Capitalism: The Transformation of the Former Soviet Bloc* (Cambridge, 2002), p. 222.

12. Lásló Andor, *Hungary on the Road to the European Union: Transition in Blue* (Westport, CT, 2000), p. 10; Mitchell Orenstein, *Out of the Red: Building Capitalism and Democracy in Postcommunist Europe* (Ann Arbor, 2001), p. 1.

13. Elena Iankova, *Eastern European Capitalism in the Making* (Cambridge, 2002), pp. 25, 185.

14. Lauri Leppik, "Social Protection and EU Enlargement: The Case of Estonia," *The Road to the European Union, Volume 2: Estonia, Latvia, and Lithuania* (Manchester, 2003), p. 144; Raivo Vetik, Gerli Nimmerfeldt, Marti Taru, and Mart Kivimäe, *Discursive Identity and EU Integration* (Glasgow, 2004), p. 6; Ian Jeffries, *The Countries of the Former Soviet Union at the Turn of the Twenty-first Century: The Baltic and European States in Transition* (London, 2004), p. 7; David Smith, "Estonia: Independence and European Integration," in David Smith, Artis Pabriks, Aldis Purs, and Thomas Lane, *The Baltic States, Estonia, Latvia and Lithuania* (London, 2002), pp. 83, 18, 21, 107.

15. Emmanuel Todd, *After the Empire: The Breakdown of the American Order* (London, 2004), p. 177.

16. Tito Boeri, Michael Burda, and Francis Kramarz, eds., *Working Hours and Job-Sharing in the EU and USA: Are Europeans Lazy? Or Americans Crazy?* (New York, 2008).

17. Jeremy Rifkin, *The European Dream: How Europe's Vision of the Future Is Quietly Eclipsing the American Dream* (New York, 2004), p. 3.

18. Even anti-Semitism in the nineteenth century was roped in by European thought as part of this broader current of anti-modernism. See the analyses of this trend and the surprising parallels to the tropes of anti-Americanism in Peter Pulzer, *The Rise of Political Anti-Semitism in Germany and Austria* (Cambridge, MA, 1988); Dan Diner, *America in the Eyes of the Germans: An Essay on Anti-Americanism* (Princeton, 1996); Andrei S. Markovits, *Uncouth Nation: Why Europe Dislikes America* (Princeton, 2007).

19. Jean-François Revel, *Anti-Americanism* (San Francisco, 2003); Wilhelm Langthaler and Werner Pirker, *Ami go home: Zwölf gute Gründe für einen Antiamerikanismus* (Vienna, 2003); Michel Albert, *Capitalism against Capitalism* (London, 1993); Andrew Kohut and Bruce Stokes, *America Against the World: How We Are Different and Why We Are Disliked* (New York, 2006); Julia Sweig, *Friendly Fire: Losing Friends and Making Enemies in the Anti-American Century* (New York, 2006).

20. Todd, *After the Empire,* p. 178.

21. Claus Offe, *Reflections on America: Tocqueville, Weber and Adorno in the United States* (Cambridge, 2005), pp. 97–100.

22. Quoted in Markovits, *Uncouth Nation,* pp. 145–46.

23. Sadar and Davies, *Why do People Hate America?,* p. 191.

24. Markovits, *Uncouth Nation.*

25. The term was first used, but only in passing, by Freud in "The Taboo of Virginity" (1918) and then with more elaboration in *Civilization and its Discontents* (*Standard Edition*, 1930, v. 21, pp. 114–15). Curiously, in his earlier writing, *Group Psychology and the Analysis of the Ego* (1921), he recognized the antagonisms between Jews and gentiles, as well as between white and black and French and German, as weighty and not just minor (*Standard Edition*, v. 18, p. 101). The phrase has been used to describe transatlantic relations also by Neil Gilbert, *Transformation of the Welfare State: The Silent Surrender of Public Responsibility* (New York, 2002), pp. 181–82, and by Garton Ash, *Free World,* p. 183.

26. I am assuming that the population described by unemployment (ages 15 to 74) is sufficiently like that used for the numbers on the disabled (20 to 64) that we can simply shift

them from one statistic to the other, and that the incarcerated population falls in the main between the ages used for unemployment statistics.

27. McKinsey and Company, *Sweden's Economic Performance 2006* (Stockholm, 2006), Exhibit 6, p. 23. Figures for 2004, when the official rate was 5.4%.

28. OECD, *Statistical Annex of the 2007 Development Co-operation Report,* Table 27. Available at http://www.oecd.org/dataoecd/52/12/1893167.xls.

29. Raymond F. Mikesell, *Economics of Foreign Aid* (New Brunswick, 2007), pp. 14–15; Jean-Sébastian Rioux and Douglas A. Van Belle, "The Influence of *Le Monde* Coverage on French Foreign Aid Allocations," *International Studies Quarterly,* 49 (2005), pp. 492, 496. In 2004, a third of French aid was used on debt, higher by far than any other Western nation other than Portugal. OECD, *Development Aid at a Glance: 2006 Edition,* table 1.3.3, pp. 26–27.

CHAPTER ONE

1. Will Hutton, "Bye Bye American Pie," *Observer,* June 30, 2002.

2. Barry Rubin and Judith Culp Rubin, *Hating America: A History* (Oxford, 2004), chapter 2.

3. ISSP, Role of Government III 1996, Variables 16, 18, 36, 24, 17, 20, 44, 22, 40, 23. Role of Government IV 2006, Variables 25, 26, 31, 33, 14, 29, 15. Most results are the sum of the first two responses and are taken from one or the other of the surveys. Germany means western Germany in those cases where the surveys distinguish.

4. OECD Stat, Public Sector, Market Regulation, Economy-Wide Regulation, Product Market Regulation, Public Ownership. Figures are for 2003.

5. Colleen A. Dunlavy, *Politics and Industrialization: Early Railroads in the United States and Prussia* (Princeton, 1994), chapters 2, 3; Timothy Dowd and Frank Dobbin, "Origins of the Myth of Neo-Liberalism: Regulation in the First Century of US Railroading," in Lars Magnusson and Jan Ottosson, eds., *The State, Regulation and the Economy: An Historical Perspective* (Cheltenham, 2001), p. 66.

6. World Bank, Doing Business Project. Available at http://www.doingbusiness.org/economyrankings/?regionid=5.

7. WDI Online, "Time to Prepare and Pay Taxes (Hours)." Data from 2007. Available at http://ddp-ext.worldbank.org/ext/DDPQQ/member.do?method=getMembers&userid=1&queryId=6.

8. Giuseppe Nicoletti et al., "Summary Indicators of Product Market Regulation with an Extension to Employment Protection Legislation," OECD Economics Department Working Papers 226, December 1999, Table 6, p. 23; Figure 4, p. 31; Figure 5, p. 34; Figure 10, p. 46. Available at http://papers.ssrn.com/so13/papers.cfm?abstract_id=201668#PaperDownload.

9. World Economic Forum, *Global Competitiveness Report 2005–2006*, Data Page 6.09, p. 558.

10. Robert A. Kagan and Lee Axelrad, "Adversarial Legalism: An International Perspective," in Pietro S. Nivola, ed., *Comparative Disadvantages? Social Regulation and the Global Economy* (Washington, DC, 1997).

11. World Bank, *Logistics Performance Index.* Available at http://info.worldbank.org/etools/tradesurvey/mode1b.asp#.

12. Pew Global Attitudes Project, "World Publics Welcome Global Trade—But Not Immigration," October 4, 2007, pp. 1, 13. Available at http://pewglobal.org/reports/pdf/258.pdf.

13. ISSP, National Identity II 2003, Variables 42, 36. Sum of the first two responses.

14. ISSP, Religion II 1998, Variable 21. Sum of first two responses.

15. John Gray, "What We Think of America," *Granta*, 77 (2002). Serious historical backing for this assertion can be found in William J. Novak, *The People's Welfare: Law and Regulation in Nineteenth-Century America* (Chapel Hill, 1996); William R. Brock, *Investigation and Responsibility: Public Responsibility in the United States, 1865–1900* (Cambridge, 1984); Jonathan R. T. Hughes, *The Governmental Habit Redux: Economic Controls from Colonial Times to the Present* (Princeton, 1991).

16. World Economic Forum, *Global Competitiveness Report 2005–2006*, Data Page 8.17, p. 606.

17. Olympia Bover et al., "Labour Market Outliers: Lessons from Portugal and Spain," *Economic Policy*, 15, no. 31 (2000).

18. Manuela Samek Lodovici, "The Dynamics of Labour Market Reform in European Countries," in Gøsta Esping-Andersen and Marino Regini, eds., *Why Deregulate Labour Markets?* (Oxford, 2000). See pp. 33 and 36, for an even more explicit statement of this point.

19. David G. Blanchflower, "A Cross-Country Study of Union Membership," Forschungsinstitut zur Zukunft der Arbeit, Discussion Paper No. 2016, March 2006, Table 1, p. 29. Available at http://ftp.iza.org/dp2016.pdf. WVS 2005, Active/Inactive Membership of Labour Unions.

20. *OECD Employment Outlook 2004*, Table 3.3, p. 145.

21. Suzanne Moore, "American Dream? It's In a Coma Now," *Daily Mail*, September 11, 2005.

22. *OECD Health Data 2007*. October 2007, Economic References, Macro-economic references, Compensation of employees, US$ purchasing power parity. Figures for 2003–05.

23. *OECD Health Data 2007* October 2007, Economic References, Macro-economic references, Average earnings of production worker. Data are for 2006. National currencies converted to PPP using the 2005 figures at World Bank, International Comparison Program. Available at http://siteresources.worldbank.org/ICPINT/Resources/summary-tables.pdf.

24. Timothy Smeeding, "Poor People in Rich Nations: The United States in Comparative Perspective," *Journal of Economic Perspectives*, 20, no. 1 (2006), Figure 2, p. 86.

25. OECD, Statistics, Share of permanent employment. Data come from 2005 and 2006. Available at http://stats.oecd.org/wbos/default.aspx?DatasetCode=TEMP_I.

26. *OECD Employment Outlook 1997*, Table 5.5, p. 138. Figures for 1995. Available at http://www.oecd.org/document/37/0,2340,en_2649_201185_31685733_119699_1_1_1,00.html.

27. Per-Ola Karlsson, Gary L. Neilson, and Juan Carlos Webster, "CEO Succession 2007: The Performance Paradox," *Strategy and Business*, 51 (2008), Exhibits 7 and 8. Preprint available at http://www.booz.com/media/uploads/CEOSuccession2007.pdf.

28. Robert Buchele and Jens Christiansen, "Do Employment and Income Security Cause Unemployment? A Comparative Study of the US and the E-4," *Cambridge Journal of Economics* (1998), 22, 117–136, Table 7. Figures from 1984-92. The Portuguese result is from Olivier Blanchard and Pedro Portugal, "What Hides Behind an Employment Rate:

Comparing Portuguese and U.S. Labor Markets," *American Economic Review,* 91, no. 1 (2001), p 190.

29. WHOSIS, Core Health Indicators, Mortality, Years of Life Lost to Injury (%). Figures for 2002. Available at http://www.who.int/whosis/database/core/core_select.cfm?strISO3_select=ALL&strIndicator_select=ALL&intYear_select=latest&language=english.

30. United Nations (UN), *Human Development Report 1995,* Table 4.3, p. 94.

31. *OECD Employment Outlook 2007,* Table F, p. 263.

32. Robert J. Gordon, "Comparing Welfare in Europe and the United States," in Barry Eichengreen et al., eds., *The European Economy in an American Mirror* (London, 2008), p. 32.

33. Michael Burda, Daniel S. Hamermesh, Philippe Weil, "The Distribution of Total Work in the EU and the US," in Tito Boeri, et al., eds., *Working Hours and Job-Sharing in the EU and USA* (New York, 2008), Table 1.4M, p. 38; Table 1.1, p. 25. Data from 2003.

34. Richard Freeman and Ronald Schettkat, "Marketization of Household Production and the EU-US Gap in Work," *Economic Policy,* 20, no. 41 (2005), Table 3, p. 14.

35. Alberto Alesina and Edward L. Glaeser, *Fighting Poverty in the US and Europe: A World of Difference* (Oxford, 2004), Table 7.3, p. 193.

36. Dean Baker, *The United States Since 1980* (Cambridge, 2007), pp. 19–21.

37. Eric Weiner, "Use Time Wisely—By Slacking Off," *Los Angeles Times,* September 11, 2007.

38. ISSP, Family III 2002, Variable 47, sum of the first two responses.

39. WVS 2005, Work Should Come First, Even if it Means Less Spare Time.

40. Betsey Stevenson and Justin Wolfers, "Economic Growth and Subjective Well-Being: Reassessing the Easterlin Paradox," May 9, 2008. Available at http://bpp.wharton.upenn.edu/betseys/papers/Happiness.pdf. Angus Deaton, "Income, Health and Well-Being Around the World: Evidence From the Gallup World Poll," *Journal of Economic Perspectives,* 22, no. 2 (2008).

41. Barry Schwartz, *The Paradox of Choice: Why More is Less* (New York, 2004); Robert J. Samuelson, *The Good Life and its Discontents: The American Dream in the Age of Entitlement* (New York, 1997); Gregg Easterbrook, *The Progress Paradox: How Life Gets Better While People Feel Worse* (New York, 2004); Robert E. Lane, *The Loss of Happiness in Market Democracies* (New Haven, 2001).

42. World Database of Happiness, Happiness in Nations. Search findings: by item type, 121C: 4-step verbal Life Satisfaction, Overview of Happiness Surveys using Item Type: 121C / 4-step verbal Life Satisfaction. The data come mainly from 2006. Available at http://worlddatabaseofhappiness.eur.nl/hap_nat/nat_fp.htm.

43. ISSP, Religion II, 1998, Variables 73, 47, sum of the first two responses.

44. WVS 2005, How Much Freedom of Choice and Control.

45. *OECD in Figures 2007*, Public Finance, Taxation. Tax Structures, pp. 58, 59. Figures for 2004.

CHAPTER TWO

1. Jean-Francois Revel, *Anti-Americanism* (San Francisco, 2003), p. 78.

2. Will Hutton, "Bye Bye American Pie," *Observer,* June 30, 2002.

3. WHO, *World Health Report 2000,* Annex, Tables 1, 5, 6, 7, 9.

4. Karen Davis et al., *Mirror, Mirror on the Wall: An International Update on the Comparative Performance of American Health Care,* Commonwealth Fund, May 2007, Figure ES-1, p. viii. Available at http://www.commonwealthfund.org/usr_doc/1027_Davis_mirror_mirror_international_update_final.pdf?section=4039.

5. Gerard F. Anderson et al., "It's the Prices, Stupid: Why the United States Is So Different from Other Countries," *Health Affairs,* 22, 3 (2003), Exhibit 3, p. 94. Figures from 2000.

6. Commonwealth Fund Commission on a High Performance Health System, *Why Not the Best? Results from the National Scorecard on US Health System Performance, 2008,* Exhibit 19, p. 34. Another study puts France lower, but Luxembourg above the United States. Chris L. Peterson and Rachel Burton, "US Health Care Spending: Comparison with other OECD Countries," *CRS Report for Congress,* 2007, Figure 20, p. 30. Available at http://digitalcommons.ilr.cornell.edu/key_workplace/311/.

7. *OECD Health Data 2008,* Health Care Resources, Health Employment, Physicians, Practicing Physicians, Density per 1,000 population. Most figures from 2006. In contrast, the UN reports much higher figures for physician density in the United States. UN, *Human Development Report 2005,* Table 6, p. 236. But since the World Bank agrees with the lower figures, I have gone with them. WDI Online, Social Indicators, Health, Physicians (per 1,000 people).

8. WHOSIS, World Health Statistics 2006, Health Systems. Most figures are from 2003.

9. OECD, *Health at a Glance 2007,* 4.7 Medical Technologies. Figures are for 2005.

10. OECD, *Health at a Glance 2007,* graphs 4.11.1, 4.12, 4.13.1 Figures are for 2004 and 2005. Heart transplant figures are for 2005. *OECD Health Data 2007,* Health Care Utilisation, Surgical Procedures, Transplants and dialyses.

11. WHO, *World Health Report 2005,* Annex Table 2B, p. 186, Child, Total. Figures from 2000–03, but Belgium is from 1992 and Denmark 1996.

12. OECD, *Health at a Glance 2007,* Health Status, Premature Mortality, p. 25. Figures are for 2004.

13. Isabelle Jourmard et al., "Health Status Determinants: Lifestyle, Environment, Health Care Resources and Efficiency," OECD Economics Department Working Papers No. 627, 2008, Table 2, p. 13. Figures for 2003 or latest year available.

14. WHO, *World Health Report, 2003,* Annex Table 4, p. 166. Figures for 2002.

15. *OECD Regions at a Glance 2007,* Graph 28.1, p. 155.

16. Ellen Nolte and C. Martin McKee, "Measuring the Health of Nations: Updating an Earlier Analysis," *Health Status,* 27, 1 (2008).

17. OECD, *Health at a Glance 2007,* Indicators 4.10.1, 4.8.1, 4.9.1. *OECD Health Data 2008,* Health Care Utilisation, Consultations, Dentists' consultations. Figures are for 2005.

18. WHOSIS, World Health Statistics 2006, Health Service Coverage. Immunization coverage among 1-year-olds, Measles. Figures are from 2004. Available at http://www.who.int/whosis/whostat2006_coverage.pdf.

19. WHO, Global Database on Body Mass Index, Detailed Data. Available at http://www.who.int/bmi/index.jsp.

20. NationMaster, Food Statistics, McDonalds Restaurants (per Capita) by Country, Number of McDonalds Restaurants per 10,000 Population. Available at http://www.nationmaster.com/graph/foo_mcd_res_percap-food-mcdonalds-restaurants-per-capita.

21. *OECD Health Data 2008*, Non-Medical Determinants of Health, Lifestyles and behaviour, Food consumption. Figures are for 2003.

22. WRI, Earth Trends Environmental Information, Energy and Resources, Data Tables, Resource Consumption, 2005, Annual per Capita Consumption (kg per person), Meat, 2002.

23. *OECD Health Data 2008,* Non-Medical Determinants of Health, Lifestyles and behaviour, Food consumption. Figures are for 2003.

24. IARC, Globocan 2002. Enter By cancer, choose disease and then countries you are interested in, Incidence, ASR(W), age-standardized world rate. Per 100,000. Available at http://www-dep.iarc.fr/.

25. U.S. figures are from American Cancer Society, *Cancer Facts and Figures, 1999*, pp. 16, 14. European figures from Eurocare, Eurocare-3, Breast cancer, Relative survival (%), by age at diagnosis, Women, All ages. The figures come from 1990 to 1994. The WinZip file with Eurocare-3 figures is available at: http://www.eurocare.it/. Results are summarized in M. Sant et al., "EUROCARE-3: Survival of cancer patients diagnosed 1990–94: Results and commentary," *Annals of Oncology,* 14 (2003), Supplement 5, pp. 72ff.

26. Gemma Gatta, et al., "Toward a Comparison of Survival in American and European Cancer Patients," *Cancer,* 89, 4 (2000), pp. 893–900; M. P. Coleman et al., "EUROCARE-3 summary: Cancer survival in Europe at the end of the 20th century," *Annals of Oncology,* 14 (2003), Supplement 5.

27. WHOSIS, Core Health Indicators, Age-standardized mortality rate for cardiovascular diseases (per 100,000 population). Data from 2002. Available at http://www.who.int/whosis/database/core/core_select.cfm.

28. *OECD Health Data 2008*. Health Status, Mortality, Causes of mortality, Acute myocardial infarction. Figures are for 2005 and, for Italy, 2003.

29. WHOSIS, Mortality Data, Mortality Profiles, choose the country and go to Causes of Death, Cerebrovascular disease, Years of Life Lost (%). Available at http://www.who.int/whosis/mort/profiles/en/index.html.

30. WHO, *World Health Report 2001,* Table 2.1, p. 24. Figures apparently from the early 1990s.

31. WHO, Health Statistics and Health Information Systems, Global Burden of Disease Estimates, Death and DALY Estimates for 2002 by Cause for WHO Member States, Age-standardized DALYs per 100,000, Neuropsychiatric Conditions. Available at http://www.who.int/healthinfo/bodestimates/en/index.html.

32. T. H. Reid, *The United States of Europe: The New Superpower and the End of American Supremacy* (London, 2004), pp. 160–61.

33. Health Consumer Powerhouse, *Euro Health Consumer Index 2007*, p. 22. Available at http://www.healthpowerhouse.com/media/Rapport_EHCI_2007.pdf.

34. Paul V. Dutton, *Differential Diagnoses: A Comparative History of Health Care Problems and Solutions in the United States and France* (Ithaca, 2007).

CHAPTER THREE

1. Timothy Smeeding, "Poor People in Rich Nations: The United States in Comparative Perspective," *Journal of Economic Perspectives*, 20, 1 (2006), Table 4, p. 79. The OECD's figures show the U.S. economy as more equal than that of Sweden, the UK, France, Italy, and Belgium before taxes and public transfers. OECD, *Sustainable Development: Critical Issues* (2001), Figure 3.A.12, p. 91. Data from late 1990s.

2. IMF, *Government Finance Statistics Yearbook 2006*, Table W5, p. 24.

3. *Benefits and Wages: OECD Indicators*, 2004 Edition, Figure 2.4, p. 83. Measured as a percent of median household income for various family models. Figures for 2001.

4. OECD, Statistics Portal, Statistics, Social and Welfare Statistics, Benefits and Wages, Net Replacement Rates (NRR) During the Initial Phase of Unemployment, 2001-2004, Net Replacement Rates for Six Family Types: Initial Phase of Unemployment, 100% of APW (average production wage), No Children, Two-Earner Married Couple, 2004. Available at http://www.oecd.org/dataoecd/25/28/34008439.xls.

5. Lyle Scruggs and Jampes P. Allan, "The Material Consequences of Welfare States: Benefit Generosity and Absolute Poverty in 16 OECD Countries," *Comparative Political Studies*, 39, 7 (2006), Table 3, p. 892. Figures are for 2000.

6. *OECD Employment Outlook 2006*, Table 3.2, p. 60. I have followed the OECD's figures here, though it must be added that, in Italy, there is also a system, the Cassa Integrazione Guadagni, for workers in certain economic sectors facing major economic difficulties, like inclement weather in the building trade. In theory, benefits here can last up to a year, but can be prolonged extraordinarily by the government. In reality, 90% of recipients use it for only three or four months. Giuseppe Bonazzi, "Italian 'Cassa Integrazione' and Post Redundancy," *Work, Employment and Society*, 4, 4 (1990), p. 578.

7. *Dagens Nyheter*, July 11, 2008, p. 6.

8. OECD Social Expenditure Database, Social Expenditure – Aggregate, Survivors, Total benefits. Figures for 2003 and in PPP terms. Available through SourceOCED at http://stats.oecd.org/brandedviewpilot/default.aspx?datasetcode=socx_agg.

9. OECD, *Babies and Bosses: Reconciling Work and Family Life* (2007), Chart 4.1, p. 72. Figures from 2003. Figures for 2001 (which are lower) are in: Willem Adema and Maxime Ladaique, *Net Social Expenditure, 2005 Edition: More Comprehensive Measures of Social Support* (Paris: OECD, 2005), Chart 4, p. 28. Available at http://www.oecd.org/dataoecd/56/2/35632106.pdf.

10. OECD, *Starting Strong: Early Childhood Education and Care* (2001), Figure 3.5, p. 88. Data from 1998 in PPP terms.

11. OECD, *Babies and Bosses*, Chart 6.4, p. 151, and Chart 6.5, p. 154. Figures are for 2004.

12. *OECD Employment Outlook: June 2001*, Table 4.7, p. 144. Figures from 1995–2000.

13. *OECD Employment Outlook: June 2001*, Table 4.8, p. 149. Figures from 1995–96.

14. OECD Social Expenditure Database, Social Expenditure—Aggregate, Public, Old Age. Figures from 2003 and in PPP terms. Available through SourceOCED at http://stats.oecd.org/brandedviewpilot/default.aspx?datasetcode=socx_agg.

15. OECD, *Pension Markets in Focus*, November 2007, Issue 4, Figure 3. Importance of pension funds relative to the size of the economy in OECD countries, 2006, % GDP, p. 6. Available at http://www.oecd.org/dataoecd/46/57/39509002.pdf.

16. Irwin Garfinkel et al., "A Re-examination of Welfare States and Inequality in Rich Nations: How In-kind Transfers and Indirect Taxes Change the Story," *Journal of Policy Analysis and Management*, 25, 4 (2006), Figure 2, p. 906.

17. Neil Gilbert, "Comparative Analyses of Stateness and State Action: What Can we Learn from Patterns of Expenditure?" in Jens Alber and Neil Gilbert, eds., *United in Diversity? Comparing Social Models in Europe and America* (Oxford University Press, forthcoming), Table 16.2.

CHAPTER FOUR

1. *OECD Health Data 2008*. Health Status, Mortality, Causes of Mortality, Assault. Figures are for 2004 and 2005.

2. Graduate Institute of International Studies, Geneva, *Small Arms Survey 2007: Guns and the City,* chapter 2, Table 2.3, p. 47, high estimates. Available at http://www.smallarmssurvey.org/files/sas/publications/yearb2007.html.

3. Jan van Dijk et al., *Criminal Victimisation in International Perspective: Key findings from the 2004–2005 ICVS and EU ICS* (The Hague, 2007), Table 18, p. 279. Figures for 2004–05. Available at http://www.unicri.it/wwd/analysis/icvs/pdf_files/ICVS2004_05report.pdf.

4. "Nicht das Tatwerkzeug ist schuld: Schiesssportverband macht mobil gegen die Waffen-Initiative," *Neue Züricher Zeitung,* February 21, 2008. For the Pro-Tell Association, see http://www.protell.ch/.

5. Murders per firearm figures calculated from UN Office on Drugs and Crime, *Ninth United Nations Survey of Crime Trends and Operations of Criminal Justice Systems,* Police, 2.2, Total recorded intentional homicide, completed; Graduate Institute of International Studies, *Small Arms Survey 2007,* chapter 2, Table 2.3, p. 47.

6. Van Dijk et al., *Criminal Victimisation in International Perspective,* Table 22a, p. 284. Figures from 2004–05.

7. Van Dijk et al., *Criminal Victimisation in International Perspective,* Table 15, p. 274; Table 16, p. 275; Table 17, p. 278. Figures for ca. 2005. Similar results from business executives: World Economic Forum, *Global Competitiveness Report 2005–2006,* Data Page 6.14, p. 563. Another survey found Americans' trust in the police to be middle of the pack, equal to the Swiss, above that of the British and Swedes, and the citizens of six other countries. CDACS, U.S. Citizenship, Involvement, Democracy Survey, 2005. Available at http://www8.georgetown.edu/centers/cdacs/cid/. The ISSP reports that the Americans consider their government better at controlling crime than anyone other than the Germans, the Finns, and the Swiss. ISSP, Role of Government IV 2006, Variable 38, sum of first two figures. Middle of the pack results in WVS 2005, Confidence: The Police.

8. *Anglo-Saxon Attitudes: A Survey of British and American Views of the World.* Available at http://www.economist.com/media/pdf/FullPollData.pdf. Van Dijk et al., *Criminal Victimisation in International Perspective,* Table 16, p. 275.

9. Franklin E. Zimring and Gordon Hawkins, *Crime Is Not the Problem: Lethal Violence in America* (New York, 1997).

10. Van Dijk et al., *Criminal Victimisation in International Perspective,* Table 8, p. 65; Table 9, p. 71; Table 10, p. 72; Table 11, p. 74. Figures for 2003–04.

11. Ed Shanahan, "Excuse Me, Is This Your Phone?" *Reader's Digest,* available at http://www.rd.com/images/content/2007/0707/cellphonereport.pdf.

12. Van Dijk et al., *Criminal Victimisation in International Perspective,* Table 12, p. 78.

13. John van Kesteren et al., *Criminal Victimisation in Seventeen Industrialized Nations: Key Findings from the 2000 International Crime Victims Survey* (The Hague, 2000), Appendix 4, table 1, p. 178. Figures from 1988–1999. Available at United Nations Interregional Crime and Justice Research Institute, Publications, 2000 Surveys: http://www.unicri.it/wwd/analysis/icvs/pdf_files/key2000i/index.htm.

14. UNICEF Innocenti Research Centre, Report Card 7, *Child Poverty in Perspective: An Overview on Child Well-Being in Rich Countries* (2007), Figure 5.3b, p. 33. Available at http://www.unicef-irc.org/publications/pdf/rc7_eng.pdf.

15. Cannabis figures are from OECD, *Society at a Glance: 2005 Edition,* Chart CO5.1, p. 89. Figures for ca. 2000. Cocaine figures are from the European Monitoring Centre for Drugs and Drug Addiction, *Statistical Bulletin 2008,* Figure GPS-20. Available at http://www.emcdda.europa.eu/stats08/gpsfig20.

16. Van Kesteren et al., *Criminal Victimisation in Seventeen Industrialized Nations,* Appendix 4, Table 26, p. 216. Van Dijk et al., *Criminal Victimisation in International Perspective,* Table 16, p. 275.

17. Will Hutton, "Bye Bye American Pie," *Observer,* June 30, 2002.

18. Van Dijk et al., *Criminal Victimisation in International Perspective,* Table 16, p. 90. Figures for 2003–04. The ISSP reveals more French and about the same number of Germans as Americans reporting public officials seeking bribes quite or very often. ISSP, Role of Government IV 2006, Variable 62.

19. UN, *Human Development Report 2002,* Table A1.1, p. 38.

20. Van Dijk et al., *Criminal Victimisation in International Perspective,* Table 14, p. 87. Figures for 2003–04.

21. Carolyn M. Warner, *The Best System Money Can Buy: Corruption in the European Union* (Ithaca, 2007), pp. 191–94.

22. World Economic Forum, *Global Competitiveness Report 2005–2006,* Data Pages 6.15, 6.16, pp. 564, 565.

23. U.S. Department of Justice, Bureau of Justice Statistics, "Homicide Trends in the U.S.: Trends by Race." Available at http://www.ojp.usdoj.gov/bjs/homicide/race.htm.

24. Figures from Brottsförebyggande rådet, *Brottslighet bland personer födda i Sverige och i utlandet* (Rapport 2005:17), pp. 37, 43. Available at http://www.bra.se/extra/measurepoint/?module_instance=4&name=1brottslsveutland.pdf&url=/dynamaster/file_archive/051214/e7dae113eb493479665ffe649e0edf57/1brottslsveutland.pdf.

25. OECD, *Society at a Glance 2006,* Chart CO2.2, p. 105.

CHAPTER 5

1. Euromonitor International, Global Market Information Database, Countries, Households and homes, Household profiles, Number of households, Households by number of rooms [5+], Historic number per '000 Households. The data come from 2007 and were converted to percentages. Available at http://www.portal.euromonitor.com/portal/server.pt ?space=Login&control=RedirectHome.

2. The European figures come from Bradford and Bingley, Press Release, May 2, 2002, "British Homes the Smallest in Europe." Available at http://www.bbg.co.uk/bbg/ir/ news/releases/consumernews/pressrelease/?id=3554908. The U.S. figure is calculated from the statement from the U.S. Department of Housing and Urban Development that 1.2 million households live in public housing (http://www.hud.gov/offices/ pih/programs/ph/index.cfm) combined with the U.S. Census Bureau's reporting that there were some 105.5 million households in the United States in 2000 (http:// quickfacts.census.gov/qfd/states/00000.html). That gives a social housing rate of 1.14% in the United States. Public spending figures for housing come from *OECD Health Data 2008*. Social Protection, Social Expenditure, Housing, Public. Figures for 2003.

3. OECD, *Society at a Glance 2006,* Chart EQ8.3, p. 83.

4. William Easterly and Tobias Pfutze, "Where Does the Money Go? Best and Worst Practices in Foreign Aid," *Journal of Economic Perspectives,* 22, 2 (2008), Table 5, p. 49.

5. WVS, Politics and Society, Confidence: The United Nations.. This has dropped significantly, however, in WVS 2005.

6. ISSP, National Identity II 2003, Variable 37. Sum of the first two responses.

7. The U.S. travel figure comes from "A New Itinerary," *Economist,* May 15, 2008. Other figures from Christophe Demunter, "Are Recent Evolutions in Tourism Compatible with Sustainable Development?" *Statistics in Focus,* 1 (2008), Tables 2 and 3. Available through Eurostat by typing keywords for the article into Quick Search at the Eurostat homepage.

8. Inbound figure from International Trade Administration, Office of Travel and Tourism Industries, 2006 Monthly Tourism Statistics, Table C, Section 1. Available at http:// tinet.ita.doc.gov/view/m-2006-I-001/table1.html. Outbound figure from the same source, US Citizen Air Traffic to Overseas Regions, Canada and Mexico, 2006. Available at http://tinet.ita.doc.gov/view/m-2006-O-001/index.html. Total visitor figures from same source, Total International Travellers Volume to and from the US, 1996-2006. Available at http://tinet.ita.doc.gov/outreachpages/inbound.total_intl_travel_volume_ 1996-2006.html.

9. Use of the definite article instead is complicated especially in German, with its many variations, and skews the results against the *FAZ,* while the search engines of the French papers do not allow searches for their equivalents in that language. Search engines often do not allow searches for "and," which was another possibility.

CHAPTER SIX

1. Titus Galama and James Hosek, *US Competitiveness in Science and Technology* (RAND National Defense Research Institute, 2008), p. xvi.

2. OECD, *Literacy in the Information Age: Final Report of the International Adult Literacy Survey* (2000), Figure 3.11, p. 42.

3. *OECD in Figures 2005*, pp 68-69, Education: Performance, Educational Attainment of Adult Population and Current Graduation Rates, %, Upper Secondary or Higher Attainment (25-64 Year-Olds), 2002.

4. OECD, *PISA 2006*, v. 2, Table 6.2c, p. 230.

5. OECD, *PISA 2006*, v. 2, Table 2.1c, p. 27.

6. Progress in International Reading Literacy Study, *PIRLS 2006 International Report*, Exhibit 1.1, p. 37. Available at http://pirls.bc.edu/pirls2006/po6_release.html.

7. National Center for Education Statistics, *Highlights from TIMMS 2007: Mathematics and Science Achievement of US Fourth- and Eighth-Grade Students in an International Context* (December 2008), Table 3, p. 7; Table 11, p. 32. Available at http://nces.ed.gov/pubsearch/pubsinfo.asp?pubid=2009001.

8. For math, the countries with more students at the bottom were Italy, Portugal, and Greece, and at the top those with fewer were Spain, Portugal, and Greece, with Italy at the same level. OECD, *PISA 2006*, v. 2, Table 2.1a, p. 24; Table 6.2a, p. 227. Level 1 and below for the lowest categories. Level 6 for the highest.

9. Yasmin Alibhai-Brown, "America Has Descended Into Madness," *Independent*, June 16, 2003.

10. OECD, *PISA 2006*, v. 2, Table 4.8a, p. 146.

11. OECD, *Knowledge and Skills for Life: First Results from PISA 2000*, p. 18.

12. Ludiger Woessmann, "How Equal are Educational Opportunities? Family Background and Student Achievement in Europe and the US," CESifo Working Paper 1162, March 2004. Table 3. Available at http://papers.ssrn.com/so13/papers.cfm?abstract_id=528209.

13. World Bank, EdStats, Country Profiles, Education Trends and Comparisons, Private sector enrollment share (%), Primary level. The figures come from 2006. Available at http://devdata.worldbank.org/edstats/cd1.asp.

14. OECD, *Education at a Glance 2008*, Table C2.4, p. 346.

15. World Bank, EdStats, Selected Topics, Private Education Expenditures, Table 2.2, Private Education Expenditures as a Percentage of Total Education Expenditures, Primary and Secondary Education. Most of the data come from 2003. Similar figures as a percentage of GDP, from 2005 in OECD, *Education at a Glance 2008*, Table B2.4, p. 240.

16. *OECD Employment Outlook: Boosting Jobs and Incomes* (2006), Figure 4.5, p. 138. Data for 2002–03.

17. OECD, *Literacy in the Information Age*, Figure 2.1, p. 14; Figure 2.3, p. 19.

18. Quoted in Philippe Roger, *The American Enemy: A Story of French Anti-Americanism* (Chicago, 2005), p. 416.

19. UNESCO Institute for Statistics, Daily newspapers: Total average circulation per 1,000 inhabitants. Data from 2004. Available at http://stats.uis.unesco.org/unesco/

TableViewer/tableView.aspx?ReportId=398. There are similar, but slightly higher, figures in World Association of Newspapers, *World Press Trends: 2001 Edition*, p. 11.

20. *Economist, Pocket World in Figures 2007 Concise Edition,* p. 46.

21. WVS 2005, Information Source: Daily Newspaper.

22. UNESCO Institute for Statistics, Libraries of institutions of tertiary education, Collections, Books: Number of Volumes. Data from 1997 to 2000. Available at http://stats.uis.unesco.org/unesco/TableViewer/tableView.aspx?ReportId=209. To calculate books per capita, population figures were used from the OECD.

23. David Fuegi and Martin Jennings, *International Library Statistics: Trends and Commentary Based on the Libecon Data* (June 30, 2004), Loans per head: 2001 snapshot. Available at http://www.libecon.org/pdf/InternationalLibraryStatistic.pdf.

24. OECD, *Literacy in the Information Age,* Figure 3.16A, p. 48. Figures for 1994–98. Though in the last week only about as many Americans had read a book as had the French. WVS 2005, Information Source: Books.

25. OECD, *Literacy in the Information Age,* Figure 3.16B, p. 48. Figures for 1994–98.

26. UNESCO, Institute for Statistics, Statistics, Data Centre, Predefined Tables, Culture and Communication, Films and Cinemas: Number, seating capacity, annual attendance, Annual Attendance per inhabitant, 1999. Available at http://stats.uis.unesco.org/unesco/TableViewer/tableView.aspx?ReportId=203.

27. Adolf Hitler, *Hitler's Table Talk, 1941–1944: His Private Conversations* (London, 2000), p. 605.

28. The Deutsche Grammophon catalogue is available at http://www2.deutschegrammophon.com/home.

29. *OECD Factbook 2007,* Quality of Life, Recreation and Culture. Figures for 2004.

30. Barry Rubin and Judith Culp Rubin, *Hating America: A History* (Oxford, 2004), pp. 38ff.

31. Emmanuel Todd, *After the Empire: The Breakdown of the American Order* (London, 2004), pp. 136–38. That he stands in a long French tradition in this respect is made clear in Roger, *American Enemy*, pp. 184ff.

32. CIA, *World Factbook.* Figures from 2008.

33. *OECD Employment Outlook 2002,* Table 2.3, p. 75. Figures for 2000.

34. UN, *Human Development Report 2007/2008,* Table 33, p. 343. Figures for 2005.

35. OECD, *Babies and Bosses: Reconciling Work and Family Life* (2007), Table 3.1, p. 45; Chart 3.4, p. 58.

36. OECD, *Babies and Bosses,* Table 2.2, p. 31.

37. UN Statistics Division, Marriages and crude marriage rates, by urban/rural residence: 2000-2004. Most figures from 2003. Available at http://unstats.un.org/unsd/demographic/products/dyb/DYB2004/table23.xls.

CHAPTER SEVEN

1. ISSP, Environment II 2000, Variables 17 (sum of first two responses), 11, 38, 12, 19, 20, 21. Relatively sanguine American opinions on global warming are found here, however: World Public Opinion.org, *International Polling on Climate Change,* December 6, 2007,

Figures 1, 2. Available at http://www.worldpublicopinion.org/pipa/pdf/dec07/CCDi-
gest_Dec07_rpt.pdf.

2. ISSP, Role of Government IV 2006, Variables 34, 17. Similar results in WVS 2005, Government should reduce environmental pollution.

3. World Economic Forum, *Global Competitiveness Report 2005–2006,* Data Page 9.04, p. 619.

4. Yale Center for Environmental Law and Policy, Center for International Earth Science
Information Network, *2008 Environmental Performance Index.* Available at http://epi.
yale.edu/Home.

5. OECD, Environmental Policy Committee, Working Group on Environmental Information and Outlooks, "Pollution Abatement and Control Expenditure in OECD Countries,"
ENV/EPOC/SE(2007)1, March 6, 2007, Table 1, p. 32. Available at http://www.oecd.org/
dataoecd/37/45/38230860.pdf.

6. OECD, *Sustainable Development,* Table 6.1, p. 161. Figures for 1998. The Swedish figure
may be underestimated, since it has fallen from previous years.

7. *OECD Factbook 2008,* Quality of Life, Transport, Road Motor Vehicles and Road Fatalities, Road Motor Vehicles, Per Thousand Population, 2006.

8. WDI Online, Development Framework, Transportation, Vehicles (per km of road). Figures mainly for 2005, but some from 2002–04.

9. WDI Online, Development Framework, Transportation, Railways, passengers carried
(million passenger-km). Figures for 2004.

10. OECD, European Conference of Ministers of Transport, *Cutting Transport CO$_2$ Emissions:
What Progress?* (2007), Annex 1, pp. 171–217. Figures used are those from UNFCCC for 2003.

11. *OECD in Figures 2005,* pp. 34–35. To calculate figures per person, population figures were
used from OECD for 2003.

12. World Metro Database. Available at: http://mic-ro.com/metro/table.html.

13. *OECD Regions at a Glance 2005,* Figure 31.2, p. 170. Figures for 2001.

14. John Pucher and Ralph Buehler, "Making Cycling Irresistible: Lessons from the Netherlands,
Denmark and Germany," *Transport Reviews,* 28, 4 (2008), Figures 1 and 2, pp. 498–99. The
walking figures and the bicycling result for Luxembourg come from a comparison of the
European figures in European Environment Agency, *Climate for a Transport Change,* Report
1 (2008), Figure 1.1, p. 31, and figures kindly compiled by Paul Schimek from the U.S. Department of Transportation Survey, Nationwide Personal Transportation Study, 2001. Available
at http://nhts.ornl.gov/. I am grateful to Professor Pucher for a preprint of his article.

15. The World Wildlife Foundation calculates that the German couple jetting off to Mexico
for a two-week holiday produces a per-person carbon footprint 30 times that of a local
vacation on the Baltic coast. "Reisefieber erwärmt Klima," http://www.wwf.de/presse/
details/news/reisefieber_erwaermt_klima/.

16. *OECD Environmental Data: Compendium 2004,* Table 5, p. 238. Figures from 2002. Population and land area figures from the CIA *World Factbook.*

17. International Energy Agency (IEA), *Oil Crises and Climate Challenges: Thirty Years of
Energy Use in IEA Countries* (2004), Figure 5–4, p. 90. Figures for 1998. Available through
SourceOECD.

18. *OECD Key Environmental Indicators 2008,* p. 19. Available at http://www.oecd.org/dataoecd/20/40/37551205.pdf.

19. Matthew Engel, "Road to Ruin," *Guardian,* October 24, 2003.

20. Jeremy Rifkin, *The European Dream: How Europe's Vision of the Future Is Quietly Eclipsing the American Dream* (New York, 2004), p. 332.

21. WDI Online, Environment, Fresh Water and Protected Areas. Figures from 2004. The UK has almost the same percent set aside.

22. *OECD Key Environmental Indicators 2008,* p. 25.

23. WRI, Earth Trends Environmental Information, Agriculture and Food, Data Tables, Food and Agriculture Overview 2005, Organic Cropland as a Percent of Total 2003. Available at http://earthtrends.wri.org/pdf_library/data_tables/agri_2005.pdf.

24. Statistics on water abstractions per unit of GDP calculated with use of *OECD Factbook 2006,* Environment and Natural Resources, Air, Water and Land, Water Consumption, Water Abstractions, Table 1. Figures from 2002 or Latest Available Year. GDP taken from IMF, World Economic Outlook Database, September 2006. Available at http://www.imf.org/external/pubs/ft/weo/2006/02/data/weoselgr.aspx.

25. *OECD Environmental Data: Compendium 2004 Edition,* Tables 2A, 2B, pp. 23–34.

26. *OECD Environmental Data: Compendium 2004 Edition,* Table 2C, pp. 35–39.

27. OECD, Environment Directorate, Working Party on Pollution Prevention and Control, "Advanced Air Quality Indicators and Reporting," ENV/EPOC/PPC(99)9/FINAL, 27 September 1999, Figures 4–3, 5–3, 6–8, 7–5, 8–7, 9–8, pp. 41, 47, 60, 73, 88, 105. Available at http://www.olis.oecd.org/olis/1999doc.nsf/linkto/env-epoc-ppc(99)9-final.

28. *OECD Environmental Data: Compendium 2004 Edition,* Tables 6A-6L, pp. 81–98. The figures are an average of measurements from the years 1999, 2000, and 2001.

29. IEA, *Oil Crises and Climate Challenges,* Figure 3–8, p. 43.

30. *OECD Environmental Data: Compendium 2004 Edition,* Table 5D, p. 217.

31. IEA, *Key World Energy Statistics 2006,* chapter 8: Energy Indicators, Selected Energy Indicators for 2004, Kg CO_2 produced per $2,000 Gross Domestic Product in Purchasing Power Parity, pp. 49-57. Available at http://www.iea.org/dbtw-wpd/Textbase/nppdf/free/2006/key2006.pdf. Another measure of the same for 2005 puts the US below Portugal and at the same level as Greece. OECD, IEA, *Oil Information (2007 Edition),* Table 7, p. II.8.

32. OECD, IEA, *CO$_2$ Emissions From Fuel Combustion, 1971–2002* (2004 edition), pp. II.46, II.49.

33. *UN Human Development Report 2007/2008,* Table 24, p. 310.

34. Rifkin, *European Dream,* p. 341.

35. OECD, IEA, *Oil Information* (2007 Edition), Table 17, p. II.29. Figures for 2005.

CHAPTER EIGHT

1. Andrew Kohut and Bruce Stokes, *America Against the World: How We Are Different and Why We Are Disliked* (New York, 2006), pp. 53–54.

2. ISSP, Role of Government IV 2006, Variable 4.

3. Pew Global Attitudes Project, "World Publics Welcome Global Trade—But Not Immigration," October 4, 2007, p. 20. Available at http://pewglobal.org/reports/pdf/258.pdf.

4. Will Hutton, *The World We're In* (London, 2002), pp. 67–70.

5. Henrik Berggren and Lars Trägårdh, *Är Svensken Människa? Gemenskap och Oberoende i det Moderna Sverige* (Stockholm, 2006).

6. Robert Putnam, *Bowling Alone: The Collapse and Revival of American Community* (New York, 2001).

7. Stephen Knack and Philip Keefer, "Does Social Capital Have an Economic Payoff? A Cross-Country Investigation," *Quarterly Journal of Economics*, 112, 4 (1997), p. 1285. The survey measured responses to whether the following behaviors could be justified: claiming government benefits you are not entitled to, avoiding fares on public transportation, cheating on taxes, keeping money that you have found, and failing to report damage accidentally done to a parked vehicle.

8. Lester M. Salamon et al., *Global Civil Society: An Overview* (Baltimore, 2003), Figure 3, p. 17. Available at http://www.jhu.edu/ftccss/publications/pdf/globalciv.pdf.

9. Douglas Baer, "Voluntary Association Involvement in Comparative Perspective," in Lars Trägårdh, ed., *State and Civil Society in Northern Europe: The Swedish Model Reconsidered* (New York, 2007), Table 3.2, p. 80. Figures for 2000. Similar results for earlier surveys in James E. Curtis et al., "Voluntary Association Membership in Fifteen Countries: A Comparative Analysis," *American Sociological Review*, 57, 2 (1992), Table 1, p. 143.

10. Michael Minkenberg, "Religious Legacies and the Politics of Multiculturalism: A Comparative Analysis of Integration Policies in Western Democracies," in Ariane Chebel d'Appollonia and Simon Reich, eds. *Immigration, Integration and Security: America and Europe in Comparative Perspective* (Pittsburgh, 2008), Tables 3.2 and 3.4, pp. 52, 56.

11. Stephan Dressler, "Blood 'Scandal' and AIDS in Germany," in Eric Feldman and Ronald Bayer, eds., *Blood Feuds: AIDS, Blood and the Politics of Medical Disaster* (New York, 1999), p. 196. West Germany, for example, imported most of its blood products during the 1980s.

12. OrganDonor.Gov, 2005 National Survey of Organ and Tissue Donation Attitudes and Behaviors. Seventy-eight percent of Americans asked about organ donation claimed that they were "likely" or "very likely" to have their organs donated after their deaths. Available at http://www.organdonor.gov/survey2005/. Eurobarometer, Europeans and organ donation, fieldwork October–November 2006, May 2007, Question: QB36: Would you be willing to donate one of your organs to an organ donation service immediately after your death? Answers: Yes. Available at http://ec.europa.eu/public_opinion/archives/ebs/ebs_272d_en.pdf. Actual donation rates for 2002 in Alberto Abadie and Sebastien Gay, "The Impact of Presumed Consent Legislation on Cadaveric Organ Donation: A Cross-Country Study," *Journal of Health Economics*, 25, 4 (2006), Figure 3, p. 607. Figures for live and cadaveric donation rates per million in 2007 in *Economist*, October 11, 2008, p. 80.

13. Jens Alber and Ulrich Kohler, "Die Ungleichheit der Wahlbeteiligung in Europa und den USA und die politische Integrationskraft des Sozialstaats," *Leviathan: Berliner Zeitschrift für Sozialwissenschaft*, 4 (2007), pp. 523–27.

14. CDACS, U.S. Citizenship, Involvement, Democracy Survey, 2005. The ISSP reports more Americans interested in politics than any Western Europeans. ISSP, Role of Government IV 2006, Variable 44. Broadly similar results in WVS 2005, Interest in Politics.
15. WVS 2005, Active/Inactive Membership of a Political Party.
16. CDACS, U.S. Citizenship, Involvement, Democracy Survey.
17. WVS, Politics and Society, Political Action. Similar results in WVS 2005, though the number participating in demonstrations appears to have dropped.
18. WVS, Perceptions of Life, Respect and Love for Parents.
19. ISSP, Social Networks II 2001, Variables 6, 10, 12, 14, 25r, 23r, 24r, 27.
20. OECD, *Society at a Glance 2005,* Chart C02.1, C02.2, p. 83. Figures from 1999–2002.
21. As measured by the percentage of private consumption devoted to restaurants and hotels. Figures in McKinsey, *Sweden's Economic Performance 2006,* Exhibit 28, p. 41. According to other numbers, however, they eat out more often than any Europeans. Erik Millstone and Tim Lang, *The Atlas of Food* (Berkeley, 2008), p. 93.

CHAPTER 9

1. Pew Global Attitudes Project, "World Publics Welcome Global Trade—But Not Immigration," October 4, 2007, p. 45. Available at http://pewglobal.org/reports/pdf/258.pdf.
2. ISSP, National Identity II 2003, Variables 63 (sum of first two responses), 9, 22, 21 (sum of first two), 20 (first two).
3. Josef Joffe, *Überpower: The Imperial Temptation of America* (New York, 2006), p. 125.
4. Dänisches Kulturinstitut, "Weihnachten in Dänemark," http://www.dankultur.de/daenemark-info/weihnachten.htm.
5. WVS, Politics and Society, War, Willingness to Fight for Country. Percentages are the highest levels for each country in surveys done from 1990 to 2000. In the WVS 2005, these results were duplicated with the Swiss now also joining the more belligerent nations, and the French and British at practically the same level as the now lower American result (63.1%).

CHAPTER TEN

1. Although I have made it a point to stick to the available comparable numbers, without spiking them with additions, it is perhaps worth pointing out that a more recent Gallup poll from May 2007 found 6% of American respondents did not believe in God (up from 4% in 2004). Available at Polling Report.com, http://www.pollingreport.com/religion.htm. The YouGov/*Economist* poll from 2008 found 9% of Americans did not believe in God. *Anglo-Saxon Attitudes: A Survey of British and American Views of the World.* Available at http://www.economist.com/media/pdf/FullPollData.pdf. In the WVS 2005, 5.3% of Americans declared God not at all important in their lives, compared to 2% of Italians and significantly higher figures for the other nations sampled there.
2. WVS, Religion and Morale, FO 34.

3. ISSP, Religion II, 1998, Variable 38.
4. WVS, Religion and Morale, F028.
5. WVS 2005, How Often Do You Attend Religious Services?
6. ISSP, Religion II, 1998, Variable 39. Sum of first two responses.
7. ISSP, Religion II, 1998, Variable 58.
8. VWS 2005.
9. Steven Pfaff, "The Religious Divide: Why Religion Seems to be Thriving in the United States and Waning in Europe," in Jeffrey Kopstein and Sven Steinmo, eds., *Growing Apart? America and Europe in the Twenty-First Century* (Cambridge, 2008).
10. Paul Rozin et al., "Attitudes Towards Large Numbers of Choices in the Food Domain: A Cross-Cultural Study of Five Countries in Europe and the USA," *Appetite*, 46 (2006), pp. 304–08. More information of this sort in Claude Fischler and Estelle Masson, *Manger: Français, Européens et Américains face à l'alimentation* (Paris, 2008).
11. WVS 2005, Thinking About Meaning and Purpose of Life.
12. WVS, Religion and Morale. FO50, FO34, FO62.
13. Tim Jensen, "Religiøs på den danske måde," *Kristeligt Dagblad,* April 11, 2005.
14. *Guardian,* October 1, 2007, p. 3.
15. Rob Blackhurst, "Britain's Unholy War over Christmas," *International Herald Tribune,* December 23–25, 2006, p. 5.
16. Timothy Garton Ash, *Free World: Why a Crisis of the West Reveals the Opportunity of Our Time* (London, 2005), p. 76.
17. Jeremy Rifkin, *The European Dream: How Europe's Vision of the Future Is Quietly Eclipsing the American Dream* (New York, 2004), p. 19.
18. When one head teacher recently tried to change this, he was told that bishops in the House of Lords and ministers would block his plans. *Observer,* September 23, 2007, p. 7.
19. *Economist,* June 2, 2007, p. 41.
20. *International Herald Tribune,* June 20, 2007, p. 3.
21. Derk-Jan Eppink, *Life of a European Mandarin: Inside the Commission* (Tielt, Belgium, 2007), p. 257.
22. Belgium, Denmark, Finland, Germany, Italy, Luxembourg, Netherlands, Norway, Sweden, Switzerland.
23. *Der Spiegel,* no.46, 2006, p. 168; *New York Times,* March 31, 2007, p. A3.
24. *FT Weekend Magazine,* July 5/6, 2008, pp. 22–23.
25. Peter Berger et al., *Religious America, Secular Europe? A Theme and Variations* (Aldershot, 2008), p. 87; U.S. Department of State, *International Religious Freedom Report, 2008,* Greece. Available at http://www.state.gov/g/drl/rls/irf/2008/108449.htm.
26. Pippa Norris and Ronald Inglehart, *Sacred and Secular: Religion and Politics Worldwide* (Cambridge, 2004), pp. 67–68.
27. ISSP, Environment II 2000, Variable 28.
28. ISSP, Environment II 2000, Variables 15 (sum of first two responses), 29 (Definitely untrue), 30, 39 (sum of last two responses).

29. OECD, *PISA 2006,* Figure 3.4, p. 132. WVS 2005. Significantly more Americans also agreed that the world is better off because of science and technology than all Europeans, though the Swiss and Germans were close.
30. ISSP, Religion II, 1998, Variables 69, 70, 71, 72, 42. Sum of first two responses.

CHAPTER 11

1. *OECD in Figures 2005*, Demography, Foreign Population, pp. 6–7; *OECD in Figures 2007*, Demography and Health, Demography.
2. Figures from Brottsförebyggande rådet, *Brottslighet bland personer födda i Sverige och i utlandet* (Rapport 2005:17), p. 62. Available at http://www.bra.se/extra/ measurepoint/?module_instance=4&name=1brottslsveutland.pdf&url=/dynamaster/ file_archive/051214/e7dae113eb493479665ffe649e0edf57/1brottslsveutland.pdf.
3. ISSP, National Identity II 2003, Variables 47 (first response), 53 (first two responses).
4. *OECD in Figures 2007*, Demography and Health, Demography; *OECD, Society at a Glance: 2006 Edition*, Chart CO2.2, p 105.
5. Randall Hansen, "Work, Welfare, and Wanderlust: Immigration and Integration in Europe and North America," in Jeffrey Kopstein and Sven Steinmo, eds., *Growing Apart? America and Europe in the Twenty-First Century* (Cambridge 2008), pp. 177–78.
6. OECD, *A Profile of Immigrant Populations in the 21st Century: Data from OECD Countries* (2008), Table 3.1, p. 82.
7. Irena Kogan, "Continuing Ethnic Segmentation in Austria," in Anthony F. Heath et al., eds., *Unequal Chances: Ethnic Minorities in Western Labour Markets* (Oxford, 2007), Table 3.2A, p. 115. In France, the only first-generation foreign men with lower university attendance rates than the French are the Maghrebin and those from Southern Europe. Table 6.A1, p. 260. The situation is different in Germany and the Netherlands.

CHAPTER TWELVE

1. Lawrence Mishel, Jared Bernstein, Sylvia Allegretto, *The State of Working America 2006/2007* (Ithaca, 2007), Downloadable tables and figures, Chapter 8, Table 8.2: Per capita income using purchasing-power parity exchange rates, 1970-2004 (2004 Dollars). Figures are for 2004. Available at: http://www.stateofworkingamerica.org/tabfig_08.html.
2. ISSP, Social Inequality III 1999, Variables 11, 34, 35, sum of first two responses. Stefan Svallfors, "Class and Attitudes to Market Inequality: A Comparison of Sweden, Britain, Germany, and the United States," in Svallfors, ed., *The Political Sociology of the Welfare State* (Stanford, 2007), Table 6.4, p. 208.
3. Timothy Smeeding, "Poor People in Rich Nations: The United States in Comparative Perspective," *Journal of Economic Perspectives*, 20, 1 (2006), Table 4, p 79; OECD, *Sustainable Development: Critical Issues* (2001), Figure 3.A.12, p 91. Data from late 1990s. John Schmitt and Ben Zipperer, "Is the United States a Good Model for Reducing Social Exclusion in

Europe?" *International Journal of Health Sciences,* 37, 1 (2007), p. 16, makes a similar claim, though it is unclear whether this refers to the enlarged EU.

4. Wojciech Kopczuk and Emmanuel Saez, "Top Wealth Shares in the United States, 1916–2000: Evidence from Estate Tax Returns," *National Tax Journal,* 58, 2/2 (2004), pp. 482–83.

5. Thomas Piketty and Emmanuel Saez, "Income Inequality in the United States, 1913–1998," *Quarterly Journal of Economics,* 118, 1 (2003), Table II, pp. 8–10; Anthony B. Atkinson and Wiemer Salverda, "Top Incomes in the Netherlands and the United Kingdom over the 20th Century," *Journal of the European Economic Association,* 3, 4 (2005), Table 2UK, pp. 899, 900. A generous slice of the most recent work done on such subjects has now been collected in A. B. Atkinson and T. Piketty, eds., *Top Incomes Over the Twentieth Century: A Contrast Between Continental European and English-Speaking Countries* (Oxford, 2007).

6. Top income tax rates have gone down in America from 70% to 35% since 1981, and in Sweden from 50% to 36% since 1975. Declining tax rates levied on those in the top percentile in Sweden are documented in Björn Gustafsson and Birgitta Jansson, "Top Incomes in Sweden During Three-Quarters of a Century: A Micro Data Approach," IZA DP No 2672, March 2007, Table 3, p. 25. In the United States: Kopczuk and Saez, "Top Wealth Shares," p. 484.

7. Jesper Roine and Daniel Waldenström, "Top Incomes in Sweden over the Twentieth Century," SSE/EFI Working Paper Series in Economics and Finance No. 602, August 15, 2005, Figure 3, p. 54; Roine and Waldenström, "The Evolution of Top Incomes in an Egalitarian Society: Sweden, 1903–2004," *Journal of Public Economics,* 92 (2008), Figure 2, p. 372. U.S. figure from Piketty and Saez, "Income Inequality in the United States," Table II, p. 10.

8. Kopczuk and Saez, "Top Wealth Shares in the United States," Table 3, pp. 454–55. The apparent date for the wealth peak of the top one-hundredth of 1923 is a typo.

9. Thomas Piketty, Gilles Postel-Vinay, and Jean-Laurent Rosenthal, "Wealth Concentration in a Developing Economy: Paris and France, 1807–1994," *American Economic Review,* 96, 1 (2006), Table 4, p. 248; Facundo Alvaredo and Emmanuel Saez, "Income and Wealth Concentration in Spain in Historical and Fiscal Perspective," Centre for Economic Policy Research, Discussion Paper Series, No. 5836, Table E1; Kopczuk and Saez, "Top Wealth Shares in the United States," Table 3, pp. 454–55.

10. Fabien Dell, "Top Incomes in Germany and Switzerland over the Twentieth Century," *Journal of the European Economic Association,* 3, 2–3 (2005), Figure 6, p. 420; Thomas Piketty and Emmanuel Saez, "The Evolution of Top Incomes: A Historical and International Approach," *American Economic Review,* 92, 2 (2006), Figure 4, p. 203.

11. F. Dell et al., "Income and Wealth Concentration in Switzerland over the Twentieth Century," in Atkinson and Piketty, eds., *Top Incomes over the Twentieth Century,* claims that few of Europe's wealthy relocate to Switzerland to escape high taxation in their native countries. But the sums that it calculates (and can calculate on the basis of Swiss tax figures) cover only a small fraction of the wealth parked in Switzerland, but outside the Swiss tax net. The 35% advance flat tax at source, for example, has been finely calibrated by the Swiss to keep the EU off their backs while being so easy to evade that only the occasional widow without benefit of tax advice would actually pay it.

12. Henry Ohlsson, Jesper Roine, and Daniel Waldenström, "Long-Run Changes in the Concentration of Wealth," United Nations University, World Institute for Development Economics Research, Research Paper No 2006/103, Table 1, p. 20. Available at http://www.wider.unu.edu/publications/working-papers/research-papers/2006/en_GB/rp2006–103/.

13. Jesper Roine and Daniel Waldenström, "Wealth Concentration over the Path of Development: Sweden, 1873–2006," IFN Working Paper No 722, 2007, Table A1, p. 31. Available at http://www.ifn.se/wfiles/wp/wp722.pdf. U.S. figures from Kopczuk and Saez, "Top Wealth Shares in the United States," Table 3, pp. 454–55.

14. Tax Justice Network, *Tax Us If You Can* (September 2005), Box 1, p. 12. Available at http://www.taxjustice.net/cms/upload/pdf/tuiyc_-_eng_-_web_file.pdf.

15. Roine and Waldenström, "Wealth Concentration over the Path of Development: Sweden," p. 19 and Table A2, p. 32.

16. Klaus Deininger and Lyn Squire, "A New Data Set Measuring Income Inequality," *World Bank Economic Review*, 10, 3 (1996), Table 1, p. 577.

17. James K. Galbraith and Hyunsub Kum, "Estimating the Inequality of Household Incomes: A Statistical Approach to the Creation of a Dense and Consistent Global Data Set," *Review of Income and Wealth*, 51, 1 (2005), Appendix A, pp. 140–141.

18. UNICEF Innocenti Research Centre, *A League Table of Child Poverty in Rich Nations*, Innocenti Report Card 1 (June 2000), Figure 1, p. 4; Figure 2, p. 7. Available at http://www.unicef-irc.org/publications/pdf/repcard1e.pdf. Similar confirmation comes from figures that measure absolute poverty defined as a percentage of U.S. posttax/posttransfer income (1991 PPP numbers). By this measure, at a 50% poverty line, France, Ireland, Italy, and the UK had higher percentages of the population in poverty, and the Netherlands only slightly below. Lane Kenworthy, "Do Social-Welfare Policies Reduce Poverty? A Cross-National Assessment," *Social Forces*, 77, 3 (1999), Table 1, p. 1,126. There is a version of this covering fewer countries in Lane Kenworthy, *Egalitarian Capitalism: Jobs, Incomes, and Growth in Affluent Countries* (New York, 2004), chapter 6. Similar figures can be found in Lyle Scruggs and James P. Allan, "The Material Consequences of Welfare States," *Comparative Political Studies*, 39, 7 (2006), Table 1, p. 884.

19. Timothy M. Smeeding and Lee Rainwater, "Comparing Living Standards Across Nations: Real Incomes at the Top, the Bottom and the Middle," in Edward N. Wolff, ed., *What Has Happened to the Quality of Life in the Advanced Industrialized Nations?* (Cheltenham, 2004), Figure 6.2, p. 170; Figure 6.6, p. 176. (Also, Luxembourg Income Study Working Paper No. 266).

20. Will Hutton, *The World We're In* (London, 2002), p. 344.

21. *OECD Factbook 2008*, Macroeconomic Trends, National Income Per Capita, Gross National Income Per Capita. Figures for 2006. Eurostat, General and Regional Statistics, Regional Statistics, Regional Economic Accounts, Regional GDP (PPS per inhabitant), Figures for 2005. Available at http://epp.eurostat.ec.europa.eu/tgm/table.do?tab=table&init=1&plugin=1&language=en&pcode=tgs00005.

22. James K. Galbraith, Pedro Conceição, and Pedro Ferreira, "Inequality and Unemployment in Europe: The American Cure," *New Left Review*, 237 (1999), pp. 45–48; James K.

Galbraith, "What is the American Model Really About? Soft Budgets and the Keynesian Devolution," *Industrial and Corporate Change,* 16, 1 (2007), pp. 10–12; James K. Galbraith, "Maastricht 2042 and the Fate of Europe: Toward Convergence and Full Employment," pp. 12–14. Friedrich Ebert Stiftung, March 2007. Available at http://library.fes.de/pdf-files/id/04340.pdf.

23. *OECD Regions at a Glance 2007,* Graph 8.2, p. 59, 9.2, p. 65, 12.2, p. 83. Figures for 2003. *OECD Regions at a Glance 2005,* Graph 11.3, p. 83. Figures for 2001.

24. Among the few I have come across is A.B. Atkinson, "Income Distribution in Europe and the United States," *Oxford Review of Economic Policy,* 12, 1 (1996), and Richard Berthoud, *Patterns of Poverty Across Europe* (Bristol, 2004).

25. Olli E. Kangas and Veli-Matti Ritakallio, "Relative to What? Cross-National Picture of European Poverty Measured by Regional, National and European Standards," *European Societies,* 9, 2 (2007), pp. 129–130. Similar information in Lee Rainwater and Timothy M. Smeeding, *Poor Kids in a Rich Country: America's Children in Comparative Perspective* (New York, 2003), chapter 11. The University of Texas Inequality Project also has done much work on such matters. James Galbraith and Enrique Garcilazo, "Pay Inequality in Europe 1995–2000: Convergence Between Countries and Stability Inside," *European Journal of Comparative Economics,* 2, 2 (2005). Some of these papers have been collected in James K. Galbraith and Maureen Berner, eds., *Inequality and Industrial Change: A Global View* (Cambridge, 2001).

26. Giovanni Peri, "International Migrations: Some Comparisons and Lessons for the European Union," in Barry Eichengreen et al., eds., *The European Economy in an American Mirror* (London, 2008), p. 188; Eurostat, *The Social Situation in the European Union, 2002,* p. 12. Available at http://ec.europa.eu/employment_social/publications/2002/ke4302567_en.pdf.

27. Jeremy Rifkin, *The European Dream: How Europe's Vision of the Future Is Quietly Eclipsing the American Dream* (New York, 2004), p. 21.

28. Pippa Norris and Ronald Inglehart, *Sacred and Secular: Religion and Politics Worldwide* (Cambridge, 2004), pp. 84–85.

29. Murder rates for 2004. Swiss figures from UN Office on Drugs and Crime, *Ninth United Nations Survey of Crime Trends and Operations of Criminal Justice Systems,* Police, 2. Crimes recorded in criminal (police) statistics, by type of crime including attempts to commit crimes, 2.2. Total recorded intentional homicide, completed, Rate per 100,000 total population, 2004, pp 3, 5, 7. Available at http://data360.org/pdf/20070531091045.Crime%20Trends.pdf. U.S. figures from FBI, *Crime in the US 2005,* Offense Data by State, Table 4. Available at http://www.fbi.gov/ucr/05cius/data/table_04.html. When the authors of the latest human development report for the United States write that, "Yet even the lowest state murder rates still exceed rates in Japan, Germany, Greece, France, Austria, Italy, Norway, Switzerland, the United Kingdom, Ireland, Spain, Sweden, and the Netherlands," they are mistaken. There are some 17 U.S. states with murder rates lower than Switzerland's. Sarah Burd-Sharps et al., *The Measure of America: American Human Development Report 2008–2009* (New York, 2008), p. 60.

30. U.S. figures from U.S. Census Bureau, Population Division, Interim State Population Projections, 2005, Table 2. Scottish figures from Alastair H. Leyland et al., *Inequalities in Mortality in Scotland 1981-2001*, Medical Research Council, Social and Public Health Sciences Unit, Occasional Paper no. 16, February 2007, Table 2.13, p 29. Available at http://www.sphsu.mrc.ac.uk/files/File/current_research/Inequalities/Inequalities_in_health.pdf. Figures for 2000 and 2001.

31. WHO, Commission on Social Determinants of Health, *Closing the Gap in a Generation: Health Equity through Action on the Social Determinants of Health,* 2008, Table 2.1, p. 32; Christopher J. L. Murray et al., "Eight Americas: Investigating Mortality Disparities Across Races, Counties and Race-Counties in the United States," *PLOS Medicine,* 3, 9 (2006), Dataset S1. Life Expectancy at Birth by County.

32. Ellen Nolte and C. Martin McKee, "Measuring the Health of Nations: Updating an Earlier Analysis," *Health Status,* 27, 1 (2008). Exhibit 5, p. 65; Joel C. Cantor, et al., *Aiming Higher: Results from a State Scorecard on Health System Performance,* The Commonwealth Fund Commission on a High Performance Health System, June 2007, Exhibit A11, p. 65. Available at http://www.commonwealthfund.org/usr_doc/StateScorecard.pdf?section=4039.

CHAPTER THIRTEEN

1. *Anglo-Saxon Attitudes: A Survey of British and American Views of the World.* Available at http://www.economist.com/media/pdf/FullPollData.pdf.

2. Death Penalty Information Center, April 2, 2007. Available at http://www.deathpenalty-info.org/FactSheet.pdf.

3. Andrei S. Markovits, *Uncouth Nation: Why Europe Dislikes America* (Princeton, 2007) p. 22. Amnesty International, Death Penalty News, June 1, 1999, p. 4. Available at http://www.amnesty.org/en/report/info/ACT53/003/1999. *UN Human Development Report 2007/2008,* Table 27, p. 322.

4. Dollar figures for military expenditure from CIA, *World Factbook.* Population statistics from OECD. Figures for 2003.

5. Jens Alber, "The European Social Model and the United States," *European Union Politics,* 7, 3 (2006), pp. 398–399. Strong support for this approach in Francis G. Castles, "Patterns of State Expenditure in Europe and America," in Jens Alber and Neil Gilbert, eds., *United in Diversity? Comparing Social Models in Europe and America* (Oxford University Press, forthcoming).

6. *OECD Health Data 2008,* Social Protection, Health Care Coverage, Private Health Insurance, Primary Private Health Insurance Coverage, and Duplicate Private Health Insurance Coverage. Figures for UK come from the latter and are for 2006. Mannheim Research Institute for the Economics of Aging, Axel Börsch-Supan et al., eds., *Health, Ageing and Retirement in Europe* (April 2005), Table 1, p 127. Available at http://www.share-project.org/t3/share/index.php?id=69.

7. OECD Health Project, *Private Health Insurance in OECD Countries* (2004), Table 2.4, p. 41. Figures from 2000. These are percentages of spending, and since health spending in the United States is high, that could mean higher actual costs per capita. And that is, indeed,

the case, though each average Swiss and Italian still pays more out of pocket than Americans. WHO, *World Health Report 2000,* Annex Table 8, pp. 192–195. Figures for 1997.

8. To judge from the following figures: A. B. Atkinson, "Income Distribution in Europe and the United States," *Oxford Review of Economic Policy,* 12, 1 (1996), Figure 6, p. 24; Andrea Brandolini and Timothy M. Smeeding, "Patterns of Economic Inequality in Western Democracies: Some Facts on Levels and Trends," *Political Science and Politics,* 39, 1 (2006), Figure 3, p. 25. Similar comparative trends in François Nielsen et al., "Exactly How Has Income Inequality Changed? Patterns of Distributional Change in Core Societies," Luxembourg Income Study Working Paper Series No. 422, May 2005.

9. Henry Ohlsson, Jesper Roine, and Daniel Waldenström, "Long-Run Changes in the Concentration of Wealth," United Nations University, World Institute for Development Economics Research, Research Paper No 2006/103, Table 2, p 23. Available at http://www.wider.unu.edu/publications/working-papers/research-papers/2006/en_GB/rp2006-103/.

10. Harold L. Wilensky, *Rich Democracies: Political Economy, Public Policy and Performance* (Berkeley, 2002), pp. 681–682. Arend Lijphart, Bernard Grofman and Matthew Shugart will be publishing a book that makes a strong case for American exceptionalism in terms of political institutions. See Arend Lijphart, "The United States: A Different Democracy," in Gary King et al. eds., *The Future of Political Science* (New York, 2009). It is hard to believe, however, that one could not, if one were willing to go to this level of detail, do something similar for, say, Italy or Switzerland. And in any case, the larger issue is what sort of typologizing one wants to be doing. A generation of scholars was lost in the trenches typologizing fascism until the entire endeavor was finally abandoned, and something similar has been the case for the welfare state, as I argue below. Rather than typologizing in a Platonic vein, looking for a never-to-be-found overlapping commonality of essences, we would be better off applying the insights of Ludwig Wittgenstein and searching out family resemblances that cluster things cheek by jowl.

11. Robin Archer, *Why is There No Labor Party in the United States?* (Princeton, 2008).

12. I draw here on Peter Baldwin, "Can We Define a European Welfare State Model?" in Bent Greve, ed., *Comparative Welfare Systems: The Scandinavian Model in a Period of Change* (London, 1996); revised version, "Der europäische Wohlfahrtsstaat: Konstruktionsversuche in der zeitgenössischen Forschung," in *Zeitschrift für Sozialreform,* 49, 1 (2003). Also on Peter Baldwin, "The Welfare State for Historians," *Comparative Studies in Society and History,* 34, 4 (October 1992).

13. (Princeton, 1985).

14. Gøsta Esping-Andersen, *The Three Worlds of Welfare Capitalism* (Cambridge, 1990).

15. Deborah Mitchell, "Welfare States and Welfare Outcomes in the 1980s," Conference on "Social Security 50 Years After Beveridge," University of York, September 27–30, 1992.

16. Francis G. Castles and Deborah Mitchell, "Three Worlds of Welfare Capitalism or Four?" Australian National University, Graduate Program in Public Policy, Discussion Paper No. 21, October 1990.

17. Richard Rose, "Is American Public Policy Exceptional?" in Byron E. Shafer, ed., *Is America Different? A New Look at American Exceptionalism* (Oxford, 1991), Table 7.5.

18. The importance of Christian Democracy was first recognized by Harold Wilensky and has more recently been taken up by others as well. Wilensky, "Leftism, Catholicism and Democratic Corporatism: The Role of Political Parties in Recent Welfare State Development," in Peter Flora and Arnold J. Heidenheimer, eds., *The Development of Welfare States in Europe and America* (New Brunswick, 1981); Kees van Kersbergen, *Social Capitalism: A Study of Christian Democracy and the Welfare State* (London, 1995); Francis G. Castles, "On Religion and Public Policy: Does Catholicism Make a Difference?" *European Journal of Political Research,* 25 (1994).

19. Maurizio Ferrera, *Modelli di solidarieta: Politica e riforme sociali nelle democrazie* (Bologna, 1993), p. 304; Ferrera, "The 'Southern Model' of Welfare in Social Europe," *Journal of European Social Policy* (1996).

20. Francis G. Castles and Deborah Mitchell, "Worlds of Welfare and Families of Nations," in Francis G. Castles, ed., *Families of Nations: Patterns of Public Policy in Western Europe* (Aldershot, 1993).

21. Maurizio Ferrera, "The Four Social Europes: Between Universalism and Selectivity," in M. Rhodes and Y. Mény, eds., *The Future of European Welfare: A New Social Contract?* (London, 1998); Heikki Niemelä and Kari Salminen, "State or Corporations: Trends of Pension Policy in Scandinavia," unpublished manuscript, January 1994.

22. Herbert Obinger and Uwe Wagschal, "Drei Welten des Wohlfahrtsstaates? Das Stratifizierungskonzept in der clusteranalytischen Überprüfung," in Stephan Lessenich and Illona Ostner, eds., *Welten des Wohlfahrtskapitalismus: Der Sozialstaat in vergleichender Perspektive* (Frankfurt, 1998).

23. Timothy B. Smith, *France in Crisis: Welfare, Inequality and Globalization Since 1980* (Cambridge, 2004).

24. Francis G. Castles, ed., *The Comparative History of Public Policy* (Oxford, 1989).

25. Fritz W. Scharpf, "Der globale Sozialstaat," *Die Zeit,* 24 (June 8, 2000); Scharpf, "The Viability of Advanced Welfare States in the International Economy: Vulnerabilities and Options," *Journal of European Public Policy,* 7, 2 (2000).

26. Gøsta Esping-Andersen, "The Comparative Macro-Sociology of Welfare States," in Luis Moreno, *Social Exchange and Welfare Development* (Madrid, 1993), p. 136.

27. Peter A. Hall and David Soskice, *Varieties of Capitalism: The Institutional Foundations of Comparative Advantage* (New York, 2001), pp. 18–21.

28. Jonas Pontusson, *Inequality and Prosperity: Social Europe vs. Liberal America* (Ithaca, 2005), pp. 3, 28, and passim.

29. Examples of a similar approach distinguishing between the English-speaking world and the Continent, not down the Atlantic: Castles, "Patterns of State Expenditure in Europe and America," and Brian Burgoon and Phineas Baxandall, "Three Worlds of Working Time: The Partisan and Welfare Politics of Work Hours in Industrialized Countries," *Politics and Society,* 32, 4 (2004). And the definitive work on income disparities at the top similarly distinguishes between the English-speaking world and Continental Europe: A.B. Atkinson and T. Piketty, eds., *Top Incomes Over the Twentieth Century: A Contrast Between Continental European and English-Speaking Countries* (Oxford, 2007).

CHAPTER FOURTEEN

1. 28,400: 30,000. WHO, *World Report on Violence and Health* (2002), Table A.9, pp. 314ff. Figures from the late 1990s.

2. Japanese per capita social spending is about 80% of the U.S. figure. OECD.StatExtracts, Social and Welfare Statistics, Social Protection, Social Expenditure—Aggregated Data, Per Head, at Current Prices and Current PPPs, in U.S. Dollars. Figures for 2003.

3. Bernard-Henri Lévy, *American Vertigo: Travelling in the Footsteps of Tocqueville* (New York, 2006), pp. 240–41.

4. Portugal's per capita income is 45% of Norway's, Mississippi's is 54% of Connecticut's. Figures taken from U.S. Census Bureau, *State and Metropolitan Data Book: 2006,* Table A-43, p. 58, and Lawrence Mishel, Jared Bernstein, Sylvia Allegretto, *The State of Working America 2006/2007* (Ithaca, NY, 2007), Downloadable tables and figures, Chapter 8, Table 8.2: Per capita income using purchasing-power parity exchange rates, 1970-2004 (2004 Dollars). Figures for 2004. Available at http://www.stateofworkingamerica.org/tabfig_08.html.

5. EU figures from the WHO, available at http://www.who.int/whosis/database/life_tables/life_tables.cfm. U.S. figures from the U.S. Census Bureau, Population Division, Interim State Population Projections, 2005, Table 2, Average Life Expectancy at Birth by State for 2000.

6. EU figures are from OECD StatExtracts, Labour, Labour Force Statistics, LFS by Sex and Age, LFS by Sex and Age—Indicators, Labour Force Participation Rate, Women. Figures for 2004. Available at http://stats.oecd.org/wbos/Index.aspx?DatasetCode=LFS_SEXAGE_I_R. U.S. figures are from U.S. Census, *State and Metropolitan Area Data Book: 2006*, Table A-29, p. 39. Figures for 2004.

7. William J. Novak, "The Myth of the 'Weak' American State," *American Historical Review,* 113, 3 (2008). I also owe the previous reference to John Stuart Mill to Novak, p. 759. See also William J. Novak, *The People's Welfare: Law and Regulation in Nineteenth-Century America* (Chapel Hill, 1996), Chapter. 6 and *passim*; William R. Brock, *Investigation and Responsibility: Public Responsibility in the United States, 1865-1900* (Cambridge, 1984).

8. Brian Doyle, *Disability, Discrimination and Equal Opportunities: A Comparative Study of the Employment Rights of Disabled Persons* (London, 1995), pp. 43–46, 68–69.

9. One of the themes pursued in Peter Baldwin, *Disease and Democracy: The Industrialized World Faces AIDS* (Berkeley, 2005).

10. John Micklethwait and Adrian Wooldridge, *The Right Nation: Conservative Power in America* (New York, 2004), p. 302.

11. Lennart J. Lundqvist, *The Hare and the Tortoise: Clean Air Policies in the United States and Sweden* (Ann Arbor, 1980).

12. Henry Aaron, "Thinking about Health Care Finance: Some Propositions," in OECD, *Health Care Reform: The Will to Change* (Paris, 1996), pp. 54–55; Elpidoforos S. Soteriades and Matthew E. Falagas, "Comparison of Amount of Biomedical Research Originating from the European Union and the United States," *British Medical Journal,* July 23, 2005, pp. 192–194.

13. To calculate the rough figure of public health spending per person covered publicly in the United States, the sum of spending on Medicare, Medicaid, and veterans' public hospital

and medical care in 2005 was divided by the sum of enrollees in Medicare and Medicaid as well as all American veterans in 2005. Medicare expenditure and expenditure on veterans' public hospital and medical care, as well as the numbers of Medicare enrollees, of people covered by Medicaid and the number of American veterans all come from the U.S. Census Bureau, *2008 Statistical Abstract*. Medicaid expenditure comes from James Marton and David E. Wildasin, "Medicaid expenditures and state budgets: past, present, and future," *National Tax Journal* (June 2007), p. 1. Available at http://www.entrepreneur.com/trade-journals/article/167976828.html. European total public health spending figures were taken from *OECD Health Data 2007*, Total expenditure on health, Public expenditure on health, Million US$, purchasing power parity, 2005. Public health spending per person was determined by taking the percentages of European populations covered by public health insurance from, *OECD Health Data 2007, October 2007*, Government/social health insurance, In-patient and acute care, % of total population. The percentages of European populations with public health coverage were multiplied by the countries' total populations to get figures of people covered by public health insurance. These figures were used to divide the total public health spending numbers to determine the amounts of public spending per person covered by public health insurance.

14. I have looked at similar themes in Peter Baldwin, "Beyond Weak and Strong: Rethinking the State in Comparative Policy History," *Journal of Policy History*, 17, 1 (2005).

15. Michael T. Halpern et al., "Association of Insurance Status and Ethnicity with Cancer Stage at Diagnosis for 12 Cancer Sites: A Retrospective Analysis," *Lancet Oncology*, 9 (2008), pp. 222–231. Much more information in a similar vein can be found in U.S. Department of Health and Human Services, Agency for Healthcare Research and Quality, *National Healthcare Disparities Report 2007*, AHRQ Publication No. 08–0041, February 2008.

16. Joel C. Cantor, et al., *Aiming Higher: Results from a State Scorecard on Health System Performance*, The Commonwealth Fund Commission on a High Performance Health System, June 2007, Exhibit 22, p. 38; figures for 2005–2006; Exhibit A11, p. 65. Figures for 2002. Available at http://www.commonwealthfund.org/usr_doc/StateScorecard.pdf?section=4039.

17. US figures are from American Cancer Society, *Cancer Facts and Figures, 1999*, p. 16. Available at http://www.cancer.org/downloads/STT/F&F99.pdf. European figures from Eurocare-3. Results are summarized in M. Sant et al., "EUROCARE-3: Survival of cancer patients diagnosed 1990–94: Results and commentary," *Annals of Oncology*, 14 (2003), Supplement 5, pp. 72ff. The WinZip file with Eurocare-3 figures is available at http://www.eurocare.it/. Figures for 1990–1994.

18. Jo Blanden et al., "Intergenerational Mobility in Europe and North America," April 2005, Centre for Economic Performance and Sutton Trust. Available at http://www.suttontrust.com/reports/IntergenerationalMobility.pdf. Gary Solon, "Cross-Country Differences in Intergenerational Earnings Mobility," *Journal of Economic Perspectives*, 16, 2 (2002).

19. These are themes explored in Robert Putnam, "*E Pluribus Unum:* Diversity and Community in the Twenty-first Century," *Scandinavian Political Studies*, 30, 2 (2007); Alberto Alesina and Edward L. Glaeser, *Fighting Poverty in the US and Europe: A World of Differ-*

ence (Oxford, 2004), chapter 6; Robert C. Lieberman, *Shifting the Color Line: Race and the American Welfare State* (Cambridge, MA, 2001); Michael K. Brown, *Race, Money and the American Welfare State* (Ithaca, 1999); Jill Quadagno, *The Color of Welfare: How Racism Undermined the War on Poverty* (Oxford, 1996).

20. That the agrarian nature of these societies in the nineteenth century was a crucial element of their styles of social policy is one of the arguments put forth in Peter Baldwin, *The Politics of Social Solidarity: Class Bases of the European Welfare State, 1875–1975* (Cambridge, 1990).

21. Figures for late 1990s in Lee Rainwater and Timothy M. Smeeding, *Poor Kids in a Rich Country: America's Children in Comparative Perspective* (New York, 2003), Figure 1.1, p. 21, Table 1.4, p. 31.

22. Assuming that the two sets of figures on amenable mortality in the following are fully comparable: Ellen Nolte and C. Martin McKee, "Measuring the Health of Nations: Updating an Earlier Analysis," *Health Status*, 27, 1 (2008). Exhibit 5, p. 65; Cantor, et al., *Aiming Higher*, Exhibit A11, p. 65. Figures for 2002–2003.

23. Stéphane Baldi, et al., *Highlights from PISA 2006: Performance of US 15-Year-Old Students in Science and Mathematics Literacy in an International Context*, U.S. Department of Education, National Center for Education Statistics, December 2007, Table 2, p. 6, Table C-12, p. 55.

CHAPTER FIFTEEN

1. Sarah Burd-Sharps et al., *The Measure of America: American Human Development Report 2008–2009* (New York, 2008), p. 13.

2. Tony Judt, "Europe vs. America," *New York Review of Books*, 52, 2 (2005).

3. James K. Galbraith, "What is the American Model Really About? Soft Budgets and the Keynesian Devolution," *Industrial and Corporate Change*, 16, 1 (2007).

4. *UK Stem Cell Initiative: Report and Recommendations* (November 2005), pp. 45–46. Available at http://www.advisorybodies.doh.gov.uk/uksci/uksci-reportnov05.pdf. Sarah Webb and Elisabeth Pain, "Navigating the Stem-Cell Research Maze," *Science*, December 1, 2006.

5. I have explored some of these themes in Peter Baldwin, "Welfare State and Citizenship in the Age of Globalization," in Andreas Føllesdal and Peter Koslowski, eds., *Restructuring the Welfare State: Ethical Issues of Social Security in an International Perspective* (Berlin, 1997); "The Return of the Coercive State? Behavioral Control in Multicultural Society," in John A. Hall et al., eds., *The Nation-State Under Challenge: Autonomy and Capacity in a Changing World* (Princeton, 2003); "Riding the Subways of Gemeinschaft," *Acta Sociologica*, 41, 4 (1998).

6. Giovanni di Stefano is a bad-boy Anglo-Italian lawyer, a discount version of Jacques Vergès, whose client list includes mass murderers and ex-dictators. He has moved into politics, founding the Radical Party of Great Britain. Apparently, in the absence of any more elaborated platform, its first target is what it considers the insanity of such needless instructions,

especially the Kit Kat example given here. "Devil's advocate: The world's most notorious lawyer defends himself," *Independent,* July 3, 2008. More examples in Alan Pearce, *Playing it Safe: The Crazy World of Britain's Health and Safety Regulations* (London, 2007).

7. Alberto Alesina et al., "Public Goods and Ethnic Divisions," *Quarterly Journal of Economics,* 114, 4 (1999).

8. Karen Davis et al., *Mirror, Mirror on the Wall: An International Update on the Comparative Performance of American Health Care,* Commonwealth Fund, May 2007, Figure 6, p. 17. Available at http://www.commonwealthfund.org/usr_doc/1027_Davis_mirror_mirror_international_update_final.pdf?section=4039.

9. James V. Dunford, et al., "Impact of the San Diego Serial Inebriate Program on Use of Emergency Medical Resources," *Annals of Emergency Medicine,* 47, 4 (2006), pp. 328–336.

10. Peter Baldwin, *Disease and Democracy: The Industrialized World Faces AIDS* (Berkeley, 2005), pp. 34–35, 258–261.

11. Quoted in Stephen P. Strickland, *Politics, Science, and Dread Disease: A Short History of United States Research Policy* (Cambridge Mass, 1972), p. 213.

12. Gary W. Phillips, *Chance Favors the Prepared Mind: Mathematics and Science Indicators for Comparing States and Nations,* American Institutes for Research, 14 November 2007, Figures 1–53, pp. 25ff. Available at http://www.air.org/publications/documents/phillips.chance.favors.the.prepared.mind.pdf. Michael O. Martin et al., *TIMMS 2007 International Mathematics Report* (Chestnut Hill, Mass, 2008), Exhibit 1.1, pp. 34–35; Michael O. Martin et al., *TIMMS 2007 International Science Report* (Chestnut Hill, Mass, 2008), Exhibit 1.1, pp. 34–35.

13. Dan Bilefsky, "Tradition of Blood Feuds Isolates Albanian Men," *International Herald Tribune,* July 10, 2008.

14. Noel Ignatiev, *How the Irish Became White* (New York, 1996); Eugen Weber, *Peasants into Frenchmen: The Modernization of Rural France, 1870–1914* (Stanford, 1976).

15. *Financial Times* August 16/17, 2008, p. 6. The Dutch and Swedish figures are from Rigmar Osterkamp and Oliver Röhn, "Being on Sick Leave: Possible Explanations for Differences of Sick-leave Days Across Countries," *CESifo Economic Studies,* 53, 1 (2007), Figure 1, p. 98.

CHAPTER SIXTEEN

1. Sarah Burd-Sharps et al., *The Measure of America: American Human Development Report 2008–2009* (New York, 2008).

2. *UN Human Development Report 2007/2008,* Table 2, p. 234, *UN Human Development Report 2006,* Table 1, p. 283.

3. Godfrey Hodgson, *The Myth of American Exceptionalism* (New Haven, 2009).

4. Burd-Sharps, *Measure of America,* Table 3.1, p. 53.

5. Burd-Sharps, *Measure of America,* pp. 4, 190, 195.

6. WHO, Commission on Social Determinants of Health, *Closing the Gap in a Generation: Health Equity through Action on the Social Determinants of Health* (2008), Table 2.1, p. 32.

The Hampstead/St Pancras figures are attributed to the WHO Commission, but are not in the report itself. *Financial Times,* August 29, 2008, p. 2.

7. Figures for general versus vocational streams are from OECD, *Education at a Glance 2005,* Table C2.1, p. 248. Figures for graduation rates are from Table A2.1, p. 44, ISCED 3A. Figures for 2003. Figures for university entry are from OECD, *Education at a Glance 2008,* Table A2.4, p. 68. Figures for 2006.

8. U.S. figures for 2005 from Burd-Sharps, *Measure of America,* US Indicator Tables, pp. 164–172. Figures from 2005. UK figures are from UK, National Statistics, ASHE Results 2007, Place of Residence by Parliamentary Constituency, Table 10.7a. Available at http://www.statistics.gov.uk/downloads/theme_labour/ASHE_2007/2007_res_pc.pdf.

9. U.S. figures from Burd-Sharps, *Measure of America,* US Indicator Tables, pp. 164–172. Figures from 2005. UK figures from UK, National Statistics, ASHE Results 2007, Place of Residence by Parliamentary Constituency, Table 10.7a.

10. Richard Berthoud, *Patterns of Poverty Across Europe* (Bristol, 2004), Table D.1 and D.2, pp. 50–53; Eurostat. Statistics, Regions and Cities, Main Tables, Regional Statistics, Regional Economic Accounts—ESA95, Disposable Income of Private Households. Figures for 2005.

CHAPTER SEVENTEEN

1. The two sides emblematically represented by Will Hutton and Robert Kagan.

2. Seymour Martin Lipset, *Continental Divide: The Values and Institutions of the United States and Canada* (New York, 1990).

3. Daniel T. Rodgers, *Atlantic Crossings: Social Politics in a Progressive Age* (Cambridge MA, 1998); Colleen A. Dunlavy, *Politics and Industrialization: Early Railroads in the United States and Prussia* (Princeton, 1994), William J. Novak, *The People's Welfare: Law and Regulation in Nineteenth-Century America* (Chapel Hill, 1996), chapter 6 and passim; William R. Brock, *Investigation and Responsibility: Public Responsibility in the United States, 1865–1900* (Cambridge, 1984).

4. Richard Rose, "Is American Public Policy Exceptional?" in Byron E. Shafer, ed., *Is America Different? A New Look at American Exceptionalism* (Oxford, 1991); Theda Skocpol, *Protecting Soldiers and Mothers: The Political Origins of Social Policy in the United States* (Cambridge MA, 1992); Neil Gilbert, *Transformation of the Welfare State: The Silent Surrender of Public Responsibility* (New York, 2002); Christopher Howard, *The Hidden Welfare State: Tax Expenditures and Social Policies in the United States* (Princeton, 1997); Jacob S. Hacker, *The Divided Welfare State: The Battle Over Public and Private Social Benefits in the United States* (Cambridge, 2002); Laura S. Jensen, *Patriots, Settlers and the Origins of American Social Policy* (Cambridge, 2003); Marc Allen Eisner, *From Warfare State to Welfare State: World War I, Compensatory State-Building, and the Limits of the Modern Order* (University Park PA, 2000); Julian E. Zelizer, *Taxing America: Wilbur D. Mills, Congress, and the State, 1945–1975* (Cambridge, 1998); Lee J. Alston and Joseph P. Ferrie, *Southern Paternalism and the Rise of the American Welfare State: Economics, Politics and Institutions, 1865–1965* (Cambridge, 1999).

5. Matthieu Leimgruber, *Solidarity Without the State? Business and the Shaping of the Swiss Welfare State, 1890–2000* (Cambridge, 2008).

6. Thomas Bender, ed., *Rethinking American History in a Global Age* (Berkeley, 2002); Thomas Bender, *A Nation Among Nations: America's Place in World History* (New York, 2006).

7. Gérard Noiriel, *Le Creuset français: Histoire de l'immigration XIXe-XXe siècles* (Paris, 1988) shows how France has been an immigrant nation almost as much as the United States.

8. Josef Joffe, "A Canvas, Not a Country: How Europe Sees America," in Peter H. Schuck and James Q. Wilson, eds., *Understanding America* (New York, 2008).

9. Louis Hartz, *The Founding of New Societies* (New York, 1964).

10. Tom W. Rice and Jan L. Feldman, "Civic Culture and Democracy from Europe to America," *Journal of Politics,* 59, 4 (1997).

11. Hans Magnus Enzensberger, *Europe, Europe: Forays into a Continent* (London, 1989), pp. 73–76.

12. Some expression of this can be found in Derk-Jan Eppink, *Life of a European Mandarin: Inside the Commission* (Tielt, Belgium, 2007).

FIGURE SOURCES

1. Economic Freedom
James Gwartney, et al., *Economic Freedom of the World, 2008 Annual Report* (Vancouver, 2008), Exhibit 1.2, p. 8. Figures from 2006. Available at http://www.cato.org/pubs/efw/efw2008/efw2008-1.pdf.

2. State Control of Enterprises
OECD Stat, Public Sector, Market Regulation, Economy-Wide Regulation, Product Market Regulation, State Control. Figures are for 2003.

3. State Ownership of Land
Kevin Cahill, *Who Owns the World: The Hidden Facts Behind Landownership* (Edinburgh, 2006). Some figures were taken directly from the book, and others had to be calculated from other figures, i.e., taking the state-owned acreage and dividing it by the total acreage. Norway's figure is an approximation. Just under half of the land in Sweden is owned by the state and large companies.

4. Labor Regulation
NationMaster, Labor Statistics, Regulation. The data come from the World Bank Group and a paper, Juan C. Botero, Simeon Djankov, Rafael La Porta, Florencio Lopez-de-Silanes, and Andrei Shleifer, "The Regulation of Labor," NBER Working Paper 9756, June 2003, available at http://elsa.berkeley.edu/~yqian/econ260b/Botero%20Regulation%20of%20Labor.pdf. The NationMaster version of the data is available at http://www.nationmaster.com/graph/lab_reg-labor-regulation.

5. Firing Flexibility
NationMaster, Labor Statistics, Regulation, Firing by Country. Same as figure 4.

6. Hiring Flexibility
NationMaster, Labor Statistics, Regulation, Hiring by Country. Same as figure 4.

7. Strike Days
International Labour Office (ILO), *2007 Yearbook of Labour Statistics*. The statistics were created with the use of Table 1A starting on p. 15 and Table 9C starting on p. 1,510. Most data from 2006.

8. Wages
OECD Health Data 2007, October 2007, Economic References, Macro-economic references, Compensation of employees, % gross domestic product. Figures for 2003–06.

9. Minimum Wages
OECD, StatExtracts, Labour, Earnings, Real Hourly Minimum Wages in USD PPP. Most data comes from 2005. Available at http://stats.oecd.org/wbos/.

10. State Minimum Wages
OECD, StatExtracts, Labour, Earnings, Real Hourly Minimum Wages in USD PPP, 2005. U.S. Department of Labor, Minimum Wage Laws in the States—Jan 1, 2007. Choose the appropriate states and look at Basic Minimum Rate (Per Hour). Available at http://www.dol. gov/esa/minwage/america.htm. U.S. wages are statutory minimum wages in US$.

11. Minimum Wage Workers
Eurostat News Release, 92/2006—13 July 2006, Minimum Wages in the EU25. Available at http:// epp.eurostat.ec.europa.eu/pls/portal/docs/PAGE/PGP_PRD_CAT_PREREL/PGE_CAT_ PREREL_YEAR_2006/PGE_CAT_PREREL_YEAR_2006_MONTH_07/3-13072006-EN-AP2.PDF. The Bureau of Labor Statistics reports that 2.7% of workers were paid at or below the minimum wage in 2004. But the highest concentration of the low paid were between 16 and 19, in other words likely to be teenage part-timers. Among workers over the age of 25, 1.7% were paid at or below the minimum wage. Bureau of Labor Statistics, Labor Force Statistics from the Current Population Survey, Table 1. Available at http://www.bls.gov/cps/minwage2004tbls.htm.

12. Part-Time Employment
OECD, *Labour Force Statistics 1985–2005*, 2006 Edition, 1. Part 1: Summary tables, Part-time employment, Part-time as percentage of employment, 2005, pp. 36–37.

13. Fatal Work Injuries
ILO, LABORSTA Internet, Yearly Statistics, 8B: Rates of occupational injuries, by economic activity. Data comes from 2002–05. The statistics are given either in terms of 100,000 workers employed or in terms of 100,000 workers insured. Available at http://laborsta.ilo.org/.

14. Vacation Time Actually Taken
Expedia.com, 2007 Vacation Deprivation Survey, Vacation days: Earned by country, minus Unused by country. Information comes from charts on Web site after you click on Expedia. com. Available at http://www.vacationdeprivation.com/survey_results.pdf.

15. Public Holidays
OECD, *Babies and Bosses: Reconciling Work and Family Life* (2007), Table 7.1, p. 172. Figures are for 2005.

16. Working Time
OECD, Statistics, Labour Productivity, Labour Productivity Levels, Average Hours Worked per Person. Figures are for 2006. Available at http://www.oecd.org/topicstatsportal/0,3398,e n_2825_30453906_1_1_1_1_1,00.html.

17. GDP per Hour Worked

OECD Stats, Estimates of Labour Productivity Levels, GDP per hour worked, current prices, US dollar, 2006. Available at http://stats.oecd.org/WBOS/Default. aspx?DatasetCode=LEVEL. For figures expressed in PPP see the following: U.S. Department of Labor, Bureau of Labor Statistics, Comparative Real Gross Domestic Product per Capita and per Employed Person: Sixteen Countries, 1960–2006, Chart 4, p. 10. Available at: http://www.bls.gov/fls/flsgdp.pdf. The result is much the same, though the U.S. drops a little in the ranking.

18. Pace of Life

Robert Levine and Ara Norenzayan, "The Pace of Life in 31 Countries," *Journal of Cross-Cultural Psychology*, 30, no. 2 (1999), p. 190.

19. Pace of Life

"Quick, Step," *Economist*, May 16, 2007. Available at http://www.economist.com/daily/chart-gallery/displaystory.cfm?story_id=E1_JTSSVSD.

20. Female Suicide

WHO, Mental health, Suicide prevention and special programmes, Suicide rates per 100,000 by country, year and sex, Females. The data come from the most recent year available as of 2008. Available at http://www.who.int/mental_health/prevention/suicide_rates/en/index.html.

21. Total Tax Revenue

Figures for total tax revenue as a percentage of GDP from OECD, *Revenue Statistics 1965–2006* (2007), Table A, p. 19. Figures for 2005. For Total tax revenue per capita, from *OECD Health Data 2008*, December 2008, Economic References, Macro-economic references, Public revenue, /capita, US$ purchasing power parity. Figures from 2005–2006.

22. Income Tax

OECD Factbook 2006, Public Finance, Taxes, Total Tax Revenue, Tables, Taxes on Income and Profits, As a Percentage of GDP, 2003.

23. Income Tax Progressivity

Adam Wagstaff et al, "Redistributive Effect, Progressivity and Differential Tax Treatment: Personal Income Taxes in Twelve OECD Countries," *Journal of Public Economics*, 72, no. 1 (1999), Table 3, p. 82. Figures from late 1980s and early 1990s.

24. Taxation of the Wealthy

OECD, *Growing Unequal: Income Distribution and Poverty in OECD Countries* (2008), Table 4.5, p. 107. Figures are for 2005. Similar figures detailing what the richest 30% paid during the 1990s are in Michael F. Förster, "Trends and Driving Factors in Income Distribution and Poverty in the OECD Area," OECD, Directorate for Education, Employment, Labour and Social Affairs, Labour Market and Social Policy Occasional Paper No. 42. Table 3.1, p. 83. Available at http://www.olis.oecd.org/OLIS/2000DOC. NSF/4f7adc214b91a685c12569fa005d0ee7/c125692700623b74c125693800385206/$ FILE/00081595.pdf.

25. Property Tax
OECD, *Revenue Statistics 1965–2006*, Table 22, p. 86. Figures for 2005. International Monetary Fund (IMF) figures are similar, though the UK is lower, while Switzerland and Iceland are higher. IMF, *Government Finance Statistics Yearbook 2006*, Table W 4, p. 18.

26. Home Ownership
"Home Sweet Home," boston.com, February 12, 2006. Available at http://www.boston.com/news/world/articles/2006/02/12/home_sweet_home/?p1=email_to_a_friend.

27. Corporate Taxes
As a percentage of GDP: *OECD in Figures 2007*, Public Finance, Taxation. Figures for 2004. Rates on corporate capital: Jack M. Mintz, "The 2007 Tax Competitiveness Report: A Call for Comprehensive Tax Reform," pp. 9–10, table 1. C.D. Howe Institute, Research Areas, Fiscal and Monetary Policy, available at http://www.cdhowe.org/pdf/commentary_254.pdf.

28. Inheritance and Gift Taxes
Der Spiegel, no 6, 2007, p. 35. Figures come from 2004.

29. Governmental Medical Spending
WHOSIS, World Health Statistics 2006, Health Systems. Figures are for 2003. Per capita numbers are at international dollar rate. Available at http://www.who.int/whosis/whostat2006_healthsystems.pdf.

30. Total Medical Spending
WHOSIS, World Health Statistics 2006, Health Systems. Figures are for 2003, International dollar rate.

31. Hospitals
WHO, Regional Office for Europe, European Health for All Database, Health Care Resources, 2003 Hospitals per 100,000. Available at: http://data.euro.who.int/hfadb/. American Hospital Association, Fast Facts on U.S. Hospitals, Total Number of All U.S. Registered Hospitals, 2004. Statistic of American hospital ratio calculated with use of 2004 American population. Available at http://www.aha.org/aha/resource-center/Statistics-and-Studies/fast-facts.html.

32. Infant Mortality
WHOSIS, World Health Statistics 2006, Health Status, Mortality, Infant mortality rate (per 1000 live births). Figures are for 2004. Available at http://www.who.int/whosis/whostat2006_mortality.pdf.

33. Male Life Expectancy
WHOSIS, World Health Statistics 2006, Health Status, Mortality, Life expectancy at birth (years), Males. Figures are for 2004.

34. Adult Male Obesity
International Association for the Study of Obesity, Prevalence of Adult Obesity, Males, Obesity, % BMI 30+. Available at http://www.iotf.org/database/documents/GlobalPrevalenceofAdultObesity30thOctober07.pdf.

35. Overweight but Not Obese Men

International Association for the Study of Obesity, Prevalence of Adult Obesity, Males, Over-weight, % BMI 25–29.9. Figures from the mid-1990s through 2006. OECD figures are similar. The percentage of the overweight is greater in the UK, Spain, Portugal, the Netherlands, Luxembourg, Italy, Iceland, Greece, Germany and Austria and at almost the same rate in Ireland and Norway. *OECD Factbook 2008*, Quality of Life, Health, Obesity.

36. Stomach Cancer Incidence

IARC, Globocan 2002. Enter By cancer, choose Stomach Cancer, and then countries, Incidence, ASR(W), age-standardized world rate. Data is on males. Available at http://www-dep.iarc.fr/.

37. Diabetes Mortality

WHO, Department of Measurement and Health Information, December 2004, Research Tools, Burden of disease statistics, Death and DALY estimates for 2002 by cause for WHO Member States, Death Rates, Table 3. Estimated deaths per 100,000 population by cause, and Member State, 2002, II. Noncommunicable diseases, C. Diabetes mellitus. Available at http://www.who.int/healthinfo/statistics/bodgbddeathdalyestimates.xls.

38. Calorie Supply

WRI, Earth Trends Environmental Information, Agriculture and Food, Data Tables, Food and Agriculture Overview 2005, Calorie Supply per Capita (kilocalories/person/day) 2002. Available at http://earthtrends.wri.org/pdf_library/data_tables/agri_2005.pdf, or if this is unavailable, start at http://earthtrends.wri.org/. Similar figures in *OECD Health Data 2008*, Non-Medical Determinants of Health, Lifestyles and Behaviour, Food Consumption.

39. Fish and Fishery Products Consumption

WRI, Earth Trends Environmental Information, Energy and Resources, Data Tables, Resource Consumption 2005, Annual per Capita Consumption (kg per person), Fish and Fishery Products, 2002.

40. Animal Products

WRI, Earth Trends Environmental Information, Agriculture and Food, Data Tables, Food and Agriculture Overview 2005, Share of Calorie Supply from Animal Products (percent), 2002.

41. Alcohol Consumption

WHO Regional office for Europe, European Health for All Database, Life Styles, Pure Alcohol Consumption, Litres per Capita, 2003. Available at http://data.euro.who.int/hfadb/. WHO, Health Topics, Alcohol Drinking, Global Alcohol Database, Global Information System on Alcohol and Health, Levels of Consumption, Recorded Adult (15+) per Capita Consumption in Litres (Total) from 1961, United States, 2003. Available at http://www.who.int/en/.

42. Smokers

WHO, Tobacco Free Initiative, Tobacco Control Country Profiles, 2003. Select the appropriate regions and countries, look at Smoking Prevalence, and look for broadest figures of smoking population (usually, Overall). Available at http://www.who.int/tobacco/global_data/country_profiles/en/.

43. All Cancers (except Non-Melanoma Skin), Incidence

IARC, Globocan 2002. Enter By cancer, choose All Sites but Non-Melanoma Skin Cancer, Incidence and then countries, Incidence, ASR(W), age-standardized world rate. Per 100,000. Data is on males. Available at http://www-dep.iarc.fr/.

44. All Cancers, Mortality

IARC, Globocan 2002. Enter By cancer, choose All Sites but Non-Melanoma Skin Cancer, Mortality and then countries, Incidence, ASR(W), age-standardized world rate. Per 100,000. Data is on males. Available at http://www-dep.iarc.fr/. Figures with similar results at: *OECD Health Data 2007*, Health Status, Mortality, Causes of mortality, Malignant neoplasms, Deaths per 100,000 population (standardised rates). Figures here are from 2001–05.

45. Breast Cancer Survival Rates

Eurocare, Eurocare-3, Breast cancer, Relative survival (%), by age at diagnosis, Women, All ages. The figures come from 1990 to 1994. The WinZip file with Eurocare-3 figures is available at: http://www.eurocare.it/. U.S. figures are from American Cancer Society, *Cancer Facts and Figures, 1999*, p. 14. Available at http://www.cancer.org/downloads/STT/F&F99.pdf.

46. Heart Disease

WHOSIS, Mortality Data, Mortality Profiles, choose the country, then look for Causes of Death, Ischaemic heart disease, Years of Life Lost (%). Data comes from 2002. Available at http://www.who.int/whosis/mort/profiles/en/index.html.

47. Stroke Mortality

WHOSIS, Mortality Data, Mortality Profiles, choose the country, then look for Causes of Death, Cerebrovascular disease, Deaths (%). Data comes from 2002. Available at http://www.who.int/whosis/mort/profiles/en/index.html.

48. Circulatory Disease Mortality

OECD Health Data 2007, October 2007, Health Status, Mortality, Causes of mortality, Diseases of the circulatory system, Deaths per 100,000 population (standardised rates). Data comes from 2001–05.

49. Plastic Surgery

NationMaster, Plastic Surgery Procedures (per Capita) by Country, 2002. Available at http://www.nationmaster.com/graph/hea_pla_sur_pro_percap-plastic-surgery-procedures-per-capita.

50. Public Employment

OECD, Public Governance and Territorial Development Directorate, *Highlights of Public Sector Pay and Employment Trends: 2002 Update*, Table 1, pp. 9–10. Data from 1998–2001. The ratios are based on 2005 population estimates. Available at http://appli1.oecd.org/olis/2002doc.nsf/43bb61 30e5e86e5fc12569fa005d004c/2bb07a986c0242ecc1256c480027f346/$FILE/JT00132606.pdf.

51. Total Government Expenditure

OECD in Figures 2005, pp. 36–37, Government Sector, 2004, Total General Government Expenditure (% of GDP). Available at http://www.oecd.org/topicstatsportal/0,3398,en_2825_497139_1_1_1_1_1,00.html.

52. Public Spending on Unemployment Benefits
OECD Health Data 2007, Social Protection, Social expenditure, Unemployment, Public, / capita US$ PPP. Data come from 2003.

53. Unemployment Benefit Replacement Rate
OECD Employment Outlook 2006, Table 3.2, p. 60. Figures from 2004. Similar results in Stephen Nickell, "Unemployment and Labor Market Rigidities: Europe versus North America," *Journal of Economic Perspectives*, 11, 3 (1997), Table 4, p. 61.

54. Long-Term Unemployment Benefit Replacement Rate
OECD Employment Outlook 2006, Table 3.2, p. 60.

55. Unemployment
OECD, StatExtracts, Standardised Unemployment Rates, 2007.

56. Male Unemployment
OECD, Statistics, Labour Force Statistics, Unemployment by Duration, 2005 Average Duration of Unemployment (in Months), Men, Total. Available at http://stats.oecd.org/wbos/default.aspx?DatasetCode=AVD_DUR.

57. Long-Term Unemployment
OECD Employment Outlook 2007, Statistical Annex, Table G, p, 265. Figures from 2006. Available at http://www.oecd.org/dataoecd/29/27/38749309.pdf.

58. Public Spending on Disability Benefits
OECD Health Data 2008, Social Protection, Social expenditure, Incapacity-related benefits, Public, /capita US$ PPP. The data come from 2003.

59. Disabled People
OECD, Statistics, Social and Welfare Statistics, search for Transforming Disability into Ability, select Transforming Disability into Ability—Selection of tables & charts, select Chart 3.1, Disability Prevalence, by Severity of Disability, as a Percentage of 20–64 Population, Late 1990s. Available at http://www.oecd.org/dataoecd/42/41/35337855.xls.

60. Public Spending on Child Care
OECD, *Babies and Bosses*, Chart 6.1, p. 135. Figures from 2003.

61. Female State Pensions
OECD, Selection of OECD Pensions at a Glance, 2005 Indicators: How Does Your Country Compare? Gross replacement rates by individual earnings level, mandatory pension programmes, women. Available at http://www.oecd.org/dataoecd/7/54/35385805.xls.

62. Retirement Income as a % of Earlier Income
OECD, *Society at a Glance: 2005 Edition*, Chart EQ4.1, p. 59. Figures for 2000.

63. Median Social Transfer Income
Luxembourg Income Study (LIS) Micro database, (2000); harmonization of original surveys conducted by the Luxembourg Income Study, Asbl. Luxembourg, periodic updating. Survey data is for year 2000 for all countries except for the Netherlands and the United Kingdom,

which are based on survey data from 1999. Social transfers recorded as missing or negative were dropped from the analysis. Social transfers expressed in PPP dollars for households. EU countries' local currencies converted into equivalent Euros at the time of data collection and then converted into PPP dollars based on conversion factors provided by the OECD. PPP conversions can be accessed at http://www.oecd.org/document/47/0,3343,en_2649_34357_362028 63_1_1_1,00.html. Mean household social transfer income, percent of households receiving social transfers, and median household social transfer income of those receiving social transfers all calculated using survey sampling weights for households. Calculations by Jamie Barron.

64. Public Social Expenditure
OECD Factbook 2005, Public Policies, Public Expenditure and Aid, Social Expenditure, As a Percentage of GDP, 2001, available at http://ocde.p4.siteinternet.com/publications/doifiles/302005041P1T087.xls.

65. Public Social Expenditure, Per Capita
OECD.StatExtracts, Social and Welfare Statistics, Social Protection, Social Expenditure— Aggregated Data, Per Head, at Current Prices and Current PPPs, in US Dollars. Figures for 2003. Available at http://stats.oecd.org/wbos/Index.aspx?datasetcode=SOCX_AGG.

66. Total Social Spending
Willem Adema and Maxime Ladaique, *Net Social Expenditure, 2005 Edition: More Comprehensive Measures of Social Support* (Paris: OECD, 2005), Table 6, p. 32. Figures from 2001.

67. Murder Rate
U.S. Department of Justice, Bureau of Justice Statistics, Reported crime in the United States, Total, Crime rate per 100,000 population, Violent crime, Murder and nonnegligent manslaughter rate, 2005. To get to the data from the United States Department of Justice homepage, under Search click on DOJ Agencies, then Bureau of Justice Statistics. Under Data for analysis, select Data Online, then Crime trends from the FBI's Uniform Crime Reports, All States and U.S. Total, State by State and national trends. Available at http://www.usdoj.gov/. European figures come from the UN Office on Drugs and Crime, *Ninth United Nations Survey of Crime Trends and Operations of Criminal Justice Systems*, Police, 2.2 Total recorded intentional homicide, completed, Rate per 100,000 total population, 2004, pp. 3–7. Available at http://data360.org/pdf/20070531091045.Crime%20Trends.pdf.

68. Gun Ownership
Martin Killias, "Gun Ownership, Suicide and Homicide: An International Perspective." Available at http://www.unicri.it/wwk/publications/books/series/understanding/19_GUN_OWNERSHIP.pdf. Wendy Cukier, "Firearms Regulation: Canada in the International Context," *Chronic Diseases in Canada*, 19, 1 (1998), p. 28, Table 2. When the sources had different figures for the same country, the higher figure was chosen. The figures for more Swiss households owning firearms than American, though not graphed here, are in Vladeta Adjacic-Gross et al., "Changing Times: A Longitudinal Analysis of International Firearm Suicide Data," *American Journal of Public Health*, 96, 10 (2006), Table 1, p. 1753. Figures from 2000.

69. Prison Population
King's College London, International Centre for Prison Studies, Roy Walmsley, *World Prison Population List* (seventh edition), Table 2, Americas and Table 4, Europe, Prison population rate (per 100,000 of national population), pp. 3 and 5. The figures come from 2005 and 2006. Available at http://www.kcl.ac.uk/depsta/law/research/icps/downloads/world-prison-pop-seventh.pdf.

70. Average Prison Time
UN, Office on Drugs and Crime, Centre for International Crime Prevention, *Seventh United Nations Survey of Crime Trends and Operations of Criminal Justice Systems, Covering the Period 1998–2000*. Choose countries and look under Prisons 18.01: Average Length of Time Actually Served in Prison (After Conviction in Months), Count, 2000. Available at http://www.nplc.lt/stat/int/7sc.pdf.

71. Police Personnel
UN, Office on Drugs and Crime, *Seventh United Nations Survey of Crime Trends and Operations of Criminal Justice Systems*. Police 1.01: Total police personnel, Rate per 100,000 inhabitants.

72. Courtesy
Neena Samuel and Joseph K. Vetter, "Uncommon Courtesy," *Reader's Digest*, July 2006. Available at http://www.rd.com/content/good-manners/2/.

73. Litigation Rate
Herbert M. Kritzer, "Lawyer Fees and Lawyer Behavior in Litigation: What Does the Empirical Literature Really Say?" *Texas Law Review*, 80, 7 (2002), p. 1982. These figures are mirrored by those produced by the World Bank, Law and Justice Institutions, International Comparison of Litigation Rates. Figures for 1990. Available at http://web.worldbank.org/WBSITE/EXTERNAL/TOPICS/EXTLAWJUSTINST/0,,contentMDK:20746049~menuPK:2036192~pagePK:210058~piPK:210062~theSitePK:1974062,00.html.

74. Property Crime
UN, *Human Development Report 2005*, Table 24, p. 297.

75. Car Theft
OECD Factbook 2006, Quality of Life, Crime, Victimisation Rates. Figures are for 2000. A more middle-of-the-pack rating for car theft for 2003–04 in van Dijk et al., *Criminal Victimisation in International Perspective*, Table 4, p. 50.

76. Assault
UN, *Human Development Report 2005*, Table 24, p. 297. Figures are from 1999. Figures for 2003–04 put the United States higher, but beneath the Netherlands, UK, and Iceland. Van Dijk et al., *Criminal Victimisation in International Perspective*, Table 13, p. 81.

77. Sexual Assault
UN, *Human Development Report 2005*, Table 24, p. 297, Table 24. Figures are for 1999.

78. Young People Fighting
UNICEF Innocenti Research Centre, Report Card 7, *Child Poverty in Perspective: An Overview on Child Well-Being in Rich Countries* (2007), Figure 5.3a, p. 33. Available at http://www.unicef-irc.org/publications/pdf/rc7_eng.pdf.

79. Ecstasy
OECD, *Society at a Glance: 2005 Edition*, Chart C05.1, p. 89. Figures for ca. 2000.

80. Opiates
UN, Office on Drugs and Crime, *2006 World Drug Report*, v. 2, Table 6.1.1, pp. 383–84. Available at http://www.unodc.org/pdf/WDR_2006/wdr2006_volume2.pdf.

81. Bribery
UN, *Human Development Report 2005*, Table 24, p. 297. Most figures are from 1999.

82. Corruption
Transparency International, 2005 Corruption Perceptions Index, available at http://www.transparency.org/policy_research/surveys_indices/cpi/2005.

83. Fraud
UN, Office on Drugs and Crime, *Seventh United Nations Survey of Crime Trends and Operations of Criminal Justice Systems*. Police 2, 2.14: Total Recorded Frauds, Rate per 100,000 Inhabitants. Figures for 1999 and 2000.

84. Total Crime
UN, *Human Development Report 2005*, Table 24, p. 297. Figures for 2005 put the U.S. rates for 10 different crimes lower than the UK, Switzerland, Ireland, the Netherlands, Iceland, Denmark, and Belgium. Van Dijk et al., *Criminal Victimisation in International Perspective*, Table 1, p. 237.

85. Robbery
UN Office on Drugs and Crime, *Eighth United Nations Survey on Crime Trends and the Operations of Criminal Justice Systems (2001—2002)*, 2. Crimes recorded in criminal (police) statistics, by type of crime including attempts to commit crimes, 2.9. Total recorded robberies, Rate per 100,000 inhabitants, 2002, pp. 42, 43. Available at http://www.unodc.org/unodc/en/data-and-analysis/Eighth-United-Nations-Survey-on-Crime-Trends-and-the-Operations-of-Criminal-Justice-Systems.html.

86. Robbery Victims
UN, *Human Development Report 2005*, Table 24, p. 297. Most figures are from 1999.

87. Non-African American Murder Rate, 2005
In 2005, with 6,379 known African American murderers out of 12,130 known offenders in the United States, 52.59% of the known murderers were African American. If we assume that the racial identity of the unknown murderers was similarly divided as the known ones, then 52.59% of the 4899 unknown offenders gives a total of 2,576 African American murderers out of the unknown ones. That gives a total of 8,955 African American murderers out of 17,029 total murderers, which means that 53% of murderers were African American

and 47% were not. If we assume that each murderer killed the same number of victims, of the 14,860 murder victims in 2005, 6984 were killed by non-African American murderers. Using the FBI's population statistic of 296,410,404, that gives a non-African American murder rate of 2.36 per 100,000 population. Federal Bureau of Investigation, *Crime in the United States 2005*, Expanded Homicide Data Table 1. Available at http://www.fbi.gov/ucr/05cius/ offenses/expanded_information/data/shrtable_01.html. FBI, Expanded Homicide Data Table 3. Available at http://www.fbi.gov/ucr/05cius/offenses/expanded_information/data/ shrtable_03.html. European figures come from the UN Office on Drugs and Crime, *Ninth United Nations Survey of Crime Trends and Operations of Criminal Justice Systems*, Police, 2. Crimes recorded in criminal (police) statistics, by type of crime including attempts to commit crimes, 2.2. Total recorded intentional homicide, completed, Rate per 100,000 total population, 2004, pp. 3, 5, 7. Available at http://data360.org/pdf/20070531091045. Crime%20Trends.pdf.

88. Living Space
European Foundation for the Improvement of Living and Working Conditions, *First European Quality of Life Survey: Social Dimensions of Housing*, Table 2, p. 23. Figures from 2003. Available at http://www.eurofound.eu.int/pubdocs/2005/94/en/1/ef0594en.pdf. The American statistic comes from Gregg Easterbrook, *The Progress Paradox: How Life Gets Better While People Feel Worse* (New York, 2004) p. 17.

89. Development Assistance
UN, *Human Development Report 2005*, Table 17, p. 278. Figures are from 2003 in 2002 dollars.

90. Total Foreign Aid
Center for Global Development, *Commitment to Development Index 2006*, Overall (Average), select 2006 spreadsheet (original 2006 methodology). The higher the number, the better the score. Available at http://www.cgdev.org/section/initiatives/_active/cdi/data_graphs.

91. Public Spending on University Education
OECD, *Education at a Glance 2006*, Table B3.2b. Figures from 2003. Available at http://www. oecd.org/document/6/0,3343,en_2649_201185_37344774_1_1_1_1,00.html.

92. Total Spending on University Education
UNESCO, Institute for Statistics, Data Centre, Predefined Tables, Education, Table 19: Finance Indicators by ISCED Level, Total Expenditure on Educational Institutions and Administration as a % of GDP, All Sources, Tertiary. Most of the data come from 2005. Available at http://stats.uis.unesco.org/unesco/TableViewer/tableView.aspx?ReportId=172.

93. University Education Attainment
OECD Factbook 2006, Education, Outcomes, Tertiary Attainment, Tables, Tertiary Attainment for Age Group 25–64, As a Percentage of the Population of that Age Group, 2003.

94. State Spending on Education
Eurostat, Data, Education and training, Education, Indicators on education finance, Expenditure on education as % of GDP or public expenditure, Total public expenditure on education as % of GDP, for all levels of education combined. Data come from 2005. Available

at http://epp.eurostat.ec.europa.eu/portal/page?_pageid=1090,30070682,1090_33076576& _dad=portal&_schema=PORTAL.

95. Total Education Expenditure
OECD Factbook 2006, Education, Expenditure on Education, Public and Private Education Expenditure, Expenditure on Educational Institutions for All Levels of Education, As a Percentage of GDP, 2002.

96. Primary Teachers' Salaries
OECD, *Education at a Glance, 2006*, Table D3.1.

97. Class Size
OECD, *Education at a Glance 2005*, Tables, Indicator D2, Table D2.1, p. 344. Figures from 2003.

98. Reading Scores
OECD, PISA, *Learning for Tomorrow's World: First Results from PISA 2003*, Figure 6.3, p. 281. Available at http://www.pisa.oecd.org/dataoecd/1/60/34002216.pdf. Reading scores for PISA 2006 were not available for the United States.

99. Variance Between Schools
OECD, *Education at a Glance 2005*, Table A6.1, p. 87.

100. Private Secondary Schools
World Bank, EdStats, Country Profiles, Education Trends and Comparisons, Private sector enrollment share (%), Secondary level. The figures come from 2006. The World Bank provides the most comprehensive figures, but does not distinguish between independent and government-dependent private schools. The OECD's figures, in contrast, are spottier in terms of which countries they cover, but make this distinction. On the other hand, while the World Bank's figures of 25% enrollment in private secondary schooling in the UK seems high, the OECD's claim of over 70% of government-dependent private schooling for upper secondary education in this country seems even further from the truth. OECD, *Education at a Glance: 2005*, Table D5.1, p. 392. Figures for 2003.

101. Footloose Young
OECD, *Education at a Glance 2007*, Table C4.3, pp. 339–40. Figures from 2005.

102. Illiteracy
UN, *Human Development Report 2005*, Table 4, p. 230. Figures for 1994–2003.

103. Daily Newspaper Titles
World Association of Newspapers, *World Press Trends: 2001 Edition*, p. 9.

104. Public Libraries
UNESCO Institute for Statistics, Public Libraries, Collections, Books: Number of Volumes. Data from the late 1990s. Available at http://stats.uis.unesco.org/unesco/TableViewer/ tableView.aspx?ReportId=207. To calculate books per capita, population figures were used from the OECD. The American statistic comes from the National Center for Education Statis-

tics, *Public Libraries in the United States: Fiscal Year 2000*, July 2002, Table 8. Figures for 2000. Available at http://nces.ed.gov/pubs2002/2002344.pdf.

105. Books Sold
Euromonitor International, Global Market Information Database, Text Search "Books and Publishing," Books and Publishing for the appropriate countries, 7.5: Units and Value by Category, Forecast Unit Book Sales by Category 2002, '000 units, Total. The ratios are based on 2005 population estimates. Available at http://www.portal.euromonitor.com/portal/server.pt ?space=Login&control=RedirectHome.

106. Book Titles in Print
The American figure of 3,106,189 book titles in print comes from *Subject Guide to Books in Print 2007–2008* (New Providence, N.J., 2007), v. 1, p. vii. The British figure of 1,110,000 book titles in print comes from *Whitaker's Books in Print 2003*, (Surrey, UK, 2003), v. 1, p. 5. The figure of 992,042 book titles in print for Germany, Austria, and Switzerland comes from *Verzeichnis Lieferbarer Bücher 2004/2005*, (Frankfurt am Main, 2004), v. 1, General Editorial Policies/Directions for Users. The French figure of 489,337 book titles in print comes from *Livres disponibles 2004, Sujets*, (Paris, 2003), v. 1, p. xiii. The Italian figure of 510,131 book titles in print comes from *Catalogo dei libri in commercio 2006, Autori e Titoli*, (Milan, 2006), Avvertenze introduttive. The number of Spanish book titles in print was estimated at 323,125 using *Libros españoles en venta, 1991* (Madrid, 1990). The Portuguese figure of 59,705 book titles in print comes from *Livros Disponíveis 1999: Títulos* (Lisbon, 1999), Introduction. To calculate the figures of book titles in print per 1,000 population, population figures were used from OECD, as close as possible to the years of the book titles in print figures. It is worth noting that the UK figures are given a major boost by the fact that a very large fraction of U.S.-published books are also published in the UK. Also, these figures assume that the books in print are written by nationals of the country in question. The often-heard complaint that U.S. publishers do not publish translations from other languages, if true, would therefore boost the proportional authorship of Americans.

107. Television Viewing
NationMaster, Television viewing (most recent) by country. Available at http://www.nationmaster.com/graph/med_tel_vie-media-television-viewing.

108. Annual World Piano Sales
U.S. International Trade Commission, David Lundy et. al., *Pianos: Economic and Competitive Conditions Affecting the U.S. Industry*, May 1999, Table 5–1, p. 5–2. Figures from 1997. Available at http://hotdocs.usitc.gov/docs/pubs/332/pub3196.pdf. To calculate the figures of annual world piano sales per 10,000 population, population figures were used from the OECD.

109. Total Michelin Restaurant Stars
The total Michelin restaurant stars were counted for major cities for 2008. Most figures come from *Michelin: Main Cities of Europe 2008*. Dublin's and London's figures come from Michelin, Complete_2008.doc, "Michelin Stars 2008." The information was provided directly by Michelin, which can be contacted at: http://www.michelin.com/portail/home/home.jsp?lang=EN. Lisbon's and Madrid's figures come from Michelin, Spain_Portugal_2008.pdf, "LISTADO DE

ESTRELLAS—2008 / ESPAÑA—PORTUGAL," provided directly by Michelin. New York's figure comes from Michelin, STARS_2008.xls, "The Michelin Guides," provided directly by Michelin. Paris's figure comes from *Michelin: France 2008*, pp. 64, 65, 69. Rome's figure comes from Michelin, Italy.pdf, "La Guida Michelin Italia 2008: Le Stelle delle Regioni," provided directly by Michelin. Vienna's figure comes from *Michelin: Österreich 2008*, p. 48. All the cities' population totals used to calculate stars per capita (except Brussels's) come from City Population, and the population totals belong to the municipalities themselves, not the larger urban areas, agglomerations, or regions. Available at http://www.citypopulation.de/. Brussels's 2007 population figure comes from Wikipedia. Available at http://en.wikipedia.org/wiki/Brussels.

110. Perfect Wines
erobertParker.com. Available with subscription at: http://www.erobertparker.com/. The countries' perfect wines were divided by the countries' 2004 wine production figures, adjusted to hundred megaliters (million liters). The wine production figures come from winebiz, Top producers of wine in the world, 2004, Wine production ML. Available at http://www.winebiz.com.au/statistics/world.asp.

111. Ticket Prices in Major Opera Houses
Ticket prices from the Web sites of the various opera houses

112. Research and Development
UN, *Human Development Report 2005*, Table 13, p. 262. Figures from 1997–2002.

113. Patents
UN, *Human Development Report 2006*, Table 13, p. 327. Figures come from 2004.

114. Nobel Prizes by Nationality
Nobel prizes by nationality of the winner: Sutton Trust, "Nobel Prizes: The Changing Pattern of Awards," September 2003, Table 2, p. 4. Available at http://www.suttontrust.com/reports/nobel.doc. Prizes by nationality of institution: Sutton Trust, "Nobel Prizes," Table 4, p. 5. Nobel prizes across the population: Nobel Laureates by Country, *Wikipedia*, available at http://en.wikipedia.org/wiki/Nobel_laureates_by_country. All the ratios are based on 2005 population statistics.

115. Women in the Work Force
World Bank, GenderStats, Summary Gender Profile, Labor force, female (% of total labor force). The figures come from 2004. Available at http://devdata.worldbank.org/.

116. Women's Income
UN, *Human Development Report 2005*, Table 26, p. 303.

117. Women in Parliaments
WDI Online, Social Indicators, Other, Proportion of seats held by women in national parliament (%). Figures from 2005.

118. Women in Leading Positions
UN, *Human Development Report 2005*, Table 26, p. 303. The figure on technical and professional workers comes from here, too.

119. Gender Division of Housework
Jeanne A. Batalova and Philip N. Cohen, "Premarital Cohabitation and Housework: Couples in Cross-National Perspective," *Journal of Marriage and Family*, 64, 3 (2002), Table 2, p. 748. The Average Division of Labor scale ranges from 1 (female does all) to 5 (male does all). The data come from 1994. Data that suggests another story is presented in Janet C. Gornick and Marcia K. Meyers, *Families that Work: Policies for Reconciling Parenthood and Employment* (New York, 2003), pp. 70–72. This, however, deals with a vaguer category of unpaid work and does not address the specific question of who does the traditional female housework activities, as do Batalova and Cohen. The latter are broadly supported by the data in Janeen Baxter, "Gender Equality and Participation in Housework: A Cross-National Perspective," *Journal of Comparative Family Studies*, 28, 3 (1997). The UN's figures has American men doing more nonmarket activities than their peers in the UK, Norway, the Netherlands, Italy, Finland, Denmark and Austria. UN *Human Development Report 2006*, Table 28, p. 379.

120. Gay Marriage-like Unions
Economist, December 2, 2006, p. 64. Plus updated information on California and Connecticut.

121. Homosexual Experiences
Durex, *Global Sex Survey 2005*, Sexual experiences you've had, A gay/lesbian/homosexual experience. Available at: http://www.durex.com/cm/gss2005Content.asp?intQid=943&intMenuOpen=.

122. Three in a Bed during Sex
Durex, *Global Sex Survey 2005*, Sexual experiences you've had, Three in a bed.

123. Nonengagement in Sexual Indulgence
Durex, *The Global Sex Survey, 2004*, Sexual indulgence. Available at: http://www.durex.com/cm/gss2004Content.asp?intQid=402&intMenuOpen=11.

124. Legal Abortions
Statistisches Bundesamt, *Statistisches Jahrbuch 2005: Für das Ausland* (Wiesbaden, 2005), International Tables, Health, Legal abortions in selected countries, per 1,000 women, 2003, p. 261.

125. Passenger Cars
WDI Online, Development Framework, Transportation, Passenger cars (Per 1000 people) Figures for 2004.

126. Road Fatalities
OECD Factbook 2006, Quality of Life, Transport, Road Motor Vehicles and Road Fatalities, Road Fatalities, Per Million Vehicles, 2004.

127. Passenger Transport by Car
OECD in Figures 2005, pp. 34–35, Transport, Passenger transport, Billion passenger-kilometres, Private cars. Figures from 2003. Ratios calculated with population statistics found in OECD Statistics, 2003.

128. Car Passenger Kilometers per Size of Country
OECD in Figures 2005, pp. 34–35. Country areas come from International Traffic Safety Data and Analysis Group (IRTAD) Database, Statistics, Exposure Data, Area of State (sq km). Figures for 2005. Available at http://cemt.org/IRTAD/IRTADPUBLIC/weng1.html.

129. Car Passenger Kilometers per Km of Road
OECD in Figures 2005, pp. 34–35. Most roadway length statistics come from CIA, *World Factbook*. Germany's length of roadways comes from IRTAD Database, Statistics, Exposure Data, Total Network Length of all Public Roads (km). Available as in figure 128.

130. Length of Railways
CIA, *World Factbook*, data created with use of country statistics, Railways: Total (km), and Population (2006). The following information on railway per square kilometer is also derived from this source.

131. Rail Freight
OECD in Figures 2005, pp. 34–35, Transport, Freight transport, billion tonne-kilometres, Rail. Figures from 2003. The figures of ton-kilometers per inhabitant were calculated with population statistics from OECD Statistics, 2003.

132. Road Freight
OECD in Figures 2005, pp. 34–35. Figures from 2003. Percentages calculated by dividing Freight transport, billion tonne-kilometres, Roads by Freight transport, billion tonne-kilometres, Total inland freight.

133. Goods Vehicles
OECD Environmental Data: Compendium 2004 Edition, Table 2C, p. 229. Data from 2002. Population figures from OECD from 2002.

134. Aircraft Departures
NationMaster, Transportation Statistics, Aircraft Departures (per Capita) by Country. Available at http://www.nationmaster.com/graph/tra_air_dep_percap-transportation-aircraft-departures-per-capita.

135. Subway Passengers
Jane's Urban Transport Systems 2006–2007, ed. Mary Webb (Surrey UK, 2006), pp. 21, 27, 29, 99, 100, 112, 113, 125, 126, 172, 174, 178, 194, 256, 278, 279, 293, 295, 328, 330, 338, 339, 347, 384, 389, 455, 456.

136. Co2 Emissions from Transport
OECD in Figures 2007, Environment, CO_2 emissions, 2005, By sector, Million tonnes of Co2, Transport, pp. 48, 49. The transport CO_2 total was divided by total CO_2 emissions from fuel combustion to get the percentage from transport.

137. Urbanized Population
WDI Online, Social Indicators, Population, Population in Urban Agglomerations over 1 million (% of total population).

138. Urban Density
Demographia World Urban Areas (World Agglomerations), March 2007, Table 6. Figures from 2000–2005. Available at: http://www.demographia.com/db-worldua.pdf. Needless to say, one can argue about how to define city sizes and thus densities, and I have done so with the compilers of the information on this Web site. Whatever the shortcomings, at least they have thought about the issues and appear to be applying their criteria consistently across the cities they study, thus making their data more reliable than more slapdash measures available elsewhere.

139. Municipal Waste
OECD Environmental Data: Compendium 2006/2007, Table 2A, p. 11. Figures from 2005. Available at http://www.oecd.org/dataoecd/60/59/38106368.pdf.

140. Recycling
Institute for Public Policy Research, "Britain Bottom of the Heap for Recycling," August 27, 2006. Data from 2003–04. Available at http://www.ippr.org.uk/pressreleases/?id=2283. U.S. Environmental Protection Agency, "Municipal Solid Waste, Recycling," available at http://www.epa.gov/msw/recycle.htm#Figures.

141. Conservation, Protected Areas
OECD Environmental Data: Compendium 2004 Edition, Table 3B, p. 142. Figures from 2003. Somewhat different figures that still bear out the point made here are in WDI Online, Environment, Freshwater and Protected Areas, Nationally protected areas (% of total land area). Figures for 2004.

142. Threatened Mammals
OECD, Statistics, Environmental Statistics, Selected Environmental Data, Threatened Species: Mammals (% of Species Known). Available at http://www.oecd.org/dataoecd/11/15/24111692.PDF.

143. Forest Cover
OECD, Statistics, Environmental Statistics, Selected Environmental Data, Forest: Forest Area (% of Land Area), available at http://www.oecd.org/dataoecd/11/15/24111692.pdf.

144. Organic Food
Rural Advancement Foundation International—USA, Michael Sligh and Carolyn Christman, "Who Owns Organic? The Global Status, Prospects, and Challenges of a Changing Organic Market," 2003, Table 2, p. 9. Figures from 2000. Denmark was assigned a range of 2.5% to 3%, so a compromise figure of 2.75% was used. Available at http://rafiusa.org/pubs/OrganicReport.pdf.

145. Pesticide Use
OECD, Statistics, Environmental Statistics, Selected Environmental Data, Land: Pesticide Use (t/km2 of Agricultural Land). Available at http://www.oecd.org/dataoecd/11/15/24111692.pdf.

146. Nitrogenous Fertilizer Use
OECD, Statistics, Environmental Statistics, Selected Environmental Data, Land: Nitrogenous Fertilizer Use (t/km2 of Agricultural Land). Available at http://www.oecd.org/

dataoecd/11/15/24111692.PDF. The more precise measure of fertilizer consumption per hectare of arable land bears out these disparities. American farmers are significantly more sparing users than anyone but the Swedes and the Danes. WDI Online, Environment, Agricultural Production, Fertilizer consumption (100 grams per hectare of arable land). Figures from 2005.

147. Intensity of Water Use
OECD Environmental Data: Compendium 2004 Edition, Table 2A, p. 65. Data from the latest available year.

148. Sulfur Oxide Emissions
OECD Environmental Data: Compendium 2004 Edition, Table 1, p. 21. Figures from 2002.

149. Airborne Particulate Matter
WDI Online, Environment, Pollution, PM10, country level (micrograms per cubic meter). The data come from 2005.

150. Organic Water Pollutant Emissions
WDI Online, Environment, Pollution, Organic water pollutant (BOD) emissions (kg per day per worker). The data come from 2002 and 2003.

151. Electricity Consumption per Capita
WRI, Earth Trends Environmental Information, Energy and Resources, Data Tables, Resource Consumption 2005, Annual Electricity Consumption per Capita (kgoe) (kilograms of oil equivalent), 2001. Available at http://earthtrends.wri.org/pdf_library/data_tables/ene5_2005.pdf.

152. Energy Consumption per Unit of GDP
OECD Environmental Data: Compendium 2004 Edition, Table 5D, p. 217. Figures for 2002.

153. Per Capita Oil Consumption
BP, *Statistical Review of World Energy 2007*, Oil consumption, Thousand barrels daily, p. 11. Figures for 2006. Available at http://www.bp.com/liveassets/bp_internet/globalbp/globalbp_uk_english/reports_and_publications/statistical_energy_review_2007/STAGING/local_assets/downloads/pdf/statistical_review_of_world_energy_full_report_2007.pdf. Population statistics taken from the OECD.

154. Oil Consumption per Unit of GDP
BP, *Statistical Review of World Energy 2007*, Oil consumption, Million tonnes, p. 12. Figures for 2006. Figures of GDP are taken from the OECD Statistics Portal.

155. Rise or Decline of Greenhouse Gas Emissions
Eurostat, *Europe in Figures: Eurostat Yearbook 2006–07*, Table 10.1, p. 272. Available at: http://epp.eurostat.ec.europa.eu/cache/ITY_OFFPUB/KS-CD-06–001/EN/KS-CD-06–001-EN.pdf.

156. Solar Energy
WRI, Earth Trends Environmental Information, Energy and Resources, Data Tables, Energy Consumption by Source 2005, Energy Consumption (as a percent of total consumption) by Source, Solar, 2001. Available at http://earthtrends.wri.org/pdf_library/data_tables/

ene2_2005.pdf. Similar figures in WDI Online, Environment, Energy Production and Use, Clean energy consumption (% of total). Figures for 2005. Also in *UN Human Development Report 2007/2008*, Table 23, p. 306.

157. Venture Capital Investment in Clean Technology Companies
Figures for venture capital investment in clean technology companies in 2006 came directly from Cleantech Network upon written request. The ratios were calculated with 2005 population statistics.

158. Nuclear Waste
OECD, Statistics, Environmental Statistics, Selected Environmental Data, Waste Generated, Nuclear Waste (t./Mtoe of TPES). Available at http://www.oecd.org/dataoecd/11/15/24111692.pdf.

159. A Great Deal of Confidence in the Government
WVS, Politics and Society, E079. Similar results in WVS 2005, Confidence: The Government

160. A Great Deal of Confidence in the Civil Service
WVS, Politics and Society, E076. Less dramatic results are found in other surveys, though again the Swedes are most distrustful, after the Italians. ISSP, Role of Government III 1996, Variable 54, sum of first two results. In 2006, the Swedes were still the most distrustful, along with the French. ISSP Role of Government IV 2006, Variable 50.

161. Shadow Economy
Friedrich Schneider and Dominik H. Enste, *The Shadow Economy: An International Survey* (Cambridge, 2002), Table 4.6, p. 38.

162. Trust in Others
Stephen Knack and Philip Keefer, "Does Social Capital Have an Economic Payoff? A Cross-Country Investigation," *Quarterly Journal of Economics*, 112, 4 (1997), p. 1285, Data Appendix, Trust. Data from the ISSP suggests that the United States falls into a middle group of trust, along with the UK, Germany, Ireland and the Netherlands, while the Scandinavian countries are high trust, and the Mediterranean nations low trust. ISSP, Citizenship 2004, Variable 46, sum of the first two figures. The more recent figures are blurrier: ISSP, Role of Government IV 2006, Variable 54, sum of first two figures.

163. Civic Organizations
Knack and Keefer, "Does Social Capital Have an Economic Payoff?" p. 1285, Data Appendix, Groups.

164. Charity
Charities Aid Foundation, "International Comparisons of Charitable Giving," November 2006, Figure 2, p. 6. Available at http://www.cafonline.org/pdf/International%20Comparisons%20of%20Charitable%20Giving.pdf.

165. Volunteer Work
Helmut K. Anheier and Lester M. Salamon, "Volunteering in Cross-National Perspective: Initial Comparisons," *Law and Contemporary Problems*, 62, 4 (1999), Table 3, p. 58. Figures for 1995–97.

166. Blood Donation
European data come from Kieran Healy, "Embedded Altruism: Blood Collection Regimes and the European Union's Donor Population," *American Journal of Sociology*, 105, 6 (2000), Table 1, p. 1638. Data for 1993. The American statistic comes from Lichang Lee, Jane Allyn Piliavin, and Vaughn R. A. Call, "Giving Time, Money, and Blood: Similarities and Differences," *Social Psychology Quarterly*, 62, 3 (1999), p. 276. They cite evidence that 40% to 45% say they have given blood at least once.

167. Voter Turnout
International Institute for Democracy and Electoral Assistance, Voter Turnout, Parliamentary Elections, Vote/VAP. Figures from the last available election, usually in the 1990s or early 2000s. Available at http://www.idea.int/vt/.

168. Frequent Discussion of Politics
WVS, Perceptions of Life, A062. Similar results in ISSP, Citizenship 2004, Variable 47.

169. Single Parent Households
OECD, Table 2.1: childreninhouseholds[1].xls, Composition of Households, 2005, Single Parent Households as a Percentage of all Households with Children. Data received directly from OECD. Data can be requested at stat.contact@oecd.org. The information will become part of OECD Family Database, which will be available at www.oecd.org/els/social/family.

170. Eating with Parents
UNICEF Innocenti Research Centre, Report Card 7, *Child poverty in perspective*, Figure 4.2a, p. 24. Statistics are approximations based on the bar graphs in the figure.

171. Talking with Parents
UNICEF Innocenti Research Centre, Report Card 7, *Child poverty in perspective*, Figure 42b, p. 25. Statistics are approximations based on the bar graphs in the figures.

172. Elderly Living in Institutions
OECD, *Society at a Glance 2002*, Annex HE: Health Indicators, Table HE10.3. Figures from the mid-1990s. Available at http://www.oecd.org/document/24/0,3343,en_2649_34637_267 1576_1_1_1_1,00.html#previous.

173. Very Proud of Own Nationality
WVS, National Identity, Citizenship, G006. The ISSP found the Austrians with most general national pride in 1995–96, the Americans in 2003–04. For domain-specific national pride, the Irish came out on top in the earlier survey, the Americans in the later one. Tom W. Smith and Seokho Kim, "National Pride in Comparative Perspective: 1995/96 and 2003/04," *International Journal of Public Opinion Research*, 18, 1 (2006), Tables 1, 2, pp. 129–30. In the WVS 2005, the Americans were less proud than the Spaniards and the Finns and at almost the same level as the British. How Proud of Nationality, sum of the first two results.

174. Convinced Atheists
WVS, Religion and Morale, F034.

175. Firm Belief in God
ISSP, Religion II, 1998, Variable 37.

176. Belief in God
WVS, Religion and Morale, F050.

177. Weekly Church Attendance
WVS, Religion and Morale, F028.

178. Christian Congregations
World Christian Database, Country/Region, Christianity, Congregations per Million, 2005.
Available with subscription at: http://worldchristiandatabase.org/wcd/esweb.asp?WCI=Res
ults&Query=239&PageSize=25&Page=1.

179. Membership in Religious Denominations
WVS, Religion and Morale, F024. On the other hand, more Americans are active members of
church or religious organizations than any Europeans. WVS 2005.

180. Catholic Church Attendance
Andrew M. Greeley, *The Catholic Myth: The Behavior and Beliefs of American Catholics* (New
York, 1990), p. 269. Figures appear to come from the 1980s.

181. Church Income
David Barrett et al, *World Christian Encyclopedia: A Comparative Survey of Churches and Religions in the Modern World* (Oxford, 2001), v 1. Statistics of income per capita were calculated
with Countryscan figures from Category 85: 2000 Churches' Income per Year (US$), pp. 838–
39, and Category 5: 2000 Population, pp. 830–31. Calculations of income per member were
done using Category 65: 2000 Affiliated Church Members, pages 834 and 835.

182. Science Does More Harm than Good
ISSP, Religion II, 1998, Variable 27. Sum of first two responses. When the same question was
repeated in 2000, in the context of a questionnaire on environmental matters, the countries
where more people think science does harm than in the U.S. were the UK, Austria, Ireland,
Spain, Portugal and Switzerland. The French were not included. ISSP, Environment II 2000,
Variable 9. Sum of the first two responses.

183. Belief in Astrology
Adherents.Com, Astrology, percentages of people who take astrology seriously. France, Germany, and United Kingdom's data come from 1982, and U.S. data from 1986. Available at
http://adherents.com/Na/Na_41.html#307.

184. Homeopathy
Peter Fisher and Adam Ward, "Medicine in Europe: Complementary Medicine in Europe,"
British Medical Journal, 309 (1994), pp. 107–111.

185. Foreign-Born Population
OECD in Figures 2005, Demography, Foreign Population, pp. 6–7. Figures for 2003.

186. Gap in Math Scores between Native-Born and Immigrants

OECD Factbook 2007, Migration, Education, Educational outcomes for children of immigrants, Tables, PISA results for children of immigrants, Share of all 15-year-old students, Points differences compared with natives, Mathematics, Unadjusted, 2nd generation. Figures from 2003.

187. Gap in Reading Scores between Native-Born and Immigrants

OECD Factbook 2007, Migration, Education, Educational outcomes for children of immigrants, Tables, PISA results for children of immigrants, PISA results for children of immigrants, Share of all 15-year-old students, Points differences compared with natives, Reading, Unadjusted, 2nd generation. Figures from 2003.

188. Increased Unemployment

OECD Factbook 2007, Migration, Labour Force and Remittances, Unemployment rates of the foreign- and the native-born, Tables, Unemployment rates of foreign- and native-born populations, Unemployment rates of foreign- and native-born populations, As a percentage of total labour force. The figures were calculated by subtracting Men, Native, 2004 from Men, Foreign born, 2004.

189. Median Income

Luxembourg Income Study (LIS) Key Figures, accessed at http://www.lisproject.org/keyfigures.htm (June 2008). LIS median income figures converted into PPP dollars. Figures are for 2000 for all countries except for the Netherlands and United Kingdom, which are for 1999. For EU members, local currencies were converted to euros at the time of data collection and then these figures were converted to PPP dollars using a conversion table provided by the OECD at http://www.oecd.org/document/47/0,3343,en_2649_34357_36202863_1_1_1_1,00.html. Calculations by Jamie Barron.

190. Resident Billionaires

Forbes, "Forbes List: The World's Billionaires 2006," eds. Luisa Kroll and Allison Fass. Sort by: Residence. Ratios calculated with 2005 population figures. Available at http://www.forbes.com/2007/03/07/billionaires-worlds-richest_07billionaires_cz_lk_af_0308billie_land.html. The following calculations regarding billionaires are based on these numbers.

191. Overall Poverty

Luxembourg Income Study, LIS Key Figures, Relative Poverty Rates, Total Population, Poverty Line (60% of Median). Figures from the late 1990s and early 2000s. Available at http://www.lisproject.org/keyfigures/povertytable.htm.

192. Richest

James B. Davies, Susanna Sandstrom, Anthony Shorrocks, and Edward N. Wolff, "The World Distribution of Household Wealth," July 2007, Table 1. Figures mainly from the late 1990s and early 2000s. Available at http://repositories.cdlib.org/cgi/viewcontent.cgi?article=1068&context=cgirs.

193. Income Inequality

LIS Key Figures, available at www.lisproject.org/keyfigures.htm.

194. Income Inequality
Klaus Deininger and Lyn Squire, "A New Data Set Measuring Income Inequality," *World Bank Economic Review*, 10, 3 (1996), Table 1, p. 577. Similar results in Miriam Beblo and Thomas Knaus, "Measuring Income Inequality in Euroland," *Review of Income and Wealth*, 47, 3 (2001), pp. 301–20; and in James K. Galbraith, "Inequality, Unemployment and Growth: New Measures for Old Controversies," *Journal of Economic Inequality*, 23 April 2008, Figure 3.

195. Distribution of Household Net Worth
Eva Sierminska, Andrea Brandolini, and Timothy M. Smeeding, "Comparing Wealth Distribution across Rich Countries: First Results from the Luxembourg Wealth Study," 7 August 2006, Table 9. Available at http://www.iariw.org/papers/2006/sierminska.pdf.

196. Low Income Population
Carles Boix, "The Institutional Accommodation of an Enlarged Europe," Table 3, p. 7. Friedrich Ebert Stiftung. It is unclear from which date the figures are, but apparently 1993. Available at http://library.fes.de/pdf-files/id/02103.pdf.

197. Absolute Poverty, European Scale
Median EU-6 equivalized income calculated using LIS Wave 5 (release 2) data. LIS Micro database, (2000); harmonization of original surveys conducted by the Luxembourg Income Study, Asbl. Luxembourg, periodic updating. Survey data is for year 2000 for all countries except for the Netherlands and the United Kingdom, which are based on survey data from 1999. Households with disposable income recorded as missing, zero, or negative were dropped from the analysis. Equivalized incomes were derived using household net disposable income and dividing by the square root of the total household size (LIS equivalization procedure). Incomes expressed in PPP dollars. EU countries' local currencies were converted into equivalent Euros at the time of data collection and then converted into PPP dollars based on conversion factors provided by the OECD. PPP conversions can be accessed at http://www.oecd.org/document/47/0,3343,e n_2649_34357_36202863_1_1_1_1,00.html. Median EU-6 income calculated in terms of PPP dollars, with a weighting procedure that took into account the survey sampling weights and the population sizes of each of the six countries. Percent below 60% EU-6 equivalized median income calculated using appropriate survey sampling weights (weights for equivalized incomes equal household weight, multiplied by household size). Calculations by Jamie Barron.

198. Absolute Poverty, U.S. Scale
Median equivalized income in the United States calculated using LIS Wave 5 (release 2) data from year 2000. LIS Micro database, (2000); harmonization of original surveys conducted by the Luxembourg Income Study, Asbl. Luxembourg, periodic updating. Survey data is for year 2000 except for the Netherlands and the United Kingdom, which are based on survey data from 1999. Households with disposable income recorded as missing, zero, or negative were dropped from the analysis. Equivalized incomes were derived using household net disposable income and dividing by the square root of the total household size (LIS equivalization procedure). Incomes expressed in PPP dollars. EU countries' local currencies were converted into equivalent Euros at the time of data collection and then converted into PPP dollars based on

conversion factors provided by the OECD. PPP conversions can be accessed at http://www.
oecd.org/document/47/0,3343,en_2649_34357_36202863_1_1_1_1,00.html. U.S. median
equivalized income and the percentage below 60% U.S. median equivalized income were
calculated using appropriate survey sampling weights (weights for equivalized incomes equal
household weight, multiplied by household size). Calculations by Jamie Barron.

199. Mean Income Ratios of Top and Bottom Quintiles
Jared Bernstein, Elizabeth McNichol, Karen Lyons, January 2006, "Pulling Apart: A State-by-
State Analysis of Income Trends," January 2006 (Center on Budget and Policy Priorities and
Economic Policy Institute), Table 2: Ratio of Incomes of Top and Bottom Fifths of Families
2001–2003 (2002 Dollars), Top-to-bottom ratio, p. 18. Available at http://www.epinet.org/
studies/pulling06/pulling_apart_2006.pdf. European figures calculated by Pierre-Yves Yanni
from World Bank, World Development Indicators 2007.

200. Population (%) under 60% of EU-6 Median Income
Luxembourg Income Study (LIS) Micro database, (2000); harmonization of original surveys
conducted by the Luxembourg Income Study, Asbl. Luxembourg, periodic updating. Survey
data is for year 2000 for all U.S. states and European countries except for the Netherlands and
the United Kingdom, which are based on survey data from 1999. Samples for all U.S. states are
representative of their respective populations, but sample sizes for smaller U.S. states can be
relatively small. Calculation procedures used in for Figure 197 (Absolute Poverty, European
Scale) applied here for U.S. states and European countries. Calculations by Jamie Barron.

201. Prisoners per 100,000 of Population
Roy Walmsley, "World Prison Population List," Home Office Research, Development and Statistics Directorate, Research Findings No. 88, p. 5. Available at http://www.homeoffice.gov.uk/rds/
pdfs/r88.pdf. U.S. Census Bureau, *State and Metropolitan Area Data Book: 2006*, Table A-26, p.
34. Figures from 2003. Available at http://www.census.gov/prod/2006pubs/smadb/smadb-06.
pdf.

202. Murders per 100,000 Population
FBI, *Crime in the United States 2004*, Table 4: Crime in the United States by Region, Geographic Division, and State, 2003–2004, Murder and non-negligent manslaughter, Rate per
100,000, 2004, pp. 76, 78, 80, 82, 84. Available at http://www.fbi.gov/ucr/cius_04/. European figures come from the UN Office on Drugs and Crime, *Ninth United Nations Survey of
Crime Trends and Operations of Criminal Justice Systems*, Police, 2. Crimes recorded in criminal
(police) statistics, by type of crime including attempts to commit crimes, 2.2. Total recorded
intentional homicide, completed, Rate per 100,000 total population, 2004, pp. 3, 5, 7. Available at http://data360.org/pdf/20070531091045.Crime%20Trends.pdf.

203. Percent of Workers Who Are Union Members
The European figures come from David G. Blanchflower, "A Cross-Country Study of Union
Membership," Forschungsinstitut zur Zukunft der Arbeit, Discussion Paper No 2016, March
2006, Table 1, p. 29. Available at http://ftp.iza.org/dp2016.pdf. U.S. Census Bureau, *State and
Metropolitan Area Data Book: 2006*, Table A-33.

204. Life Expectancy at Birth in Years
European statistics come from UN, *Human Development Report 2002*, Table 1, p. 149. Figures for 2000. Statistics for U.S. states come from U.S. Census Bureau, Population Division, Interim State Population Projections, 2005, Table 2. Figures for 2000. Available at http://wonder.cdc.gov/WONDER/help/populations/population-projections/MethodsTable2.xls.

205. Unemployment Rate
OECD, StatExtracts, Standardised Unemployment Rates, 2005. U.S. Census Bureau, *2008 Statistical Abstract*, State Rankings, Unemployment Rate, 2005. Available at http://www.census.gov/compendia/statab/ranks/rank25.xls.

206. Defense Spending
CIA, *World Factbook*, Military Expenditures—Percent of GDP. Most figures are from 2001–2005.

207. Armed Forces
International Institute for Strategic Studies, *Military Balance 2007* (Abingdon, UK, 2007), pp. 28, 103, 107, 110, 116, 119, 123, 129, 136, 141, 148, 156, 164, 167, 173, 175. Ratios calculated with use of population figures from Population Reference Bureau, *2006 World Population Data Sheet*. Available at http://www.prb.org/pdf06/06WorldDataSheet.pdf.

208. Percent of Population with Health Care Coverage
This graph is only broadly illustrative. Data for the U.S. is sketchy and available only for the years indicated at the data points where the connector line changes direction. No data is implied for the points in between. Nor was data available for the same years for all countries. *Source Book of Health Insurance Data 1963* (New York, 1963), Percentage of United States Population With Some Form of Health Insurance Protection, Percent, p. 10. U.S. Census Bureau, *Income, Poverty, and Health Insurance Coverage in the United States: 2005* (August 2006), Table C-1, p. 60. Available at http://www.census.gov/prod/2006pubs/p60–231.pdf. *OECD Health Data 2007*, Social Protection, Health care coverage, Government/social health insurance, In-patient and acute care, % of total population; and Social Protection, Health care coverage, Private health insurance, Primary private health insurance coverage, % of total population. Germany's figure was added to its Government/social health insurance figure to get the percentage of people covered by health insurance.

209. Enrollment in Tertiary-Level Education
UNESCO Institute for Statistics, World Education Indicators, Participation in Education, Gross Enrollment Ratios by sex, Tertiary, Both sexes. Data range from 1970 to 1995. Available at http://www.uis.unesco.org/statsen/statistics/indicators/i_pages/IndGERTer.asp. UNESCO Institute for Statistics, Table 14. Data range from 2000 to 2005. Available at http://stats.uis.unesco.org/unesco/TableViewer/tableView.aspx?ReportId=167. No data available between 1995 and 2000.

210. Annual Hours Worked per Person Employed
Angus Maddison, *The World Economy: A Millennial Perspective* (OECD; Paris, 2001), Table E-3, p. 347.

211. Catastrophic Death
Injury: WHO, Health Statistics and Health Information Systems, Global Burden of Disease Estimates, Deaths and DALY Estimates for 2002 by Cause for WHO Member States, Estimated Deaths per 100,000 Population, 2002. Murder: U.S. Department of Justice, Bureau of Justice Statistics, Reported crime in the United States, Total, Crime rate per 100,000 population, Violent crime, Murder and nonnegligent manslaughter rate, 2005. Available at http://www.usdoj.gov. UN Office on Drugs and Crime, *Ninth United Nations Survey of Crime Trends and Operations of Criminal Justice Systems*. Figures from 2004. Available at http://data360.org/pdf/20070531091045.Crime%20Trends.pdf. *Eighth United Nations Survey on Crime Trends and the Operations of Criminal Justice Systems (2001—2002)*. Figures from 2002. Available at http://www.unodc.org/unodc/en/data-and-analysis/Eighth-United-Nations-Survey-on-Crime-Trends-and-the-Operations-of-Criminal-Justice-Systems.html. Suicide: *OECD Health Data 2008*, Health Status, Mortality, Causes of Mortality, Intentional Self-Harm. Figures from 2005 or 2006. Supplemented by WHO, *World Report on Violence and Health* (2002), Table A.9, pp. 314ff. Figures from the late 1990s.

212. Human Development Index Trends
UN Human Development Report 2007/2008, Table 2, p. 234.

INDEX